Sentence Comprehension as a Cognitive Process

Sentence comprehension – the way we process and understand spoken and written language – is a central and important area of research within psycholinguistics. This book explores the contribution of computational modelling to the field, showing how computational models of sentence processing can help scientists in their investigation of human cognitive processes. It presents the leading computational model of retrieval processes in sentence processing, the Lewis and Vasishth cue-based retrieval model, and proposes a principled methodology for parameter estimation and model comparison/evaluation using benchmark data to enable researchers to test their own models of retrieval against the present model. It also provides readers with an overview of the last 20 years of research on the topic of retrieval processes in sentence comprehension, along with source code that allows researchers to extend the model and carry out new research. Comprehensive in its scope, this book is essential reading for researchers in cognitive science.

SHRAVAN VASISHTH is Professor of Linguistics at the University of Potsdam. He is also a chartered statistician (Royal Statistical Society).

FELIX ENGELMANN obtained his PhD in linguistics from the University of Potsdam (2016). He is a data scientist and entrepreneur, currently based in Berlin. His published research applies diverse computational methods to the modelling of human language processing and language acquisition.

Sentence Comprehension as a Cognitive Process

A Computational Approach

Shravan Vasishth
University of Potsdam

Felix Engelmann
University of Potsdam

CAMBRIDGE
UNIVERSITY PRESS

University Printing House, Cambridge CB2 8BS, United Kingdom

One Liberty Plaza, 20th Floor, New York, NY 10006, USA

477 Williamstown Road, Port Melbourne, VIC 3207, Australia

314–321, 3rd Floor, Plot 3, Splendor Forum, Jasola District Centre,
New Delhi – 110025, India

103 Penang Road, #05–06/07, Visioncrest Commercial, Singapore 238467

Cambridge University Press is part of the University of Cambridge.

It furthers the University's mission by disseminating knowledge in the pursuit of
education, learning, and research at the highest international levels of excellence.

www.cambridge.org
Information on this title: www.cambridge.org/9781107133112
DOI: 10.1017/9781316459560

© Shravan Vasishth and Felix Engelmann 2022

This publication is in copyright. Subject to statutory exception
and to the provisions of relevant collective licensing agreements,
no reproduction of any part may take place without the written
permission of Cambridge University Press.

First published 2022

A catalogue record for this publication is available from the British Library.

Library of Congress Cataloging-in-Publication Data
Names: Vasishth, Shravan, 1964– author. | Engelmann, Felix, 1982– author.
Title: Sentence comprehension as a cognitive process : a computational
approach / Shravan Vasishth, Felix Engelmann.
Description: New York : Cambridge University Press, 2022. |
includes bibliographical references and index.
Identifiers: LCCN 2021024706 (print) | LCCN 2021024707 (ebook) |
ISBN 9781107133112 (hardback) | ISBN 9781107589773 (paperback) |
ISBN 9781316459560 (epub)
Subjects: LCSH: Grammar, Comparative and general–Sentences–Psychological
aspects. | Psycholinguistics. | Computational linguistics. |
BISAC: LANGUAGE ARTS & DISCIPLINES / Linguistics / General |
LANGUAGE ARTS & DISCIPLINES / Linguistics / General
Classification: LCC P295 .V38 2021 (print) | LCC P295 (ebook) | DDC 401/.9–dc23
LC record available at https://lccn.loc.gov/2021024706
LC ebook record available at https://lccn.loc.gov/2021024707

ISBN 978-1-107-13311-2 Hardback

Cambridge University Press has no responsibility for the persistence or accuracy
of URLs for external or third-party internet websites referred to in this publication
and does not guarantee that any content on such websites is, or will remain,
accurate or appropriate.

Contents

List of Figures	*page* ix
List of Tables	xvii
Foreword by Richard L. Lewis	xx
Preface	xxiii
Acknowledgements	xxiv

1	**Introduction**	**1**
	1.1 Working Memory in Theories of Sentence Comprehension	2
	1.2 Prediction in Sentence Processing	6
	1.3 Working Memory and Prediction as Explanations for Processing Difficulty	7
	1.4 Current Beliefs about Constraints on Sentence Comprehension	7
	1.5 Some Gaps in the Sentence Processing Literature	8
	1.5.1 The Relative Scarcity of Computationally Implemented Models	8
	1.5.2 A Focus on Average Behaviour and Neglect of Individual-Level Differences	10
	1.5.3 The Absence of High-Precision Studies	11
	1.5.4 Unclear Desiderata for a Good Model Fit	11
	1.6 The Goals of This Book	16
	1.6.1 Providing Open Source Model Code	17
	1.6.2 Modelling Average Effects as Well as Individual Differences	17
	1.6.3 Developing a Set of Modelling and Empirical Benchmarks for Future Model Comparison	18
	1.7 Looking Ahead	19
2	**Dependencies in Sentence Comprehension**	**21**
	2.1 Memory Processes in Sentence Comprehension	21
	2.2 Dependency Completion in Sentence Processing	23
	2.3 Subject-Verb Non-Agreement Dependencies	26
	2.4 Subject-Verb Number Agreement	31
	2.5 Reflexives and Reciprocals	38
	2.5.1 Individual-Level Effects in the Dillon et al. Design	44
	2.5.2 A Sensitivity Analysis on the Ungrammatical Agreement and Reflexives Conditions Using Informative Priors	44
	2.6 Concluding Remarks	47
3	**The Core ACT-R-Based Model of Retrieval Processes**	**49**
	3.1 ACT-R	49
	3.2 The Lewis and Vasishth (2005) Model	52
	3.2.1 A Priori Predictions of the Model	54

v

vi   Contents

| | | 3.2.2 | Comparison of the LV05 Prediction Space with the Results of the Jäger et al. Meta-analysis | 60 |

3.2.2 Comparison of the LV05 Prediction Space with the Results of the Jäger
     et al. Meta-analysis   60
3.3 A More Principled Approach to Parameter Estimation   63
    3.3.1 Bayesian Parameter Estimation   64
    3.3.2 Approximate Bayesian Computation   66
3.4 Concluding Remarks   69

4   An Extension of the Core Model: Modelling Prominence and
    Multi-associative Cues   71
4.1 Incorporating Prominence and Multi-associative Cues   72
    4.1.1 Item Prominence   74
    4.1.2 Multi-associative Cues   84
    4.1.3 Implementation of Item Prominence and Multi-associative Cues   89
    4.1.4 Multi-associative Cues   90
    4.1.5 Prominence   93
4.2 A Simulation of the Meta-analysis Studies   94
    4.2.1 Data   95
    4.2.2 Method   95
    4.2.3 Results   98
4.3 Discussion   103
    4.3.1 Distractor Prominence   107
    4.3.2 Multi-associative Cues   108

    Appendices
4.A Key Terms and Concepts   111
4.B List of Experiments Included in the Simulations   113
4.C Model Specifications   114

5   An Extension of the Core Model: Modelling the Interaction of
    Eye-Movement Control and Parsing   116
5.1 The EMMA/ACT-R Reading Model   118
5.2 Replication of Salvucci (2001)   119
    5.2.1 Data   119
    5.2.2 Model   120
    5.2.3 Analysis   120
    5.2.4 Results   122
    5.2.5 Discussion   122
5.3 The Extended EMMA/ACT-R Model   122
    5.3.1 Surprisal   124
5.4 Simulations on the Potsdam Sentence Corpus   125
    5.4.1 Data   126
    5.4.2 Model   127
    5.4.3 Results   128
    5.4.4 Discussion   131
5.5 General Discussion   132
    5.5.1 Comparison with E-Z Reader   132
    5.5.2 Future Prospects   134

Contents   vii

Appendices
5.A Root-Mean-Square Deviation   136
5.B Linear Regression Analysis   136

6 Reanalysis and Underspecification in Sentence Comprehension: Modelling Eye Movements 140

6.1 Introduction   140
6.2 Modelling Reanalysis: Memory and Expectation Processes in Parsing   141
    6.2.1 Memory and Expectation in Relative Clauses   141
    6.2.2 Simulation: Modelling the Staub (2010) Data   143
    6.2.3 Results   144
    6.2.4 Discussion   145
6.3 Modelling Underspecification: The Adaptive Interaction between Parsing, Eye-Movement Control, and Working Memory Capacity 148
    6.3.1 Good-Enough Parsing   148
    6.3.2 Simulation: Modelling the von der Malsburg and Vasishth (2013) Experiment 153
    6.3.3 Results   154
    6.3.4 Discussion   157
6.4 General Discussion   160

7 Competing Accounts of Interference in Sentence Processing 161

7.1 The Direct-Access Model   161
7.2 Comparing the Predictive Performance of the Models   164
    7.2.1 Inhibitory Interference   164
    7.2.2 Relative Clauses in Chinese   167
    7.2.3 Discussion   170
7.3 Encoding Interference in Agreement Attraction   171
    7.3.1 An Evaluation of the Nairne Proposal   173
    7.3.2 Model Comparison   174
    7.3.3 Discussion   175
7.4 Summary   176

8 Modelling Sentence Comprehension Deficits in Aphasia 178

8.1 Theories and Models of Sentence Comprehension Deficits   178
    8.1.1 Timing Deficit   179
    8.1.2 Reduction in Memory   180
    8.1.3 Intermittent Deficiency   181
    8.1.4 Weakened Syntax   182
    8.1.5 Slow Syntax   183
    8.1.6 Lexical Integration Deficit   184
    8.1.7 Lexical Access Deficits   184
    8.1.8 A Comparison of Theories of Impaired Processing, and Their Relation to Theories of Unimpaired Processing 185
8.2 Modelling Individual-Level Differences   187
    8.2.1 Mapping ACT-R Parameters to Sources of Deficits   189
    8.2.2 Simulations   191
    8.2.3 Results   192
    8.2.4 Discussion   195

viii   Contents

8.3	Competing Models of Retrieval in Aphasia	197
	8.3.1 Materials	197
	8.3.2 Results and Discussion	198
8.4	Concluding Remarks	198

9   Future Directions   200

9.1	Developing Implemented Computational Models	200
9.2	An Excessive Focus on Average Behaviour	200
9.3	Creating Higher-Precision Benchmark Data-Sets for Model Evaluation and Comparison	201
9.4	Developing Better Criteria for Evaluating Model Fit	202
9.5	In Closing	202

Bibliography	203
Index	221

Figures

1.1   A schematic summary of the Roberts and Pashler (2000) discussion regarding what constitutes a good fit of a model to data. The data are represented by the circle (the estimated mean) and the vertical uncertainty interval, and the model predictions by the diagonal parallel lines. If a model predicts a positive correlation between two variables x and y, strong support for the model can only be argued for if both the data and the model predictions are highly constrained: the model must make predictions over a narrow range, and the data must have low uncertainty associated with it.   12

1.2   A demonstration of Type M and S error. Low power studies will yield overestimates and/or incorrect signs whenever a result is significant.   14

1.3   The five possible outcomes when using the null region or "region of practical equivalence" method for decision-making (Kruschke, 2015). Outcomes A and B are inconsistent with the quantitative predictions of the theory; C and D are inconclusive; and E is consistent with the quantitative theoretical prediction. Figure reproduced from Vasishth and Gelman (2019).   16

2.1   A schematic illustration of the fan effect. Searching for an object that is grey and a square (the target item) is more difficult when competing items have one or more features matching cues used for identifying the target item.   22

2.2   Inhibitory interference effects (sorted in increasing order by magnitude) in reading studies by Van Dyke and colleagues. The grey vertical lines show the 95% credible interval for the meta-analysis estimate of the effect.   28

2.3   Distribution of power (paired, two-sided t-test) assuming that the effect has normal distribution with mean 13 and standard deviation 6, the standard deviation ranges from 75 to 100 ms, and the subject sample size is 60.   29

ix

x   List of Figures

2.4   Visualization of two conditions in the Cunnings and Sturt (2018) experiment and the predictions of the cue-based retrieval model. The verb *shattered* attempts to retrieve an item in memory that is a direct object and has the property "is shatterable". In both the (a) and (b) conditions shown, the direct object (which is the target noun that should be retrieved) matches the direct object retrieval cue. However, in (b), the distractor noun matches the "is shatterable" cue. As a consequence, in (b), both the target and distractor nouns enter into a race, and whichever item is non-deterministically retrieved is the winner of the race. This race process leads to a faster reading time at the verb *shattered* in (b) vs. (a).   31

2.5   Subject-verb number agreement effects in ungrammatical sentences (reading studies). Shown are the means (sorted by increasing magnitude of the effect) and 95% confidence intervals that were either computed from publicly available data or derived from published estimates.   34

2.6   The role of case marking in agreement attraction configurations. The figure is reused here under a CC-BY4.0 license and is available from https://doi.org/10.6084/m9.figshare.11440854.v1.   35

2.7   Target match number agreement effects in reading studies.   36

2.8   Summary for total reading time of the Dillon et al. (2013) comparisons for ungrammatical sentences involving agreement and reflexives. The sample size was 40 participants. The upper plot shows the posterior distributions of the facilitatory interference effect in agreement and reflexives, and the lower plots show the individual-level estimates of the effect, with 80% and 95% credible intervals.   42

2.9   Summary for total reading time of the Jäger et al. (2020) comparisons for ungrammatical sentences involving agreement and reflexives. The sample size was 181 participants. The upper plot shows the posterior distributions of the facilitatory interference effect in agreement and reflexives, and the lower plots show the individual-level estimates of the effect, with 80% and 95% credible intervals.   43

3.1   Figure 1 of Lewis and Vasishth (2005). The figure shows the representation of chunks (maximal projections of phrases) that constitute a syntactic tree. The figure is copyrighted by Wiley, and is reused with permission, license number 4782371233287.   53

3.2   Figure 2 of Lewis and Vasishth (2005). The figure shows the processing cycle of the parsing algorithm. The figure is

List of Figures xi

copyrighted by Wiley, and is reused with permission, license
number 4782380063983. 53

3.3 Spreading activation according to ACT-R/LV05 in the four
conditions shown in Example 21. Line weights indicate the
amount of spreading activation from a cue to an item. Black oval
boxes represent a feature match. Grey oval boxes indicate features
matching an "overloaded" cue (MASC in b), and white boxes
indicate a mismatch. The figure is by Engelmann and Vasishth
(2019); available at https://doi.org/10.6084/m9.figshare.9305456
under a CC-BY4.0 license. 55

3.4 An illustration of a race process involving two distributions that
represent retrieval time distributions of two items. When the two
distributions have similar means (Figure A), the distribution of the
retrieval times of the winner (which may differ from trial to trial)
will have a distribution with a mean that is lower than the mean of
the two distributions involved in the race (statistical facilitation).
When one distribution has a much smaller mean than the other
distribution's mean (Figure B), the distribution of the winner's
retrieval times will have the same mean as that of the distribution
of the item with the smaller mean. 58

3.5 Prediction space for the interference effect in ACT-R in
target-match (circles, solid line) and target-mismatch
configurations (triangles, broken line). Interference is plotted in
terms of the difference in mean retrieval latencies between the
interference (labelled distractor-match) and the no-interference
(labelled distractor-mismatch) condition, and as a function of the
latency factor F. Positive values indicate longer mean retrieval
latencies in the interference condition (*inhibitory interference*) due
to cue-overload (fan effect) from a partially matching distractor;
negative values indicate shorter mean retrieval latencies in the
interference condition (*facilitatory interference*) due to retrievals
of the partially matching distractor on trials where the distractor is
highly activated and hence fast. Each individual data point
represents the mean interference effect of 6,000 iterations with
one out of 10,980 different parameter settings (each in
target-match and target-mismatch configurations; i.e., there are
21,960 data points plotted in total). Each parameter setting is a
combination of the following parameter values: latency factor
$F \in \{0, 0.01, \ldots, 0.6\}$, noise parameter $ANS \in \{0.1, 0.2, 0.3\}$,
maximum associative strength $MAS \in \{1, 2, 3, 4\}$, mismatch
penalty $MP \in \{0, 1, 2\}$, retrieval threshold $\tau \in \{-2, -1.5, \ldots, 0\}$. 59

3.6 A *Beta*(2, 6) prior on the latency factor. 68

xii   List of Figures

3.7   The posterior distributions of the latency factor parameters for agreement and reflexive conditions using the original Dillon et al. (2013) data (40 participants, 48 items) and our own Jäger et al. (2019) replication data (181 participants, 48 items).   69

3.8   The posterior predictive distributions of the facilitatory interference in ungrammatical agreement and reflexive conditions, derived using the posterior distributions of the latency factor parameter.   70

4.1   Predictions of ACT-R for the four conditions shown in Example (22). Line weights indicate the amount of spreading activation from a cue to an item. Black oval boxes represent a feature match. Grey oval boxes indicate features matching an "overloaded" cue (MASC in b), and white boxes indicate a mismatch.   73

4.2   Predicted target-match and target-mismatch interference effects (distractor-match minus distractor-mismatch) as a function of distractor prominence (p_distr ranging from $\{-3, \ldots, 5\}$ when target prominence is zero (mean of 10,000 iterations with parameters $F = 0.2, ANS = 0.2, MAS = 2, MP = 0$). Positive values indicate longer mean retrieval latencies (inhibition) in the interference condition due to cue overload (fan effect). Negative values indicate shorter mean retrieval latencies (facilitation) in the interference condition due to retrievals of the distractor on trials where the distractor is highly activated and hence fast. The points where the vertical line intersects with the curves represent standard LV05 predictions.   76

4.3   Mechanisms underlying the effect of distractor prominence in target-mismatch configurations. The x-axis in each panel shows increasing distractor prominence (with target prominence $= 0$). The panels from top left are: (1) Mean activation of target and distractor at retrieval event in interference (distractor-match) and no-interference (distractor-mismatch) condition (the sign of the activation value – negative or positive – has no special meaning in ACT-R). (2) Proportion of distractor retrievals over multiple iterations (retrieval probability). Values above 0.5 indicate higher retrieval probability for the distractor than the target (misretrievals). (3) Mean retrieval latencies (of most activated item at retrieval). (4) Mean interference effect as the difference in retrieval latencies between interference and no-interference condition. Positive values mean inhibitory interference (longer latencies when distractor matches); negative values mean facilitatory interference (short latencies due to misretrievals when distractor mismatches). The vertical lines mark locations of (a) low interference due to low prominence; (b) LV05 equivalence at prominence $= 0$ (equal activation of target and distractor in interference condition); (c) maximal facilitatory interference effect due to misretrievals; (d) low interference due to latencies close to zero.   78

4.4   Mechanisms underlying the effect of distractor prominence in target-match configurations. The x-axis in each panel shows increasing distractor prominence (with target prominence $= 0$). The panels from top left are: (1) Mean activation of target and distractor at retrieval event in interference (distractor-match) and no-interference (distractor-mismatch) condition (the sign of the activation value – negative or positive – has no special meaning in ACT-R). (2) Proportion of distractor retrievals over multiple iterations (retrieval probability). Values above 0.5 indicate higher retrieval probability for the distractor than the target (misretrievals). (3) Mean retrieval latencies (of most activated item at retrieval). (4) Mean interference effect as the difference in retrieval latencies between interference and no-interference condition. Positive values mean inhibitory interference (longer latencies when distractor matches); negative values mean facilitatory interference (short latencies due to misretrievals when distractor mismatches). The vertical lines mark locations of (a) low interference due to low prominence; (b) maximal inhibitory interference effect due to increased fan; (c) equal activation of target and distractor in interference condition: lower fan effect due to statistical facilitation; (d) zero interference effect because of equal strength of fan effect and facilitation due to misretrievals of the highly activated distractor; (e) maximal facilitatory interference effect due to misretrievals; (f) low interference due to latencies close to zero.   80

4.5   Spreading activation in conditions labelled distractor-match (c) and distractor-mismatch (d) conditions in target-mismatch configurations when cues are cross-associated. Line weight and box shading indicate the amount of spreading activation added to an item due to a feature match. Dashed lines represent spreading activation to a cross-associated feature.   86

4.6   Predicted target-match and target-mismatch interference effects (distractor-match minus distractor-mismatch) as a function of the cross-association level c. Lines and shaded area show mean and range of the effect, respectively, for parameter values of the latency factor F ranging from 0.2 to 0.4, and distractor prominence

xiv List of Figures

ranging from $-0.5, 0, 0.5$, running 5,000 iterations each; other parameters were fixed as $ANS = 0.2, MAS = 2, MP = 0$. Positive values indicate longer mean retrieval latencies (inhibition) in the interference condition due to cue-overload (fan effect). Negative values indicate shorter mean retrieval latencies (facilitation) in the interference condition due to misretrievals of the distractor. 87

4.7 Standard target-mismatch/distractor-match condition without cross-associated cues. 90

4.8 Target-mismatch/distractor-match condition when cues are cross-associated. 92

4.9 Number of studies included in the Jäger et al. (2017) meta-analysis and in the simulations, grouped by dependency type and distractor prominence status (studies are listed in Table 4.6 in the Appendix). 96

4.10 Mean interference effects from simulations with LV05 and the extended model, labelled LV05+IP+MAC, for target-match and target-mismatch configurations of the meta-analysis, grouped by dependency type (studies are listed in Table 4.6 in the Appendix). The behavioural data is shown as mean effect estimates with 95% credible intervals as reported in Jäger et al. (2017). 99

4.11 Mean interference effects from simulations with LV05 and the extended model, labelled LV05+IP+MAC, for target-match (top panel) and target-mismatch configurations (bottom panel) in the Jäger et al. (2017) meta-analysis, grouped by distractor prominence level within dependency types (studies are listed in Table 4.6 in the Appendix). The behavioural data is shown as raw means with additional smaller points representing individual studies. The target-mismatch plot in non-agreement subject-verb dependencies does not contain data because no data were available at the time of the meta-analysis. However, Cunnings and Sturt (2018) have recently found evidence consistent with the predictions of the model; in two experiments, they obtained an estimated mean of -22 ms with a 95% credible interval of $[-4, -42]$, and in a second experiment, a mean of -19 ms, $[-40, 1]$. 100

4.12 Reading time data and simulation results of LV05 and the extended model, labelled LV05+IP+MAC, for interference effects in target-match and target-mismatch configurations of four individual studies: Kush and Phillips (2014), (Jäger et al., 2015, Exp. 1), (Sturt, 2003, Exp. 1), and (Cunnings and Felser, 2013, Exp. 2, participants with low working memory). 102

5.1 Replication of Salvucci (2001) on the Schilling Corpus. Effects of word frequency on gaze, first, and single fixation duration, and on

List of Figures

xv

	the rate of skipping a word, fixating it once, and fixating it more than once. Grey solid lines represent experimental data, black dotted lines show Salvucci's simulation results, and black dashed lines show the replication results. Lexical frequency is divided into classes 1 (lowest) to 5 (highest).	123
5.2	A schematic figure illustrating the Time Out mechanism in the case of object vs. subject relatives. In an object relative, if the integration of the relative clause verb is still in progress while the encoding of the word following it has already completed, time out initiates an attention shift to the word to the left of the currently fixated one (Time Out regression). Once the integration of the relative clause verb has finished, the `exit-time-out` rule returns the model into the state of continuing fixating in the reading direction.	128
5.3	Shown are the predictions of Model 2 (EMMA, dotted lines) vs. Model 7 (EMMA+rs_2, dashed lines) vs. experimental data (grey solid lines) for the Potsdam Sentence Corpus. The figure shows means of early (first row) and late measures (second row) as a function of frequency class. Each row shows reading time durations on the left and probabilities on the right side.	131
5.4	Coefficients and 95% confidence intervals for predictors surprisal and retrieval estimated by linear regression. Predictors were log frequency, length, log retrieval, and surprisal. Coefficients are plotted along the y-axis for surprisal on the left side and retrieval on the right side. Regressions were carried out on the simulated data of all six EMMA models (shown on the x-axis); 95% confidence intervals that do not cross 0 indicate statistical significance at $\alpha = 0.05$.	137
6.1	Model predictions for reading times in subject- and object-relative clauses.	145
6.2	Predicted first-pass regressions from the model for subject- and object-relative clauses.	146
6.3	Proportions of sentence rereading by working memory capacity in the data of von der Malsburg and Vasishth (2013).	152
6.4	Predicted gaze durations by source activation at ambiguous and unambiguous attachments.	155
6.5	Predicted time out proportions by source activation at ambiguous and unambiguous attachments.	156
6.6	Predicted proportions of sentence rereading by source activation at ambiguous and unambiguous attachments.	156
6.7	Predicted attachment proportions by source activation at ambiguous and unambiguous attachments.	157

xvi   List of Figures

7.1 A schematic illustration of the direct-access model. For sentences like (38a), the model assumes that once a search is initiated in memory using a set of retrieval cues (here, subject and animate), one of two events can happen. Either the correct item is retrieved from memory, or the incorrect item, which matches some of the retrieval cues, is misretrieved. In the case of a misretrieval, either processing ends with a misretrieval, or a reanalysis step is initiated that leads to a correct retrieval. This reanalysis step costs time, and therefore leads to slowdowns in processing on average.   163

7.2 A comparison of observed sample means with the posterior predictive distributions of the activation-based model, and the direct-access model. The figure is adapted from the online materials available from a StanCon 2017 conference talk by Bruno Nicenboim and Shravan Vasishth, which are under a CC-BY 4.0 licence.   166

8.1 Marginal distributions of each of the three parameters for subject relatives in controls (solid lines) vs. IWA (dotted lines). The vertical line shows the default setting for the respective parameter.   193

8.2 Marginal distributions of each of the three parameters for object relatives in controls (solid lines) vs. IWA (dotted lines). The vertical line shows the default setting for the respective parameter.   193

8.3 Shown are the differences between the two models in expected pointwise log density for each data-point. Points above the zero line show an advantage for the activation-based model, and points below the zero line an advantage for the direct-access model. The darkness in the hexagons represents density, with darker hexagons representing more dense data-points. The figure is under a CC-BY 4.0 license, https://doi.org/10.6084/m9.figshare .12114075.v1.   199

Tables

2.1 Nested contrast coding to investigate the effect of intrusion in grammatical and ungrammatical agreement and reflexive constructions. The contrast *dep* is the main effect of dependency type (agreement or reflexive). The abbreviation *intr.au* means intrusion (interference effect) in agreement dependencies, ungrammatical; *intr.ag* stands for intrusion (interference effect) in agreement dependencies, grammatical; *intr.ru* refers to intrusion (interference effect) in reflexive dependencies, ungrammatical; *intr.rg* stands for intrusion (interference effect) in reflexive dependencies, grammatical.　41

2.2 Summary of the sensitivity analysis investigating the effect of incorporating prior knowledge from mildly uninformative priors; a meta-analysis of existing reading data on ungrammatical agreement and reflexives; and the model predictions in Engelmann et al. (2020). The dependent measure in the analysis is total fixation time and the posterior estimates are back-transformed to the ms scale from log ms. The priors are shown in the ms scales.　47

3.1 Results of the Jäger et al. (2017) meta-analysis showing mean effect estimates $\hat{b}$ with Bayesian 95% credible intervals in the Estimates column. The range specified by a 95% credible interval contains the true value of the estimated parameter with 95% certainty, given the model and the data. A positive interference effect means inhibition, a negative one facilitation. Results are compared with the predictions of cue-based retrieval as implemented in the LV05 ACT-R model, and the additional contributions of the extensions *item prominence* (IP) and *multi-associative cues* (MAC), which are discussed in Chapter 4.　62

4.1 Possible feature combinations exhibited by correct antecedents of English reflexives, reciprocals, and Chinese *ziji*.　85

4.2 Root-mean-square deviation between modelling results and observed data, averaged within dependency type and model (best

xvii

xviii   List of Tables

values in bold). The superscript *no dec* means that the decay
parameter is set to 0.   97

4.3 Estimated values for prominence parameter in the LV05+IP+MAC
model with decay for three prominence levels.   99

4.4 Shown here is the terminology used in the present chapter in
relation to cue-based retrieval and interference in dependency
resolution.   111

4.5 Shown here is the terminology used in the extension of the
cue-based retrieval model (continued from previous page).   112

4.6 List of experiments included in the simulations.   113

4.7 List of experiments included in the simulations (continued from
previous page).   114

4.8 Model parameters, their default values, and the values used in the
simulation of the studies in the meta-analysis.   115

5.1 Frequency classes used in the analyses of the Schilling Corpus
(SC) and Potsdam Sentence Corpus (PSC).   120

5.2 Fit and parameter estimates for all simulations. The interpretation
of the data are discussed in the Results and Discussion sections.   121

5.3 Linear regression results for predictors retrieval and surprisal   138

6.1 ACT-R/EMMA parameter values.   141

7.1 Model comparison using K-fold cross-validation for the Gibson
and Wu 2013 data. Shown are the differences in $\widehat{elpd}$, along with
standard errors of the differences. In a comparison between a
model A vs B, a positive $\Delta\widehat{elpd}$ favours model A.   169

7.2 Model comparison using k-fold cross-validation for the Vasishth et
al. (2013) replication of the Gibson and Wu (2013) study.   170

7.3 Comparison of the 10 sets of hierarchical models. Shown are the
differences in $\widehat{elpd}$ between (a) the standard hierarchical model and
the homogeneous variance mixture model; (b) the feature
percolation model and the homogeneous variance mixture model;
and (c) the homogeneous vs. heterogeneous variance mixture
model. Also shown are standard errors for each comparison. If the
difference in $\widehat{elpd}$ is positive, this is evidence in favour of the
second model. The pairwise model comparisons are transitive.
These comparisons show that the heterogeneous variance mixture
model has the best predictive performance.   175

8.1 A matrix showing how the models relate to each other along
dimensions of the three working-memory related events – delays,
forgetting (or failure to retrieve), and misretrieval – that have been
investigated in sentence comprehension research.   186

8.2 The number of participants in subject/object relatives (SR/OR) for
which nondefault parameter values were predicted, in the subject

	vs. object relative tasks, respectively; for goal activation (GA), default action time (DAT), and noise (ANS) parameters.	194
8.3	Discrimination ability of hierarchical clustering on the combined data for subject/object relatives. Numbers in bold show the number of correctly clustered data points. The bottom row shows the percentage accuracy.	195

Foreword by Richard L. Lewis

In reading a draft of this remarkable book, I was reminded of the title that Allen Newell chose for his contribution to a meeting celebrating the scientific contributions of Herbert Simon: "Putting It All Together". Newell was both acknowledging Simon's putting so much together under bounded rationality, but also looking forward to the theoretical integration made possible by models of cognitive architecture. What Shravan Vasishth and Felix Engelmann have offered us is perhaps the most comprehensive and integrated attempt yet to put it all together in sentence processing in a way that begins to do justice to its rich, cross-linguistic empirical details.

I'll point out below a few of my favourite contributions to integration that appear in the book. But I first want to draw the reader's attention to another thread running through all of the chapters – and one that is perhaps even more important than the specific details of the models, explanations, and empirical analysis that is focus of each chapter.

That thread is a sharp critique of our current practices in empirical and theoretical psycholinguistics. Indeed, the first two chapters do not read like the expected triumphant summary of 20 years of empirical research confirming effects of similarity-based interference and other predictions of our early sentence processing models. On the contrary, it is a sobering taking-stock of the empirical record and current methodological practice through the lens of what we have too slowly come to understand about what is required to make progress. And what is required is quite often much larger amounts of carefully collected data, rigorous statistical analysis, and multiple alternative model testing. In short, this book and the work it reports is part of the larger movement throughout the psychological and cognitive sciences that is helping us to wake up to the reality of just how challenging our science really is. In the case of psycholinguistics, we take for granted that we can infer internal cognitive and linguistic structure from movements of the eyes and hands and tongue and lips or fluctuations in electrical potentials on the scalp. Why did we think that task would be easier than it in fact is?

But along with this sobering critique, the book also takes us on a kind of joy ride – letting us experience the joy of a few real advances and interesting ideas that help us see a little bit further ahead. My own favourites include the detailed comparison of different retrieval models (concluding with a rejection of the specific model in Lewis and Vasishth, 2005), the model-based accounts of individual differences and pathologies (paralleling a renaissance across the field ranging from areas such as computational psychiatry to cognitive aging), and the beginnings of explicit models of adaptive eye movements that start to do justice to the flexible and highly adaptive nature of human language comprehension.

On a more personal note, it is a unique privilege as a scientist to be able to look back to a collaboration that started over 20 years ago, and to see how far the work has come. I cannot believe the good fortune I had to cross paths with Shravan when he was a prodigious graduate student in linguistics and I was a young professor in computer science at Ohio State. The ideas we explored in the early ACT-R models of parsing were really an evolution and combination of insights of George Miller, Noam Chomsky, and John Anderson. And by now what is generously referred to in the book as the Lewis and Vasishth model is really the Vasishth and colleagues model. But in the end, scientific ideas do not belong to any of us – they belong to the field, and individuals and teams are but stewards.

Of course there are many gaps, weaknesses, and shortcomings in the pages that follow. But unlike most scientific books, a great many of them are documented by the authors themselves! And so I am reminded of another colourful quote (attributed to Warren McCulloch), one that Allen Newell enjoyed using when advancing his candidate integrated theories: "Don't bite my finger, look where I'm pointing." Vasishth and Engelmann are pointing the way to a better science of sentence processing, and we'd do well to take a look in their direction. I especially hope that new students joining the field will do so, and be inspired to take us down ambitious and imaginative new paths towards integrated and deeply explanatory theory.

Preface

The early work of Richard L. Lewis in the 1990s set the stage for the work reported in the present book. Rick's research on developing a language processing model within the SOAR architecture (Lewis, 1993) evolved into a sharper focus on developing process models of dependency completion in sentence comprehension. He initiated the use of the cognitive architecture ACT-R to model proactive and retroactive interference effects (Lewis, 1996). The first major elaboration of these ideas appeared in Lewis and Vasishth (2005) and Lewis et al. (2006). In the late 1990s and early 2000s, both Julie Van Dyke and the first author of the present book were Rick's PhD students. Since then, quite a lot of evidence has accumulated that is consistent with Rick's original insight that dependency completion time (retrieval time in ACT-R parlance) in sentence processing is affected by similarity-based interference. However, some important counterexamples to this proposal have also emerged, and there are some important empirical details relating to retrieval processes that may not be explainable by the general mechanisms posited within ACT-R (Anderson et al., 2004) or other memory architectures. We discuss several of these counterexamples in detail in the present book. More generally, the present book takes stock of the computational modelling done in this context and situates the modelling within some (but not all) of the important scientific questions in sentence processing research that are actively under consideration today. We hope that this book will be useful to researchers seeking to build on the work presented here and to develop the next generation of computational models of sentence processing.

xxiii

Acknowledgements

The following researchers made important contributions to the computational modelling presented in this book during the time that they were doing their PhD or postdoctoral research with the first author.

- Ms. Paula Lissón was the lead on the aphasia modelling work on the comparison of the models of retrieval processes in aphasia (Lissón et al., 2021).
- Ms. Dorothea Pregla developed the German data-set on individuals with aphasia and controls as part of her PhD dissertation; in future work, this will serve as benchmark data for evaluating some of the models discussed in this book.
- Ms. Daniela Mertzen carried out several large-sample experiments on interference as part of her PhD dissertation work. These will serve as benchmark data for model evaluation in future work.
- Mr. Himanshu Yadav, Dr. Garrett Smith, and Dr. Dario Paape helped develop extensions of the Approximate Bayesian Computation approach reported here.
- Dr. Garrett Smith developed the new principled approach for determining lexical features (Smith and Vasishth, 2020).
- Prof. Dr. Lena Jäger: Co-authored the meta-analysis (Jäger et al., 2017) that forms the empirical basis for some of the model evaluations reported in this book, and co-developed the prominence and multi-associative cues extension of the core model, as reported in Engelmann et al. (2020).
- Prof. Dr. Bruno Nicenboim: Developed the implementation of the direct-access model, as reported in Nicenboim and Vasishth (2018).
- Prof. Dr. Titus von der Malsburg: Provided the empirical basis for modelling underspecification and reanalysis (von der Malsburg and Vasishth, 2013), as discussed in Chapter 6.
- Mr. Paul Mätzig: Carried out the model development and simulations reported in Mätzig et al. (2018).

Acknowledgements

- Prof. Dr. Pavel Logačev implemented and tested several models relating to attachment ambiguities and underspecification (Logačev and Vasishth, 2015; Logačev and Vasishth, 2016).
- Dr. Umesh Patil: Carried out the model development and simulations reported in Patil et al. (2016a).

For comments, helpful feedback, and advice over the years, we would like to thank the following people: Serine Avetisyan, Douglas Bates, Michael Betancourt, Adrian Brasoveanu, Bob Carpenter, Pyeong Wang Cho, Ian Cunnings, Brian Dillon, Jakub Dotlačil, Ralf Engbert, Julie Franck, Hiroki Fujita, Andrew Gelman, Matt Goldrick, Robert Grant, Sandra Hanne, Lena Jäger, Reinhold Kliegl, Dave Kush, Sol Lago, Anna Laurinavichyute, Richard L. Lewis, Tal Linzen, Paula Lissón, Pavel Logačev, Paul Mätzig, Daniela Mertzen, Mitzi Morris, Bruno Nicenboim, Dario Paape, Dan Parker, Umesh Patil, Colin Phillips, Dorothea Pregla, Maxmilian Rabe, Milena Rabovsky, Daniel Schad, Pia Schoknecht, Scott Sisson, Garrett Smith, Patrick Sturt, Whitney Tabor, Matt Tucker, Julie Van Dyke, Mick van het Nederend, Hedderik van Rijn, Sashank Varma, Titus von der Malsburg, Matt Wagers, Jan Winkowski, and Himanshu Yadav. Elna Haffner and Junilda Petriti helped prepare the index, and Junilda Petriti checked for formatting and other errors and inconsistencies. Some of the data that formed the basis for modelling came from our own lab, but a lot of other data came from Adrian Staub, Brian Dillon, Sol Lago, Matt Wagers, Matt Tucker, Julie Franck, Patrick Sturt, Ian Cunnings, Roger Levy, Frank Keller, and Ted Gibson (among others). The openness and transparency of these scientists is greatly appreciated. Colin Phillips and Ted have also been very supportive colleagues over the years, despite many scientific disagreements between us. Sashank Varma reviewed the final draft of this book and made very important suggestions for improvement, which we have tried to implement in the final version of this book. Our apologies if we have forgotten anyone.

This book was generously funded by the Volkswagen Foundation through an *Opus Magnum* award (grant number 89 953) to Shravan Vasishth. The grant allowed the first author to take a two-year sabbatical from teaching to concentrate on research and writing. Shravan Vasishth also thanks his wife and son for their patience over the last few years.

1 Introduction

A large body of work in cognitive science is concerned with understanding the constraints on human language comprehension and production. Although questions about language processing fall within the relatively narrow confines of psycholinguistics, there are deep connections between language processing and independently developed research on memory processes within cognitive psychology. This book is about a particular set of computational models of sentence comprehension processes (Engelmann et al., 2020; Lewis and Vasishth, 2005) that seek to explain how one particular conception of working memory constraints comes into play when we comprehend a sentence. The aim is to use an independently developed process model of human information processing (ACT-R) to account for some of the cognitive processes that unfold when a sentence is read or heard. Because of the narrow focus of the work presented here, our discussion of alternative computational modelling approaches will be cursory. This is in no way intended to diminish the importance of these approaches; we feel that approaches such as connectionist modelling and non-linear dynamical systems-based models add great theoretical value to the field and deserve a fuller treatment.

In fact, even within theories that assume working memory constructs in sentence comprehension, this book summarizes only one particular research thread. The work reported here should be seen as a modest contribution towards a broader, longer-term goal: developing competing theories and models of sentence comprehension or parsing processes that can be quantitatively compared against high-quality benchmark empirical data. In an effort to foster reproducibility, and to allow others to use and extend the computational models presented here, all the associated data and code for this book have been made available from the following repository:

https://vasishth.github.io/RetrievalModels

In the next few subsections, we quickly survey some important aspects of previous research on sentence processing, focussing on two important and closely related ideas: the role of working memory constraints and the role of predictive processing.

2   Introduction

1.1   Working Memory in Theories of Sentence Comprehension

Theoretical and empirical research in sentence comprehension spans a broad range of topics; for comprehensive reviews of the classical theory, see Frazier (1987a) and Pickering and Van Gompel (2006), and for a discussion of some of the recent theoretical developments, see Traxler (2014). Historically, there have been two broad classes of empirical phenomena that have been studied: the effect on comprehension difficulty of complexity (syntactic or semantic/pragmatic) and of ambiguity.

Miller and Chomsky (1963) were among the first to investigate the role of syntactic complexity in sentence processing by indirectly invoking a limit on working memory capacity. They developed a measure of structural complexity that was meant to correlate with memory limitations (Miller and Chomsky, 1963, 480–482): the ratio between the non-terminal and terminal nodes in the tree representation of a sentence (i.e., a global ratio) was taken as a measure of "the amount of computation per input symbol that must be performed" (Miller and Chomsky, 1963, 480). For example, the ratio of non-terminals to terminals in a sentence like *That John failed his exam surprised Mary* is higher than for the extraposed (and easier to process) version *It surprised Mary that John failed his exam.* In related work, Yngve (1960) proposed the depth hypothesis, which stated that the depth of embedding of a phrase was a major predictor of processing complexity. This line of work on complexity continues to be expanded on today.

The double centre-embedding construction is a classic example that illustrates this shift in emphasis from limits on working memory capacity to the constraints imposed on the predictive process. Janet Fodor is cited in Frazier (1985) as noticing that in English, complex multiple centre embeddings are easier to process when the middle verb is missing (i.e., when the sentence is ungrammatical), compared to when the sentence has the correct syntactic structure. Consider the following sentences:

(1)   a.   *The apartment that the maid who the service had sent over was well decorated.

   b.   The apartment that the maid who the service had sent over *was cleaning every week* was well decorated.

The middle verb phrase *was cleaning every week* is missing in (1a), rendering the sentence ungrammatical (ungrammaticality is marked with an asterisk, following linguistic convention); compare the ungrammatical sentence with its grammatical counterpart (1b). In an acceptability rating study, Gibson and Thomas (1997) found similar ratings for both sentences, a surprising outcome given that the first sentence is outright ungrammatical. Gibson and colleagues invoked storage overload when holding predictions in memory:

the increased storage cost of holding items in memory is assumed to lead the parsing system to forget a previously generated prediction of an upcoming verb phrase. Gibson's storage cost proposal would predict similar behaviour across languages; however, it seems that German behaves differently from English. In a set of seven reading studies (self-paced reading and eyetracking while reading), Vasishth et al. (2010) found that in English, reading time at the region following the final verb phrase was shorter in the ungrammatical vs. grammatical constructions. This finding from English is consistent with the Gibson and Thomas proposal. However, Vasishth et al. (2010) found the opposite pattern in German: the region after the final verb phrase was read *slower* in the ungrammatical vs. grammatical sentences. This pattern for German has been replicated, and similar patterns were found for Dutch (Frank et al., 2015), but see Bader (2016) for results inconsistent with this claim about German. Vasishth et al. (2010) suggested that German speakers may be able to hold predictions of upcoming verb phrases in memory better than English speakers, because verb phrases in German embedded clauses are always in the last position. German speakers get more exposure to verb-final constructions than English speakers; this is assumed to allow German speakers to maintain predictions for upcoming verbs in German better than English speakers reading English. The explanation is therefore grounded in experience, not some inherent working memory capacity difference between German and English speakers. Incidentally, the ability to maintain predictions seems to be linked to the properties of the language: when German and Dutch speakers who speak fluent English read sentences in English, they no longer show German/Dutch-like behaviour, and behave like English native speakers, reading ungrammatical sentences faster (Frank et al., 2015). This differentiated pattern of responses conditional on the language being currently used suggests that the probabilistic knowledge about syntactic predictions may not transfer across the languages spoken by an individual; if this conclusion turns out to be correct, it would be an interesting avenue of research in bilingualism, where research often presupposes transfer effects across languages.

Some of the other recent empirical work on reading that is concerned with the role of prediction in processing complex syntactic structures is Levy et al. (2012, 2013), Levy and Keller (2013), Vasishth et al. (2018), and Linzen and Jaeger (2016). However, working memory limitations may also play a role independent of the constraints imposed by predictive processing. For example, Safavi et al. (2016) showed that in Persian, readers tended to forget highly predictable particles in verb-particle constructions; this is unexpected under the probabilistic prediction accounts. Further, Husain et al. (2014) found that strong predictions about upcoming materials could override forgetting effects, but weak predictions did not.

4   Introduction

Working memory limitations have also been invoked to explain the effect of ambiguity on comprehension ease. For example, Frazier proposed two heuristic principles that guide parsing decisions. These were mainly directed at explaining so-called garden-path sentences, which are characterized by a local ambiguity in the syntactic structure that is resolved later in the sentence, leading to a possible misparse.

The first principle is Minimal Attachment, which stipulates: "Choose the structurally simplest analysis (the one with the fewest additional nodes)." An example is:

(2)   The lawyer knew the answer was wrong.

Here, the parser initially assumes incorrectly that *the answer* is the object of *knew*, because this is a simpler structure than the correct one, in which a missing complementizer *that* appears after *knew*:

(3)   The lawyer knew that the answer was wrong.

The second heuristic principle was Late Closure: "Integrate current input into current constituent (when possible)." An example sentence is:

(4)   After the student moved the chair broke.

Frazier suggested that Minimal Attachment and Late Closure are reflexes of a constrained capacity working memory system. Regarding Late Closure, (Frazier, 1979, p. 39) writes:

> It is a well-attested fact about human memory that the more structured the material to be remembered, the less burden the material will place on immediate memory. Hence, by allowing incoming material to be structured immediately, Late Closure has the effect of reducing the parser's memory load.

Similarly, regarding Minimal Attachment (Frazier, 1979, p. 40) writes:

> [T]he Minimal Attachment strategy not only guarantees minimal structure to be held in memory, but also minimizes rule accessing. Hence, [Minimal Attachment is also an "economical" strategy] in the sense that [it reduces] the computation and memory load of the parser.

The minimal attachment proposal has an interesting twist. Swets et al. (2008) showed that task demands can modulate whether participants engage in any attachment at all. In other words, participants may be engaging in underspecification, and one possible explanation for why they underspecify may have to do with working memory limitations. To understand the phenomenon of underspecification, consider the triplet of sentences shown in (5):

(5)   a. Low attachment:
       The son of the princess who scratched herself in public was terribly humiliated.

1.1 Working Memory in Theories of Sentence Comprehension 5

b. High attachment:
The son of the princess who scratched himself in public was terribly humiliated.

c. Globally ambiguous:
The maid of the princess who scratched herself in public was terribly humiliated.

Under the classical account, discussed for example in Frazier and Rayner (1982), the parser should find it easier to complete low attachment than high attachment (compare 5a and 5b) to minimize effort as discussed above, and in the globally ambiguous case (5c), the parser should automatically take the route of least effort and make a low attachment. As a consequence, the globally ambiguous condition should show the same processing difficulty as the low attachment condition. Surprisingly, the relative clause in the globally ambiguous condition has been found to be read *faster* than in the low attachment condition (Traxler et al., 1998); this phenomenon is called the ambiguity advantage.

Swets and colleagues suggested that the ambiguity advantage could be due to an underspecification process under different task demands. To show this, they carried out a self-paced reading study, asking participants to read sentences like (5). They asked different kinds of questions about these sentences, changing the complexity and frequency of the questions in a between-participants design. Forty-eight participants were asked questions about relative clause attachment on every experimental trial. An example question for the above set of example sentences is *Did the maid/princess/son scratch in public?* A second group of 48 participants was asked superficial questions. An example for the above sentences is *Was anyone humiliated/proud?* A third group of 48 participants was asked superficial questions only occasionally (once every 12 trials). Swets and colleagues found that an ambiguity advantage was observed when questions were superficial, but no ambiguity advantage was observed when the questions were about the relative clause attachment (here, the globally ambiguous and low attachment conditions patterned together, as the classical theory by Frazier would predict). Thus, when participants do not need to engage deeply with the target sentences, they may engage in more superficial processing, to the extent that they may not even build completely connected syntactic structure. Although the driver of underspecification here is externally imposed task demands, working memory limitations may also be an additional factor. In a Spanish reading study using eyetracking, von der Malsburg and Vasishth (2013) suggested that low working memory capacity participants may underspecify more often in the face of temporary ambiguity; also see Traxler (2007).

6   Introduction

1.2   Prediction in Sentence Processing

In his Syntactic Prediction Locality Theory (Gibson, 1998) and his subsequent Dependency Locality Theory, Gibson (2000) formalized the idea that the parser predicts upcoming material, and that there are limits on how much information can be stored. Storage cost has empirical support from several studies; examples are the double centre-embedding work on English by Gibson and Thomas (1997), discussed above, and a Hindi eyetracking corpus study (Husain et al., 2015). A very different perspective on predictive processing was developed through the work of Jurafsky (1996), Hale (2001), and Levy (2008), among others; the assumption here is not that prediction is constrained by working memory limitations, but rather by an underlying probabilistic grammar representation. As a sentence is processed incrementally, an essentially parallel, or ranked parallel set of possible continuations is predicted, and as one transitions from one word to the next, the change in the probability mass of the predicted continuations indexes processing difficulty. Briefly put, rare continuations are hard to process. These prediction-oriented theories represent a distinct class of account that has two characteristics: it has no need for any constraints imposed by working memory, and it only focusses on "forward-looking processes", i.e., predictions about upcoming material. Extreme forms of prediction theories assume, implicitly or explicitly, no limit on the number of proposed continuations (i.e., massively parallel predictions); for discussion, see Boston et al. (2011). Contrast this with the discussion about ambiguity resolution above, where the focus was on the constraints on accessing previously encountered material. For example, when an attachment site for a relative clause is searched for by the parser, the search is directed towards accessing previously processed material. Such "backward-looking processes" could be subject to somewhat different constraints than "forward-looking processes".

Explicit rejections of working-memory based accounts of sentence comprehension difficulty come from the connectionist modelling literature; these can also be seen as a class of prediction-based models. For example, MacDonald and Christiansen (2002) wrote an important critique of Just and Carpenter (1992), who had claimed that high- and low-working memory capacity individuals process sentences differently. Just and Carpenter present data showing that high capacity participants exhibit smaller differences in object vs. subject relative clause difficulty than low-capacity participants.[1] MacDonald and Christiansen argued that the differences in processing difficulty attributed to inherent capacity differences may be due to an interaction between experience

---

[1] It is worth noting here as an aside that capacity was measured using the Daneman and Carpenter (1980) reading span task, which may index experience with language rather than inherent capacity per se (Wells et al., 2009).

1.4 Current Beliefs about Constraints on Sentence Comprehension

with language and biological (neural architectural) factors that have nothing to do with the capacity of a separate working memory system.

1.3 Working Memory and Prediction as Explanations for Processing Difficulty

In summary, memory load and limits on working memory capacity are candidate explanation for certain aspects of language processing, but certain other aspects of processing have a better explanation in terms of probabilistic predictive processes. Much of the inspiration for memory explanations came, either directly or indirectly, from work in cognitive psychology. Decay and similarity-based interference are two key constructs that have been invoked in psycholinguistics in one form or another; these ideas come from research on memory in psychology (Brown, 1958; Keppel and Underwood, 1962; Peterson and Peterson, 1959; Waugh and Norman, 1965). This connection between sentence comprehension difficulty and research on decay and/or interference has been explored in detail by Lewis (1993, 1996), Gibson (2000), and Just and Carpenter (1992). The critical role that prediction plays in human sentence processing was recognized quite early in connection with formal theories of parsing, as discussed in Resnik (1992). The seminal work of Jurafsky (1996) laid the foundations for the use of probabilistic grammatical knowledge in explaining sentence comprehension difficulty; this line of thinking resulted in another important paper by Levy (2008).

1.4 Current Beliefs about Constraints on Sentence Comprehension

Given the above short (and incomplete) survey, some of the broad tentative conclusions that the last 60 years of work on sentence processing can be summarized as follows. Of course, not everyone will agree with this summary; but in our opinion, the claims listed below are relatively well supported by the literature.

(i) The parser builds incremental structural (syntactic) representations during online processing, although the parser may also, under certain circumstances, engage in underspecification of structure or track only local collocational frequencies (Frazier and Rayner, 1982; Swets et al., 2008; Tabor et al., 2004; Traxler et al., 1998).

(ii) The parser probabilistically predicts upcoming material (Hale, 2001; Levy, 2008).

(iii) What is retained in memory and what is predicted during parsing is probably constrained by a working memory component (Gibson, 1998, 2000; Husain et al., 2014, 2015; Safavi et al., 2016).

8   Introduction

(iv) Experience with language affects our probabilistic knowledge of language, and consequently, our comprehension (MacDonald and Christiansen, 2002; Wells et al., 2009).

1.5   Some Gaps in the Sentence Processing Literature

Although the last 60 years have seen significant advances in our understanding of sentence comprehension processes, we see several major gaps in existing work (there may be others; these are just the ones that stood out for us during the modelling work reported here).

1.5.1   The Relative Scarcity of Computationally Implemented Models

The first gap is that, instead of making computational/mathematical modelling the basis for theory development, the field has largely relied on verbally stated models of comprehension processes. This has led to a great deal of vagueness in theory development. Verbally stated theories have the great advantage that nascent ideas can be quickly sketched out. Indeed, computational models usually begin with an informal statement of the key intuitions. In psycholinguistics, researchers stop too often at the verbal theorizing stage and never attempt to implement their models. There are of course exceptions to this: some examples of implemented models are listed below.

(i) Connectionist models: Engelmann and Vasishth (2009); Frank (2009); Linzen and Leonard (2018); MacDonald and Christiansen (2002); Rabovsky and McRae (2014).
(ii) Constraint-based models: McRae et al. (1998).
(iii) Probabilistic parsing models: Hale (2001); Levy (2008); Rasmussen and Schuler (2017).
(iv) Dynamical systems approaches: Cho et al. (2017); Smith et al. (2018); Tabor et al. (2004); Vosse and Kempen (2000).
(v) Computational cognitive models of underspecification: Logačev and Vasishth (2016).
(vi) Models of decision processes in parsing: Hammerly et al. (2019); Parker (2019).

As an aside, we note that, with some rare exceptions, one major problem with much of the modelling has been the lack of publicly available reproducible code that allows the reader to independently evaluate or extend the published model.

Despite the fact that several serious attempts exist at implementing theories as computational models, many theoretical proposals remain unimplemented. Except for the simplest of ideas, it is generally not sufficient to stop at verbal

1.5 Some Gaps in the Sentence Processing Literature

statements. This is because informally stated theories usually have hidden degrees of freedom that allow the researcher to explain away or simply ignore counterexamples. Computational implementations force the researcher to confront the distance between theory and data. Although computational models also have hidden degrees of freedom, these are usually easier to see.

An example of the problems that arise in verbally stated theories comes from the Dependency Locality Theory (Gibson, 2000). Originally, a central tenet of the theory was that only new discourse referents can disrupt dependency completion; in previous work, this point was explicitly brought up by showing that a pronoun, which introduces a given or easily inferable referent, causes less disruption than a newly introduced discourse referent (Warren and Gibson, 2005). Moreover, in the classic description of the model (Gibson, 1998) and in its follow-up revision (Gibson, 2000), the following assumption is adopted: "Although processing all words probably causes some integration cost increment, it is hypothesized here that substantial integration cost increments are caused by processing words indicating new discourse structure" (Gibson, 1998, 12). However, in Gibson and Wu (2013), previously introduced (old) discourse referents are assumed to lead to increased dependency completion cost in exactly the same way that new discourse referents do (Hsiao and Gibson, 2003), without any discussion about the change in the assumptions of the model. This change is actually not an inherently important one for the theory, because one could have easily assumed from the outset that all intervening discourse referents (regardless of whether they are new or old) cause processing difficulty. Nevertheless, the example illustrates that model predictions can be "computed" (in the researcher's mind) without noticing that the model assumptions have changed. A further disadvantage of verbally stated theories is that no quantitative predictions can be derived. This affects the kinds of scientific questions one can ask, and the way that one frames one's predictions. With verbally stated theories, we can only ask questions of the type "Does this effect exist or not?" This kind of framing makes it irrelevant whether the effect is 2 ms or 200 ms in magnitude. As discussed in Section 1.5.4, ignoring the magnitude of the expected effect has important consequences for inference. By contrast, a quantitative modelling approach allows us to focus on how the empirical estimates (and the uncertainty associated with these estimates) match up with the range of predictions from the computational models of interest.

A commonly heard objection to computational modelling is that we don't yet know enough about the process of interest to implement it; a related objection is that an implemented model will miss crucial aspects of the cognitive process of interest. These objections are valid, to some extent. But models should be seen as useful lies that help us see the range of possibilities that could constitute truth (Epstein, 2008). As the word itself suggests, a model is rarely intended to accurately capture every single aspect of reality. The criticism that a model fails

10 Introduction

to capture this or that detail points to an important limitation of the model, but is not a reason to abandon the entire enterprise of model development (Smaldino, 2017).

In contrast to sentence comprehension research, within other areas adjacent to cognitive science – artificial intelligence and mathematical/cognitive psychology – the development of different computational cognitive architectures and frameworks has flourished and has had a major and positive impact on our understanding of the phenomena under study. This is because it is well-understood in these areas that computational models allow the scientist to build detailed process models of human cognitive processes and to investigate the quantitative predictions arising from these models. Prominent examples from classical artificial intelligence research are the SOAR (Laird, 2012) and ACT-R (Anderson et al., 2004) architectures; in psychology, the E-Z Reader (Reichle et al., 2003, 2009) and SWIFT (Engbert et al., 2005; Rabe et al., 2020; Richter et al., 2006) models of eye-movement control stand out as examples of comprehensive architectural frameworks of a particular cognitive process of interest (reading). Cognitive psychology has a rich tradition of such models: the working memory models by Oberauer and Kliegl (2006), Lewandowsky et al. (2008), the 4CAPS architecture (Just et al., 1999; Just and Varma, 2007; Varma, 2016) (www.ccbi.cmu.edu/4CAPS/), and other models (Busemeyer and Diederich, 2010; Farrell and Lewandowsky, 2018; Lee and Wagenmakers, 2014; Lewis, 2000). By contrast, in the narrower field of sentence processing, not as much effort has gone into developing comprehensive architectures; an interesting exception is CC READER (Just and Carpenter, 1992; Just and Varma, 2002).

1.5.2 A Focus on Average Behaviour and Neglect of Individual-Level Differences

The second gap in current work is that the vast majority of the empirical and modelling work has focussed on explaining average behaviour. Researchers have pointed out that the excessive focus on modelling average behaviour is problematic; for example, see the discussion in Kidd et al. (2018).

As Blastland and Spiegelhalter (2014) put it, "The average is an abstraction. The reality is variation." The average response is not sufficiently informative about the true nature of the cognitive process of interest. The focus should be on understanding the causes for average as well as the individual-level behaviour; this will lead to a better understanding of the systematic reasons that lead speakers/comprehenders to show differentiated behaviour. Individual differences have been investigated in some sentence processing studies (e.g., Just and Carpenter, 1992; MacDonald and Christiansen, 2002; Van Dyke et al., 2014), but the field would benefit from making this a routine part of the investigation of the causes of processing difficulty.

1.5.3   The Absence of High-Precision Studies

The third gap in the literature is the absence of properly powered experimental studies. The proliferation of underpowered studies has led to a range of invalid inferences in the literature. The term "invalid inference" here doesn't mean the inferences don't reflect the truth, but rather that they are not supported by the statistical analyses. The most egregious example of invalid inferences is concluding that the null hypothesis is true when the p-value is greater than 0.05.

The underlying reasons for the proliferation of underpowered studies is easy to work out. First, researchers are incentivized to publish "big news" papers as fast as possible; this encourages small sample "microstudies" that seem to lead to groundbreaking discoveries. Second, many of the early discoveries in psycholinguistics were large effects that didn't even need an experiment to establish. An example is the strong garden-path sentence *The horse raced past the barn fell*; one can "feel" the oddness of the sentence even without doing an experiment. Another example is the late closure example mentioned above, *After the student moved the chair broke*; one immediately senses that something is wrong with this sentence. Processing difficulties in such easily discernible effects can be reliably detected even with relatively modest sample sizes. For example, the classic garden-path study by Frazier and Rayner (1982) had only 16 subjects, and 16 items for a four-condition late-closure design, and 16 items for a four-condition minimal attachment design (the late closure/minimal attachment manipulation was between items). This sample size might have been sufficient to detect large effects. But such a sample size is certainly too small to investigate predictability (Vasishth et al., 2018) or memory effects (Jäger et al., 2017, 2020; Mertzen et al., 2020a). For investigations of such subtle phenomena in sentence comprehension, there has been no systematic attempt to assess whether sample sizes used for classical garden-path effects would suffice. The consequence has been that a lot of the data published in psycholinguistics is likely to come from underpowered studies. As we discuss in Section 1.5.4, this has very bad consequences for theory development.

1.5.4   Unclear Desiderata for a Good Model Fit

In psycholinguistics, there are no general standards on how to quantify a good model fit. Sometimes root mean squared deviation is used; this quantifies the average deviation from the observed value. But there are better approaches. We discuss two important criteria below that we feel are appropriate for modelling work in psycholinguistics; both are related and are fundamentally graphical in nature.

The Roberts and Pashler (2000) Criteria In an influential paper, Roberts and Pashler (2000) pointed out that a quantitative model's fit to the data

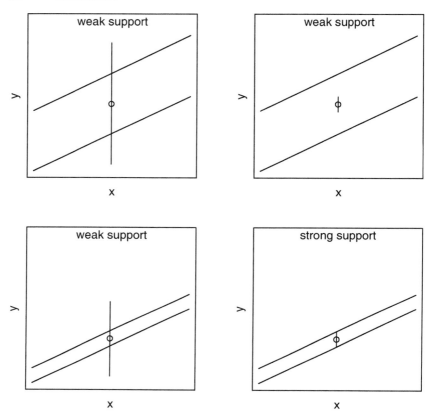

Figure 1.1 A schematic summary of the Roberts and Pashler (2000) discussion regarding what constitutes a good fit of a model to data. The data are represented by the circle (the estimated mean) and the vertical uncertainty interval, and the model predictions by the diagonal parallel lines. If a model predicts a positive correlation between two variables x and y, strong support for the model can only be argued for if both the data and the model predictions are highly constrained: the model must make predictions over a narrow range, and the data must have low uncertainty associated with it.

is only convincing when two conditions are met. First, the model must make sufficiently constrained predictions. Second, the data should have low uncertainty. These criteria are illustrated in the schematic plot shown in Figure 1.1. The two diagonal lines illustrate a hypothetical range of correlations between two variables x and y that are predicted by some model. The uncertainty (variability) in the correlation can be high or low. High variability is shown by widely

1.5 Some Gaps in the Sentence Processing Literature 13

separated lines and amounts to a relatively unconstrained prediction from the model. Roberts and Pashler (2000) make the point that a model's predictions are not going to be impressive if they allow just about any outcome. A more tightly limited prediction will pose a stringent test for the theory. Similarly, a good fit to a model's predictions will be unimpressive and unconvincing if the data have high uncertainty; in practice, what high uncertainty means is that the standard error of the estimated effect is large.

Thus, for a model fit to be convincing, two conditions must be satisfied: the model must make highly constrained predictions and the data must deliver estimates with low uncertainty.

Why Is High Uncertainty Undesirable in the Estimate from the Data? It seems obvious enough that a model should not allow any possible empirical outcome; such a model is not particularly useful because it can "explain" any outcome. Examples from psychology of models that can predict any outcome are discussed in Roberts and Pashler (2000). It is less clear intuitively why empirical estimates of effects need to be measured with precision. As researchers, we are trained to only check whether an effect is statistically significant or not; it is considered irrelevant whether the standard error of the effect is large or not. Here, we show why the precision of the estimate (roughly speaking, the standard error) is a crucial component when evaluating theoretical predictions. The *p*-value is in most cases useless, especially when considered as the sole piece of information from a data analysis (Wasserstein and Lazar, 2016). The limitations of using *p*-values alone for inference is by no means a new insight, but it has been generally ignored in psychology and linguistics.

Estimates of an effect that have high uncertainty (wide standard errors) are also studies that are likely to be underpowered. This has all the bad consequences that come with low power, most dramatically Type M and S errors (Gelman and Carlin, 2014). Type M(agnitude) error refers to an overestimation of the effect magnitude, and Type S(ign) error refers to an incorrect sign (incorrect relative to the predicted or expected effect). Both types of error occur when power is low, as the following simulation demonstrates. Suppose that a true effect in a reading time experiment has magnitude 20 ms, and that standard deviation is 150 ms. In such a situation, a paired *t*-test with a sample size of 26 yields 10% power. If one were to repeatedly run an experiment with this sample size, as shown in the upper part of Figure 1.2, apart from there being many null results, *all* significant results will be either overestimates or will have the wrong sign (or both). By contrast, as shown in the lower part of the figure, when power is high (say, 80% or higher), most significant effects will be close to the true value.

Overestimates or effects with possibly the wrong sign are problematic for the modeller, because the target for modelling itself is misleading.

14   Introduction

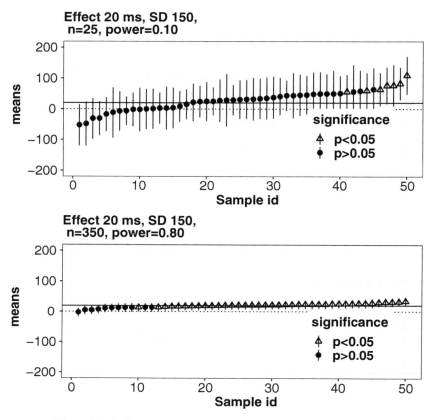

Figure 1.2 A demonstration of Type M and S error. Low power studies will yield overestimates and/or incorrect signs whenever a result is significant.

The Type M/S error issue is not just a theoretical statistical point; it has real practical consequences. For example, consider the eyetracking studies reported in Levy and Keller (2013). These studies claim to show evidence for surprisal effects (Hale, 2001; Levy, 2008), but seven replication attempts, including one higher powered study (100 participants vs. the original 28 participants) consistently failed to reproduce the claimed effect (Vasishth et al., 2018). It is quite possible that many such underpowered studies form the basis for theory development in psycholinguistics. We return to this point later when carrying out model evaluations on published interference effects.

Apart from the incorrect inferences that arise due to Type M/S error, another major problem in psycholinguistics is statistically incorrect inferences based on null results. Null results under repeated sampling can only be interpreted

1.5 Some Gaps in the Sentence Processing Literature

if there is a demonstration of sufficient statistical power (Hoenig and Heisey, 2001) computed before conducting the studies. In the past, power has never been considered in such studies, but the situation has improved in recent years (e.g., Stack et al., 2018). This point about null results in low-power experiments is demonstrated in the upper part of Figure 1.2. If a researcher were to run an experiment with 10% power repeatedly, they would usually get a null result. Accepting the null result would be a mistake here, because the true estimate is not zero; it is just impossible to detect accurately using statistical significance as a criterion for discovery. Such incorrect inferences are quite common in psycholinguistics. The problems with such misinterpretations have been brought up repeatedly in the psychology literature (e.g., Cohen, 1962). But these problems with incorrect inferences from low power studies have generally have been ignored; a likely reason for this misuse of statistical theory is the cursory statistical education usually available in psycholinguistic curricula.

The Freedman-Spiegelhalter Approach In Bayesian approaches to clinical trials, an approach for evaluating predictions exists that is closely related to the Robert and Pashler criteria discussed above.[2] Simply put, the proposal is to posit a range of predicted values and then compare the estimates from the data with this predicted range. This method is discussed in Freedman et al. (1984) and Spiegelhalter et al. (1994). In recent years, this idea has been re-introduced into psychology by Kruschke (2014) as the region of practical equivalence (ROPE) approach.

The essential idea behind interpreting data using a ROPE is summarized in Figure 1.3. Assume that we have a model prediction spanning $[-36, -9]$ ms (Jäger et al., 2020). If we run our experiment until we have the same width as the predicted range (here, $36 - 9 = 27$ ms), then there are five possible uncertainty (confidence) intervals that can be observed; see Figure 1.3. The observed interval can be:

A. to the right of the predicted interval.
B. to the left of the predicted interval.
C. to the right of the predicted interval but overlapping with it.
D. to the left of the predicted interval but overlapping with it.
E. within the predicted range.

Only situation E shows complete consistency with the quantitative prediction. A and B are inconsistent with the model prediction; and C and D are inconclusive. There is a sixth possibility: one may not be able to collect data with the desired precision, and in that case, the observed interval could overlap

---

[2] The following section is from Vasishth and Gelman (2019), which is available under a CC-BY 4.0 Attribution International license.

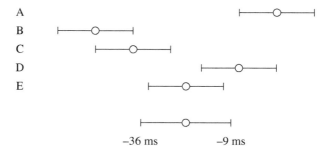

Figure 1.3 The five possible outcomes when using the null region or "region of practical equivalence" method for decision-making (Kruschke, 2015). Outcomes A and B are inconsistent with the quantitative predictions of the theory; C and D are inconclusive; and E is consistent with the quantitative theoretical prediction. Figure reproduced from Vasishth and Gelman (2019).

with the predicted range but may be much wider than it (here, the width of the predicted range is 27 ms). That would be an uninformative, low-precision study.

In contrast to the ROPE approach described above, what models in psycholinguistics usually predict is the sign of an effect, but not the magnitude or the uncertainty. This is one reason why null hypothesis significance testing is so popular: the question whether an effect is "present" vs. "absent" is easily answered by looking at the *p*-value.

But a prediction like "the effect is present" is not particularly useful because this implies that an effect with estimated mean 500 ms that is statistically significant would be consistent with the prediction just as well as a significant 5 ms effect. However, a 5 ms effect may have no special relevance for theory development.

If one really insists on using language like "the effect is present/absent," a more conservative way to proceed is to run the study until a Bayes factor of 10 (either in favour of the null or the alternative) is achieved. This is generally a more conservative approach than using the *p*-value with a cut-off of 0.05 because the bar for drawing a binary conclusion is much higher. Here, the fact that Bayes factor can be highly sensitive to the prior specification complicates the interpretation of a Bayes factor-based analysis. See Nicenboim and Vasishth (2016); Nicenboim et al. (2021) for discussion of the underlying theory of Bayes factors and its application in psycholinguistics.

1.6 The Goals of This Book

This book is a first attempt to address the gaps discussed in the previous section from a very particular perspective. In the following pages, we will spell out a theory of sentence processing (Lewis and Vasishth, 2005) that uses (or is inspired by) a specific cognitive architecture, ACT-R (Anderson et al., 2004), which has been designed for modelling general cognitive processes. ACT-R is a reasonable choice for a framework because it is a mature architecture that has been widely used in artificial intelligence, human-computer interaction, psychology, and other areas of cognitive science to model human information processing (for examples, see the literature listed on the home page for the architecture: http://act-r.psy.cmu.edu/).

It is important to keep in mind that this is not a book about sentence processing models in general, but about one particular class of models, those relating to retrieval processes. The reader should therefore not be surprised to find that the discussion focusses on one kind of modelling approach.

1.6.1 Providing Open Source Model Code

One of the great failures of psycholinguistics has been that model code, as well as experimental data, are rarely made public (there have been, of course, some exceptions, particularly in recent years). A major goal of this book is to help change this unfortunate culture. This book can be seen as providing the reader with a complete report of all the modelling work on retrieval processes that we have done between 2005 and 2020. All the code and data associated with the modelling reported here can be reproduced by the reader, and extended and used to test novel predictions of the models. Of course, we recognize that code rot – the slow deterioration and increasing unusability of software over time – is inevitable. It is highly likely that five years from now the code provided will not work as expected, unless the reader can obtain the ACT-R, lisp, R, and Stan versions we used in creating the models. Even if the code fails to run some years from now, our hope is that at least the code can be adapted or rewritten to reproduce and extend the models presented here.

If the reader intends to run the code in this book, they should install ACT-R 6.0 and the R packages indicated in the source files for the book available from the GitHub repository (https://vasishth.github.io/RetrievalModels).

1.6.2 Modelling Average Effects as Well as Individual Differences

The book will discuss the modelling of both average effects and of individual differences. Specifically, we will illustrate how we could investigate (a) the influence of individual differences in working memory capacity on parsing; (b) the role of parsing strategy, including task-dependent underspecification; (c) the interaction between individual working memory capacity, grammatical knowledge, and parsing; (d) the interaction between the eye-movement control system and sentence comprehension; and (e) how individual-level differences

18   Introduction

in the behaviour of individuals with aphasia might be explained in terms of model parameters.

1.6.3 Developing a Set of Modelling and Empirical Benchmarks for Future Model Comparison

A further goal of the book is to provide the next generation of researchers with a synthesis of the modelling and empirical work that followed the publication of the article by Lewis and Vasishth (2005). Our hope is that others will be able to build and improve on the present work, either falsifying or extending the empirical support for the model claims and thereby advancing our understanding of the important open theoretical issues, or developing competing models that can outperform the ones presented here. Some attempts at developing competing models that aim to outperform the models presented in the present book already exist (Cho et al., 2017; Parker, 2019; Rasmussen and Schuler, 2017; Smith et al., 2018). One problem common to all these models is that they take up one or two empirical phenomena of interest (a common choice is subject vs. object relatives, usually in English). This often leads to overfitting the model to a very narrow set of facts. A remarkable number of modelling studies (including our own!) limit themselves to narrow topics like relative clause processing. What is missing in the field is a set of benchmark empirical tests that a model can be evaluated on in order to demonstrate superior fit to data, relative to some baseline model. As a first step towards developing such a benchmark, we provide in one place the data-sets from reading studies on interference effect that happen to be publicly available.

Because the modelling reported here was carried out over many years (most of the work was done between 2005 and 2020), many computational challenges had to be overcome. For example, the ACT-R architecture itself is continuously evolving independently of the sentence processing architecture we work with. These version changes in ACT-R necessitated a near-complete rewrite of the modelling constructs. As a consequence, the original Lewis and Vasishth model's underlying machinery also changed in subtle ways. This evolution of ACT-R will remain a challenge for future researchers. A further problem that we encountered was that lisp is not a widely used programming language anymore; this makes the ACT-R model less accessible to researchers interested in using it. Fortunately, researchers have recently developed viable alternative implementations in python (Brasoveanu and Dotlačil, 2020), which may be easier to maintain and develop further. The lesson to be learnt here is that developing a sustainable code base, and preventing code rot, is a major challenge in any large programming project like this one, and the user/reader needs to be aware of this limitation and to be patient when adapting or using legacy code. One insight to be gained here is that perhaps some compromises are necessary in order to make the theoretical machinery more accessible to the wider community. It is possible to investigate the core principles of the model without implementing a fully fledged model; this can be done by using code written in the programming language R. We provide such an implementation, along with a Shiny app that allows the reader to compute simple effects without doing any coding at all.[3]

Another issue we faced was that we studied different research problems piecemeal. For example, a model integrating eye-movement control and parsing is reported in Chapter 5, but this model has not been regression-tested with the core phenomena discussed in Chapter 4 or other chapters. Future generations working on this framework could (and should) develop a more systematic testing framework, so that empirical coverage is incremental in the sense that the model's performance on all previously modelled data-sets and phenomena is evaluated again when exploring an extension of the architecture.

One further area where the present work fell short was that modelling should ideally always be comparative; a baseline model is necessary to evaluate a particular model's relative performance. In more recent work, reported in Chapters 7 and 8, we have attempted to shift the focus towards evaluating competing models' performance on the same data-set. In future work, this should be standard practice. For example, an alternative competing model of eye-movement control and parsing would be very useful in order to better understand the relative performance of the model presented in Chapter 5.

Regarding the data used in this book, we focus almost exclusively on reading data, from self-paced reading or self-paced listening, and eyetracking studies. This is because we primarily set out to model the reading process; an exception is the modelling of visual world data reported in Patil et al. (2016a). We chose reading times as a convenient starting point because the Lewis and Vasishth (2005) model delivers predictions in terms of retrieval time and retrieval accuracy, and dependent measures in reading studies (e.g., fixation durations, comprehension accuracy) map relatively straightforwardly to this measure. We will therefore not discuss the large body of research using other methods such as electroencephalography (EEG) and the visual world paradigm. It is of course important to develop computational models that can be related to data that come from these methods. We hope that future generations will take up that task.

1.7   Looking Ahead

It may be useful to briefly summarize the structure of the remainder of this book. Chapter 2 reviews the range of empirical phenomena that form the basis for a large chunk of the modelling, and discusses the published empirical findings

---

[3] https://engelmann.shinyapps.io/inter-act/

20 Introduction

regarding these phenomena. One of the key takeaways from this chapter is that published studies on these phenomena are likely to be underpowered and therefore not sufficiently informative. Chapter 3 presents the core ACT-R model, as developed in the Lewis and Vasishth (2005) paper; Chapters 4 and 5 summarize two recent extensions. The first extension (Chapter 4) modifies the core model to account for linguistic prominence of items in memory and for so-called multi-associative cues. The second extension (Chapter 5) integrates an eye-movement control model (EMMA, a simplified version of the E-Z Reader model) with the parsing model and evaluates its performance. Chapter 6 then presents an evaluation of the model incorporating eye-movement control on psycholinguistic data on reanalysis and underspecification effects, and shows how individual differences in capacity can be explained by the model. One important question that needs to be answered is: how does the Lewis and Vasishth model fare in comparison to a competing model of retrieval processes? This is the topic of Chapter 7, which covers a model evaluation, using an implementation of the direct-access model of McElree as a baseline. Finally, Chapter 8 discusses the model's ability to explain individual-level differences in deficits in sentence comprehension in aphasia. The concluding chapter takes stock of the achievements and limitations of the work presented in the preceding chapters.

2 Dependencies in Sentence Comprehension

2.1 Memory Processes in Sentence Comprehension

Cognitive psychology has a rich history of investigating human memory processes. A typical experiment in cognitive psychology might involve getting participants to study pairs of words in succession and then asking them to recall the second word given the first, or to recall the first word given the second. Using such experimental paradigms, psychologists have developed many theories about how human memory works. For sentence processing, especially interesting are theories explaining why we forget material that we have previously seen.

A dominant explanation for forgetting is interference: the association between multiple items in memory leads to competition among them and the subsequent inability to retrieve the correct item. Anderson (1974) suggested that interference is affected by the total number of associated links in memory; he refers to this number as the fan. The larger the fan, the greater the interference. Following Dillon (2011), we will refer to the processing difficulty arising from the fan effect as *inhibitory interference*. Figure 2.1 shows a schematic illustration of the fan effect. Suppose an experiment is carried out where a participant is shown a grey circle, triangle, and square, and the participant's task is to identify the grey square. The participant initiates a search, looking for an object that is grey and a square; these are the cues used for a search. Because there are three items that match the cue grey, the fan is three. Here, identifying the target object (the grey square) will be slower compared to a case where the circle and triangle are not grey.

Apart from interference arising from the fan effect, many other interesting generalizations have emerged from the study of memory in psychology. Some that seem to be important for sentence processing are the following:

(i) Recency and primacy effects (Gibson et al., 1996; Nairne, 1988)
(ii) Pro- and retroactive interference (Keppel and Underwood, 1962; Lewis, 1996; Watkins and Watkins, 1975)
(iii) Misretrieval of items from memory (Patson and Husband, 2016)

22   Dependencies in Sentence Comprehension

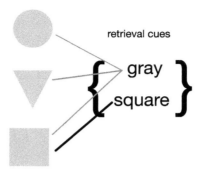

Figure 2.1 A schematic illustration of the fan effect. Searching for an object that is grey and a square (the target item) is more difficult when competing items have one or more features matching cues used for identifying the target item.

(iv) Reactivation of the memorial representation due to repeated accesses from memory (Vasishth and Lewis, 2006)
(v) Richer encoding of an item in memory leading to easier access, due to increased prominence (Hofmeister, 2007, 2011; Hofmeister and Vasishth, 2014)
(vi) Shared features between multiple items in memory, degrading memory representations (Nairne, 1990; Oberauer and Kliegl, 2006; Vasishth et al., 2017a).

Despite this apparently rich connection between sentence processing and the findings of cognitive psychology, it is reasonable to question whether these generalizations from psychology have anything to do with constraints on sentence processing. A priori, the answer could well be: not much. Unlike memorizing unrelated items in a psychology experiment, the words that appear in a sentence occur in a particular context: syntax, semantics, pragmatics, discourse, gesture, prosody, and possibly also facial expressions together impose structure and add context in a way that cannot be compared to simple list memorization and recall. For example, consider a task where a participant is asked to memorize word pairs like

(6) reporter-hired, editor-admitted, article-write

The word associations that the participant would build up in reading these words without any surrounding context will be quite different from the situation when one reads them in a full sentence:

2.2 Dependency Completion in Sentence Processing 23

(7) The editor who hired the reporter to write the article admitted his mistake

What is similar between word pair memorization and the above sentence is that associations between the same sets of words need to be built. But the differences from word pair memorization stand out: the nature of the associations between the words in the sentence is much richer and more constrained compared to the association in the word pair context. The word associations within a sentence are clearly grounded in a lifetime of experience with the real world and with the grammar of the language in question.

Seen in this way, a priori it seems unlikely that generalizations about memory derived from having participants memorize random lists of words could apply to a structured information processing task such as sentence comprehension. Nevertheless, psycholinguists have investigated the possibility that these generalizations about memory processes also come into play in sentence parsing. Under this view, some, but not all, aspects of the memory system are assumed to affect syntactic structure building and interpretation.

In the next section, we survey the literature on how constraints on memory might play a role in the formation of dependencies between words in a sentence context.

2.2 Dependency Completion in Sentence Processing

Who did what is a central component of comprehending the meaning of a sentence. We will refer to the process of connecting co-dependents for interpretation as dependency completion. This can be seen as a word-association process not unlike the one studied in memory research in psychology, but with the crucial difference that the associations lead to the construction of structured representations.

Completing a dependency crucially involves retrieving a co-dependent element that resides in memory in a heightened state of activation, usually because it has been read or heard in the recent past. This retrieval process is widely assumed to be driven by a cue-based, content-addressable search (McElree et al., 2003). For example, the verb *slept* would generally require an animate subject; one retrieval cue here would therefore be animacy. Another example is number marking on the auxiliary verb; the sentence *The key is on the table* has a singular-marked auxiliary verb which, due to the subject-verb number agreement constraint in English, needs a singular-marked subject.

In such retrieval situations, if more than one noun is present that has a feature that matches the retrieval cue, retrieving the correct noun has been argued to become more difficult. Here, we will refer to the correct target for retrieval as the target noun, and the interfering noun or nouns as the distractor(s).

24   Dependencies in Sentence Comprehension

As discussed by Lewis (1996), there are in principle two possible serial order configurations for the target and the distractor(s): the distractor noun can intervene between the target and the verb, or the distractor can precede the target noun. Following the terminology from memory research in cognitive psychology, Lewis (1996) refers to these configurations as proactive and retroactive interference, respectively. As an example, consider the eyetracking study by Van Dyke and McElree (2011). As shown in Example 8, the critical region is the verb *compromised*. Assuming that this verb takes an animate noun as subject, at the verb the animate subject *attorney* must be retrieved. In (8b), the animate distractor noun *witness* appears before the target noun, leading to a proactive interference configuration. The baseline condition here is (8a), which has an inanimate distractor noun *motion*. Retroactive interference arises in (8d) because the distractor *witness* appears between the target noun and the verb; the baseline condition here is (8c).

(8)   a. Proactive interference: Low interference
           The judge / who had declared that / the **motion** / was inappropriate
           / realized that the **attorney** / in the case / **compromised** …

       b. Proactive interference: High interference
           The judge / who had declared that / the **witness** / was inappropriate
           / realized that the **attorney** / in the case / **compromised** …

       c. Retroactive interference: Low interference
           The **attorney** / who the judge realized / had declared that / the
           motion / was inappropriate / **compromised** …

       d. Retroactive interference: High interference
           The **attorney** / who the judge realized / had declared that / the
           witness / was inappropriate / **compromised** …

In the above example, interference is argued to lead to slowdowns at the verb. Pro- and retroactive configurations can also lead to facilitatory effects, if there is a partial match with a proper subset of the retrieval cues triggered at a verb. An example is the study by Wagers et al. (2009). The authors investigated ungrammatical sentences that can lead to illusions of grammaticality due to a partial feature match between plural number marking on the distractor noun and the verb's plural feature. The distractor *musicians* (in the proactive interference condition 9b) and *cells* (in the retroactive condition 9d) can lead to an illusion of grammaticality, leading to faster reading times at the auxiliary (relative to the respective baseline conditions).

(9)   a. Proactive interference, distractor mismatch
           *The musician who the reviewer praise so highly will …

2.2 Dependency Completion in Sentence Processing 25

   b. Proactive interference, distractor match
     *The musicians who the reviewer praise so highly will ...
   c. Retroactive interference, distractor mismatch
     *The key to the cell (unsurprisingly) were rusty from many years
     of disuse
   d. Retroactive interference, distractor match
     *The key to the cells (unsurprisingly) were rusty from many years
     of disuse

Apart from the work mentioned above, pro- and retroactive interference configurations have not been systematically studied in sentence processing; this is an important gap in the literature on interference.

We turn next to a typology of linguistic dependencies that have been investigated in the reading literature. We limit the discussion to work on reading (self-paced reading and eyetracking) because the mapping between reading time and the predictions of the models under consideration in this book is relatively straightforward to define.

Primarily because there is empirical data available from reading studies on these dependency types, we will focus on three basic classes of dependency:

(i) **Subject-verb non-agreement dependencies**. These dependencies involve the grammatical subject of a verb. A simple example would be *The senator read the report*. Here, *senator* is subject of the verb *read*. The reason these are referred to as "non-agreement" dependencies is to distinguish them from subject-verb dependencies in which the verb has an overt number marking that must match that of the subject (at least in subject-agreement languages).

(ii) **Subject-verb number agreement**. As mentioned above, here, the verb carries number marking that must (in the languages considered here, usually English) agree with that of the subject. A classic example is *The keys to the cabinets are on the table*, where the key dependency is that between *keys* and *are*. These subject-verb number agreement constructions are treated separately from the subject-verb non-agreement dependencies because they behave very differently, and the empirical data pose some interesting problems for sentence processing models (especially the ones presented in this book).

(iii) **Reflexives and reciprocals**. These dependencies arise between antecedents and reflexives like English *herself* or Mandarin *ziji*; and reciprocals like English *each other*. These dependencies are special because they involve the binding theory, a central construct in linguistic theory; empirically, what's interesting is that they seem to show distinct patterns of dependency completion time than the other types mentioned above.

26   Dependencies in Sentence Comprehension

2.3   Subject-Verb Non-Agreement Dependencies

Julie Van Dyke has carried out a comprehensive set of experiments which suggest that inhibitory interference effects arise when a grammatical subject needs to be connected to a verb and one or more other nouns in memory share certain features with the subject noun.

As an example, consider the self-paced reading study carried out by Van Dyke and McElree (2006). They showed participants sentences like (10). Before participants saw the target sentence, they were either asked to memorize three words, here *table, sink, truck* (memory-load condition) or not asked to memorize any words (no-memory-load condition). Every sentence was followed by a question like *Did the guy live by the sea?*

(10)   a.   No-interference condition
              It was the boat that the guy who lived by the sea sailed in two sunny days.

        b.   Interference condition
              It was the boat that the guy who lived by the sea fixed in two sunny days.

In the memory-load condition, participants showed longer reading times at the word *fixed* vs. *sailed*; by comparison, in the no-load condition, no difference was seen between the two words. Van Dyke and McElree's conclusion was that this effect was due to increased similarity-based interference at the verb *fixed*: the reader had to retrieve the subject *boat*, but also had three interfering words in memory (*table, sink, truck*) that could potentially be subjects of the verb *fixed*. These interfering words cause slowdowns in the dependency-completion at the verb. As the authors put it (p. 163): "Reading times for … the locus of the interference manipulation … provided the critical test of our retrieval interference hypothesis. We found clear support for retrieval interference from the significant effect of interference and the significant interaction in this region, which revealed that the interference effect was linked to the difference between the two sentence types in the Load conditions."

One difficulty here is that the claim above is based on a statistically non-significant result (the interaction has min $F'(1,68) = 1.44$, $p = 0.23$; 56 participants), and the interaction between load and interference also failed to show an effect in a subsequent attempt by Van Dyke et al. (2014) (estimate -10 ms, $SE = 15$; 65 participants). In the Van Dyke et al. (2014) paper, there isn't enough information to determine whether the direction of the effect is identical to that of the original study. In a recent larger-sample replication attempt involving English (Mertzen et al., 2020a), we failed to find an interaction between load and interference in total reading time, although we do see some evidence for the interaction in first-pass reading time. Mertzen et al. (2020a)

2.3 Subject-Verb Non-Agreement Dependencies

also carried out eyetracking experiments in parallel on German and Russian, but these languages didn't show any evidence of the expected interaction in any eyetracking dependent measure.

In subsequent work, Van Dyke (2007) conducted eyetracking reading studies in which sentences like (11, 12) were shown. The labels on each sentence type are explained below.

(11) a. LoSyn, LoSem
        The worker was surprised that the resident who was living near the dangerous warehouse was complaining about the investigation.

     b. HiSyn, HiSem
        The worker was surprised that the resident who said that the neighbour was dangerous was complaining about the investigation.

(12) a. HiSyn, LoSem
        The worker was surprised that the resident who said that the warehouse was dangerous was complaining about the investigation.

     b. LoSyn, HiSem
        The worker was surprised that the resident who was living near the dangerous neighbour was complaining about the investigation.

This experiment had a 2×2 factorial design which varied whether a noun (*warehouse/neighbour*) that appears between a subject-verb dependency (*resident–was complaining*) was a grammatical subject (High Syntactic interference) or not (Low Syntactic interference), and was animate (High Semantic interference) or not (Low Semantic interference). The research question was the following: when a subject-verb dependency is to be completed at the verb phrase *was complaining*, can a distractor noun (such as *neighbour*) that overlaps in syntactic and semantic features with the grammatical subject (*resident*) cause greater difficulty in completing the dependency at the verb? Van Dyke found that syntactic interference effects occurred earlier than semantic interference effects: when the distractor noun was in subject position inside the relative clause (compared to non-subject position), an interference effect showed up earlier compared to the case where the distractor noun was animate. This suggests that syntactic cues may have priority or may be weighted more heavily than semantic cues.

As mentioned above, Van Dyke and McElree (2011) also investigated interference in proactive and retroactive configurations (see Example 8 above), and argued that retroactive interference effects are stronger than proactive interference effects.

All the experiments by Van Dyke and colleagues investigated sentences with a subject-verb dependency, where the retrieval cues were either syntactic or semantic in nature: in other words, the target noun was either a grammatical

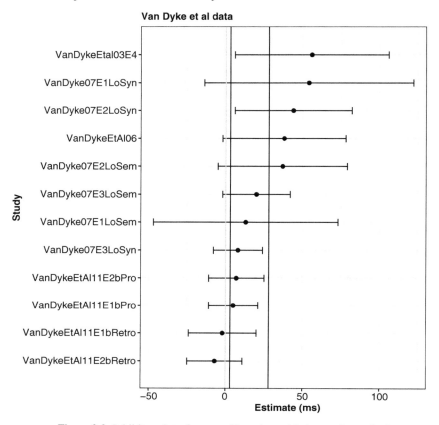

Figure 2.2 Inhibitory interference effects (sorted in increasing order by magnitude) in reading studies by Van Dyke and colleagues. The grey vertical lines show the 95% credible interval for the meta-analysis estimate of the effect.

subject or object, or animate or inanimate. Jäger et al. (2017) assembled the estimates and standard errors for all the studies carried out by Van Dyke and colleagues. As shown in Figure 2.2, these studies tend to show a consistent pattern: with some exceptions, when a distractor noun is present that has features matching the retrieval cues of the verb, an increase in processing time (reading time) is observed. We can summarize these results by computing the posterior distribution of the effect, using a random effects meta-analysis; see Jäger et al. (2017) for details. The meta-analysis shows that the presence of a distractor increases reading time at the verb by 13 ms, with a 95% credible interval of [3,28] ms. Note, however, that a recent pair of eyetracking

2.3 Subject-Verb Non-Agreement Dependencies

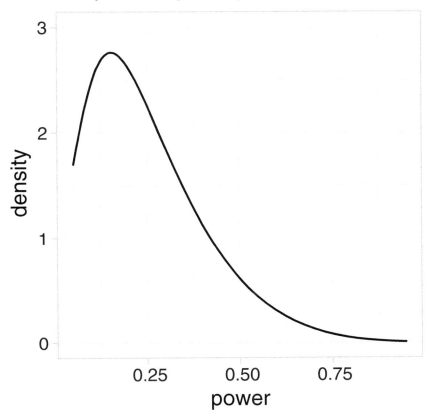

Figure 2.3 Distribution of power (paired, two-sided t-test) assuming that the effect has normal distribution with mean 13 and standard deviation 6, the standard deviation ranges from 75 to 100 ms, and the subject sample size is 60.

experiments by Cunnings and Sturt (2018) investigating fan effects found no evidence for inhibitory interference.

Such a failure to find interference effects is no surprise; if the true effect really is in the range [3,28] ms, as Van Dyke's work suggests, then, assuming a standard deviation of 75 ms for reading times (eyetracking or self-paced reading) and a sample size of 60 participants, power is in the range from 6% to 81% (see Figure 2.3 for the power distribution, assuming that standard deviation ranges from 75 to 100 ms and subject sample size is 60). Given that sample sizes are often much lower than 60 participants, power is probably much lower. For example, Cunnings and Sturt had 48 participants; such a sample size would result in power in the range from 6% to 72% for a standard deviation of 75.

30   Dependencies in Sentence Comprehension

Thus, with such small sample sizes, an absence of an interference effect is not possible to interpret.

A widely accepted explanation for the inhibitory interference effects is that the retrieval cue cannot uniquely identify the target noun, and this leads to increased processing difficulty due to spreading activation; this is the so-called fan effect (Anderson et al., 2004).

Interestingly, in certain situations, subject-verb dependency configurations can also show facilitatory interference. One plausible explanation for this is a so-called race process (Raab, 1962) triggered by a partial feature match: a subset of the retrieval cues triggered at the verb match with a distractor noun and another subset of cues match with the target, leading to a race process that results in an occasional misretrieval of the distractor (Logačev and Vasishth, 2015; Nicenboim and Vasishth, 2018). The race process is discussed further in Section 3.2.1.

For example, evidence for such a facilitatory interference effect in grammatical subject-verb dependencies comes from Cunnings and Sturt (2018). They conducted two eyetracking (reading) studies in which they manipulated the plausibility of the correct dependent of the verb and the plausibility of the distractor noun. They showed that when the correct dependent is implausible, the distractor's plausibility influences reading time at the verb is faster when the distractor is a plausible subject of the verb. Faster total reading times are observed at the verb *shattered* in (13a) compared to (13b). In their experiment 1, the facilitation effect at the verb was estimated to be -22 ms, $[-4, -42]$, and in experiment 2, it was -19 ms, $[1, -40]$.

(13)   a. What Sue remembered was the letter that the butler with the cup accidently shattered today in the dining room.

       b. What Sue remembered was the letter that the butler with the tie accidently shattered today in the dining room.

One explanation for this facilitation is in terms of a lognormal race (although this is not how Cunnings and Sturt explain it): the verb *shattered* searches for a subject noun with the property "can be shattered", and in some trials ends up incorrectly retrieving the noun *cup* as the subject; the correct subject is *letter*. Thus, the observed facilitation could be explained by assuming occasional misretrievals of the distractor due to a partial feature match. The process of partial matching leading to occasional misretrievals is graphically summarized in Figure 2.4.

Subject-verb dependencies have also been investigated in the context of number agreement. Here, the retrieval cue of interest is number marking: at least in English, the subject must agree in number with the verb. Dependencies involving number agreement exhibit some interesting peculiarities, as we discuss next.

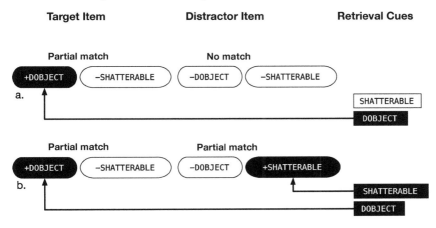

Figure 2.4 Visualization of two conditions in the Cunnings and Sturt (2018) experiment and the predictions of the cue-based retrieval model. The verb *shattered* attempts to retrieve an item in memory that is a direct object and has the property "is shatterable". In both the (a) and (b) conditions shown, the direct object (which is the target noun that should be retrieved) matches the direct object retrieval cue. However, in (b), the distractor noun matches the "is shatterable" cue. As a consequence, in (b), both the target and distractor nouns enter into a race, and whichever item is non-deterministically retrieved is the winner of the race. This race process leads to a faster reading time at the verb *shattered* in (b) vs. (a).

2.4 Subject-Verb Number Agreement

It is well-known that sentences such as (14a) can lead to an illusion of grammaticality. The sentence is ungrammatical because of the lack of number agreement between the subject *key* and the auxiliary *are*. Note that the second noun, *cabinets*, and the auxiliary *are* agree in number, but no syntactic agreement is possible between these two elements.

(14) a. *The key to the cabinets are on the table.

b. *The key to the cabinet are on the table.

32   Dependencies in Sentence Comprehension

Many sentence comprehension studies have shown that the illusion has the effect that the auxiliary *are* is read faster in (14a) compared to the equally ungrammatical sentence (14b); in the latter case, the second noun (*cabinet*) is singular and does not agree with the auxiliary in number.

In sentence comprehension, one explanation for the agreement attraction effect is in terms of cue-based retrieval. Wagers et al. (2009) suggested that when the parser encounters the verb, the mismatch between the expected number of the verb and the actual number marking triggers a retrieval process. In the above example, the verb triggers a search for a plural-marked noun that is the subject of the verb. This leads to occasional misretrievals of the only plural marked noun in the sentence, *cabinets*. An obvious problem with this account is that it seems unlikely that the reader interprets the sentence to mean that the cabinets are on the table; of course, such an objection assumes that the reader is engaged in fully interpreting the sentence, which itself may be a questionable assumption (Ferreira et al., 2002; Sanford and Sturt, 2002); we return to the question of underspecification later (Chapter 6). Note that the explanation for subject-verb number agreement conditions is the same as that for Cunnings and Sturt's data for their sentences (13 above). One important difference between the Wagers et al. design and that of Cunnings and Sturt is that in the latter it is very plausible that the reader incorrectly retrieves the distractor as a subject (although Cunnings and Sturt did not check whether readers did in fact misinterpret the sentence). It is not clear whether such a misretrieval occurs in subject-verb number agreement.

Another possible explanation for the agreement attraction effect is in terms of the feature overwriting model of Nairne (1990). In Example (14b), both the nouns are marked singular, whereas in Example (14a) the nouns have different number marking. As discussed in Villata and Franck (2016), the similarity in number of the two nouns in (14b) could be the underlying cause for increased processing difficulty compared to (14a). The identical number marking in (14b) could lead to increased confusability between the two nouns, leading to longer reading times at the moment when a subject noun is to be accessed at the auxiliary verb. The feature overwriting model of Nairne (1990) formalizes this idea. To quote (p. 252): "*An individual feature of a primary memory trace is assumed to be overwritten, with probability F, if that feature is matched in a subsequently occurring event. Interference occurs on a feature-by-feature basis, so that, if feature b matches feature a, the latter will be lost with probability F.*" This proposal can be formalized as a hierarchical mixture model (Vasishth et al., 2017a), as we discuss in Section 7.3.

A third explanation for agreement attraction is in terms of the Marking and Morphing (MM) model; this model is intended to explain effects in production rather than comprehension. Under the MM model, attraction arises due to ambiguous encoding of the number marking on a subject phrase (e.g., Eberhard

2.4 Subject-Verb Number Agreement

et al., 2005). In MM, number is considered to be a continuum and not a binary value. The feature "plural" from the distractor noun (i.e., the attractor) spreads activation to the root node of the subject noun phrase, causing it to become more "plural". The extent to which the subject noun phrase becomes plural depends on factors such as the number of distractor nouns with the plural feature, and how near they are to the subject noun phrase's root node in the syntactic tree. Hammerly et al. (2019) provide an implementation of MM that seeks to explain grammaticality judgement data in terms of a drift diffusion process (Ratcliff, 1978). In the Hammerly et al. implementation, the basic explanation for ungrammatical agreement attraction configurations being judged grammatical erroneously is a slower rate of evidence accumulation in favour of the correct and incorrect dependency completion. This model has not yet been extended to explain reading times, and it is not clear whether under this model attraction is limited to retroactive interference designs and not proactive (Avetisyan et al., 2020), but it is an interesting proposal that needs further development.

Related evidence for an encoding account for agreement attraction comes from Paape et al. (2020). This work presents empirical evidence from Eastern Armenian that the number feature percolates to the grammatical subject from both the distractor noun as well as the verb. Paape and colleagues implement a series of competing computational models and show that the model that best explains the data is one that allows feature overwriting on the grammatical subject.

These different theories/explanations for the agreement attraction effect are not necessarily mutually exclusive; any combination of these theories, or possibly all of them, could together explain the data. Such hybrid models have not yet been developed or tested; developing them is an interesting direction for future research.

As shown in Figure 2.5, there is remarkable variability in agreement attraction data, but the posterior distribution of the effect has mean -22 ms, with 95% credible interval $[-37, -9]$ ms, which is consistent with an overall facilitation effect. These estimates are remarkably consistent with the facilitatory effects observed in the two experiments by Cunnings and Sturt (2018) (-22 ms, $[-4, -42]$ ms, and -19 ms, $[1, -40]$ ms). As discussed earlier, Cunnings and Sturt's experiments involved a plausibility manipulation, not the number feature; this could mean that such facilitatory effects are a hallmark of configurations in which the features on the item targeted for retrieval don't fully match all the retrieval cues.

Almost all the data displayed in Figure 2.5 comes from languages like English and Spanish (an exception is Tucker et al., 2015, who investigated Arabic). English and Spanish have relatively impoverished case marking systems. What happens if the grammatical subject and object are unambiguously case-

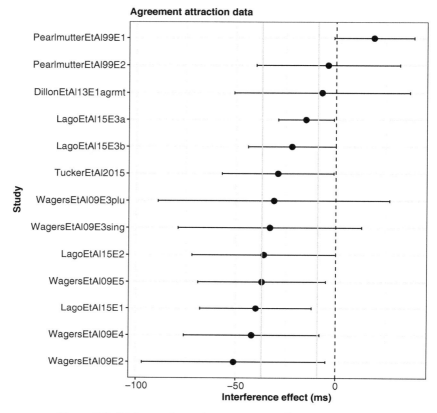

Figure 2.5 Subject-verb number agreement effects in ungrammatical sentences (reading studies). Shown are the means (sorted by increasing magnitude of the effect) and 95% confidence intervals that were either computed from publicly available data or derived from published estimates.

marked? If case marking allows the parsing system to sufficiently distinguish between the nouns, the agreement attraction effect should be weakened when the nouns have distinctive case marking. Avetisyan et al. (2020) tested this hypothesis using Armenian, a language with subject-verb agreement and rich case marking. In a series of experiments (forced choice and self-paced reading), they found that although distinctive case marking on subject and object nouns led to facilitation in processing, there was no indication that distinctive case marking attenuates the agreement attraction effect. One explanation offered by Avetisyan et al. (2020) for the absence of an interaction between case marking and agreement attraction is cast in terms of predictive parsing processes. As

2.4 Subject-Verb Number Agreement

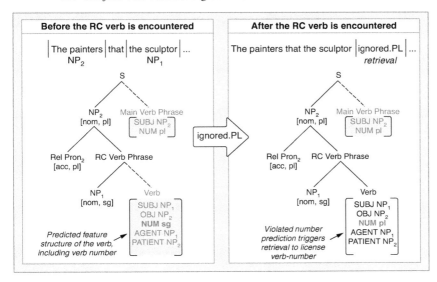

Figure 2.6 The role of case marking in agreement attraction configurations. The figure is reused here under a CC-BY4.0 license and is available from https://doi.org/10.6084/m9.figshare.11440854.v1.

shown schematically in Figure 2.6, once the nouns have been read, the parser predicts a verb phrase with the subject and object subcategorization features already linked to the previously processed nouns. For example, if the reader encounters a sentence like *The painters that the sculptor...*, a singular-marked verb is predicted, but the subcategorization frame of the verb is already filled with the indices corresponding to the subject and object nouns. Now, if a plural-marked verb is encountered, only the number marking of the predicted chunk needs to be modified to integrate the verb with the predicted verb phrase chunk. After that integration, agreement attraction may happen in the manner that Wagers et al. (2009) suggest. If case marking only plays a role during prediction, as suggested above, this may explain why Avetisyan et al. find no indication that distinctive case marking attenuates the agreement attraction effect.

The number attraction examples discussed in Figure 2.6 involve ungrammatical sentences. Grammatical versions of the number agreement configuration have also been investigated. Examples are shown in the following.

(15)   a.   The keys to the cabinet are on the table.
       b.   The keys to the cabinets are on the table.

Here, the general claim in the reading literature (Lago et al., 2015) is that no difference is seen between the two conditions. If we examine the estimates

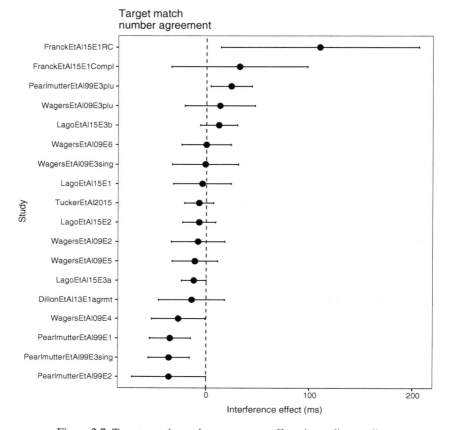

Figure 2.7 Target match number agreement effects in reading studies.

from these studies, we again see a wide range of variability, with all possible outcomes being observed; see Figure 2.7. The mean of the posterior distribution of this effect (the reading time at the auxiliary in (15b) minus the reading time at the auxiliary in (15a) across all these studies (some studies used the post-critical region) is −7 ms, with 95% credible interval [−17, 4] ms.

Based on the studies from their lab, Wagers and colleagues conclude that there is no difference in processing in the two grammatical agreement attraction conditions shown in (15a, 15b). Wagers et al. explain this null effect as follows. The subject noun predicts a verb with a particular number marking, and this prediction is validated when the verb is encountered. In such a situation, no retrieval process is triggered. This proposal has some difficulties. A great deal of work on English (Bartek et al., 2011; Gibson, 2000; Grodner and Gibson, 2005) has consistently shown that even in grammatical constructions, a retrieval

2.4 Subject-Verb Number Agreement

process is triggered. It seems implausible that retrieval is not triggered only in this one particular case, where the number feature is involved.

How strong is the evidence for the null results reported in the Dillon et al., Wagers et al., and Lago et al. studies? When p-values are greater than 0.05, this is not necessarily evidence that the null hypothesis is true. As discussed in Section 1.5.4, when power is low, it is hardly surprising that repeated experiments show null results. This point has somehow been lost in the course of translating statistical theory to psychological and linguistic applications. Instead of concluding that they have no evidence for an effect, researchers will incorrectly conclude that "absence of evidence is evidence of absence."

What would have happened if statistical power were higher than in the studies mentioned above? The Dillon et al., Wagers et al., and Lago et al. studies generally have small sample sizes, leading to power far below 80%. Nicenboim et al. (2018) increased power by increasing sample size to 185 subjects and by increasing the strength of the interference manipulation. Their design involved grammatical German sentences with number interference. Here, a subject noun and a verb always have two nouns intervening between them. In the high-interference condition, all three nouns match the number feature that is on the verb; in the low-interference condition, only the subject noun has the number feature that is on the verb. Thus, this design seeks to increase the magnitude of the number interference effect by increasing the fan, that is, by increasing the number of nouns that match the retrieval cues.

(16) a. HIGH INTERFERENCE

Der   **Wohltäter**,   der   den   Assistenten
The.sg.nom philanthropist, who.sg.nom the.sg.acc assistant

        des   Direktors **begrüsst hatte**,   sass   später im
(of) the.sg.gen director   **greeted   had.sg**, sat.sg later   in the

Spendenausschuss.
donations committee.

'The philanthropist, who had greeted the assistant of the director, sat later in the donations committee.'

b. LOW INTERFERENCE

Der   **Wohltäter**,   der   die   Assistenten
The.sg.nom philanthropist, who.sg.nom the.pl.acc assistant(s)

        der   Direktoren **begrüsst hatte**,   sass   später im
(of) the.pl.gen director(s) **greeted   had.sg**, sat.sg later   in the

Spendenausschuss.
donations committee.

'The philanthropist, who had greeted the assistants of the directors, sat later in the donations committee.'

38 Dependencies in Sentence Comprehension

This larger-sample study suggests that the magnitude of the cue-based retrieval effect in grammatical sentences involving number agreement may be smaller compared to the effect observed in ungrammatical agreement attraction configurations. Nicenboim et al. demonstrate that if the number of distractor nouns is increased from one to two, a small interference effect can be observed at the verb *begrüsst hatte*, 'greeted had', in sentences like (16a) compared to (16b). The authors found that with two distractors present, the interference effect is approximately 9 ms with a 95% credible interval of 0–18 ms. What could be the reason for the smaller interference effect in this case? Nicenboim et al. argue that feature percolation (the mechanism assumed in the MM model) and cue-based retrieval may be acting in opposite directions. It follows that if one increases the magnitude of the interference effect, the effect should be detectable. This proposal has yet to be tested with new experimental designs and is an interesting avenue for future research.

2.5   Reflexives and Reciprocals

Sturt (2003) carried out an eyetracking study that investigated the processing of direct object reflexives. He suggested that when the parser encounters a reflexive, in the first moments of processing, the antecedent is chosen using principle A of the binding theory (Chomsky, 1981). This implies that if any other noun phrases are present that are not syntactically licensed as antecedents of the reflexive, these would never be considered as possible antecedents even if the gender marking on the reflexive matches these noun phrases. Two examples are shown below to illustrate the two basic configurations that have been studied in the literature. These examples are adapted from Sturt's paper.

(17)   a. Proactive
           Jonathan/Jennifer remembered that the surgeon had pricked himself with a used syringe needle.
       b. Retroactive
           The surgeon who Jonathan/Jennifer met had pricked himself with a used syringe needle.

Example (17a) shows a proactive interference configuration: the reflexive *himself* requires the subject of the local clause, that is, *surgeon*, as the legal antecedent. However, the proper noun *Jonathan* matches in gender with the reflexive. Under the Sturt account, in the first moments of processing, compared to the baseline where the distractor noun (e.g., *Jennifer*) doesn't match the gender of the reflexive *himself*, the masculine-marked distractor noun *Jonathan* would never be considered as an antecedent. Example (17b) shows a retroactive interference configuration: the distractor noun *Jonathan* appears between the subject, which is the antecedent of the reflexive, and the reflexive *himself*.

2.5 Reflexives and Reciprocals

In both configurations, one can investigate the effect of the distractor noun by comparing sentences that either have a masculine distractor noun such as *Jonathan*, or a feminine distractor noun such as *Jennifer*. Sturt found no evidence that the reflexive was mistakenly associated with the distractor noun at the earliest moments of processing, that is, in first-pass reading times. As Sturt puts it (p. 542), "Principle A of the binding theory operates at the very earliest stages of processing; ... the gender of the ungrammatical antecedent [the distractor noun] had no effect on early processing, although it affected processing during later stages." In other words, at the earliest moments of processing, based on these null results, reflexives are assumed to be immune to the effects of interference.

Recall that earlier we had seen in subject-verb dependencies that interference effects are robustly seen. In the grammatical subject-verb dependencies investigated by Van Dyke and colleagues, we robustly see inhibitory effects, and in ungrammatical subject-verb dependencies with number agreement between the distractor and verb, we see a relatively clear indication of facilitation effects. Since the majority of these studies involve self-paced reading, we cannot say whether these inhibitory and facilitatory effects reflect the earliest moments of processing. An exception is the eyetracking study by Van Dyke (2007); but here, too, first-pass reading time seems to show no interference effects (see Figure 2.2). However, in a recent larger-sample eyetracking study involving English, Mertzen et al. (2020a) did find the predicted inhibitory interference effects in first-pass reading times.

Is the processing of reflexives different from those of subject-verb constructions? The answer would be yes if interference effect was seen in subject-verb agreement constructions but not in reflexive constructions. In particular, at the earliest moments of processing (e.g., in first-pass reading times), we would expect to see interference effects in subject-verb constructions but not in reflexives. Dillon et al. (2013) were the first to directly compare interference effects in these two dependency types (their experiment 1). They compared subject-verb number agreement constructions with reflexives. See (18, 19).

Number agreement conditions:

(18) a. Grammatical
         The new executive who oversaw **the middle manager** apparently
         was dishonest about the company's profits

      b. Grammatical
         The new executive who oversaw the middle managers apparently
         was dishonest about the company's profits

      c. Ungrammatical
         *The new executive who oversaw the middle manager apparently
         were dishonest about the company's profits

40   Dependencies in Sentence Comprehension

    d. Ungrammatical
    *The new executive who oversaw **the middle managers** apparently **were** dishonest about the company's profits

Reflexive conditions:

(19) a. Grammatical
      The new executive who oversaw **the middle manager** apparently doubted **himself** on most major decisions

      b. Grammatical
      The new executive who oversaw the middle managers apparently doubted **himself** on most major decisions

      c. Ungrammatical
      *The new executive who oversaw the middle manager apparently doubted **themselves** on most major decisions

      d. Ungrammatical
      *The new executive who oversaw **the middle managers** apparently doubted **themselves** on most major decisions

Dillon generously gave us the data from his study. This allowed us to determine whether, in early vs. late measures, any difference is seen between agreement and reflexives. We first defined nested contrasts (in grammatical and ungrammatical sentences separately) as shown in Table 2.1; for more details on contrast coding, see Schad et al. (2020b). Note that Dillon and colleagues used a different contrast coding than we did (main effects and interactions of grammaticality and intrusion); the details of these differences are discussed in Jäger et al. (2020). Our contrast coding was designed to directly test the predictions of the Lewis and Vasishth (2005) model.

We analyzed all dependent measures that have been invoked as indexing early processes in the dependencies considered in this chapter: first-pass reading time and regression probability (Dillon et al., 2013), and regression path duration (Cunnings and Sturt, 2018). As shown in Figure 2.8, the only clear effect is in total reading times in ungrammatical agreement dependencies. None of the dependent measures that is claimed to index early processes shows any effects in either agreement or reflexive dependencies. Thus, from these data at least, there is no reason to believe that interference effects *ever* occur in early measures in *any* dependency, as claimed by Sturt (2003). It is therefore not clear why reflexive processing is seen as special and different from any other dependency. One could conclude that all dependencies uniformly show an absence of interference effects in early measures.

In their paper, Dillon and colleagues argue that reflexives and agreement attraction constructions exhibit different interference profiles in ungrammatical constructions. In order to argue for a difference between agreement and

2.5 Reflexives and Reciprocals

Table 2.1. *Nested contrast coding to investigate the effect of intrusion in grammatical and ungrammatical agreement and reflexive constructions. The contrast* dep *is the main effect of dependency type (agreement or reflexive). The abbreviation* intr.au *means intrusion (interference effect) in agreement dependencies, ungrammatical;* intr.ag *stands for intrusion (interference effect) in agreement dependencies, grammatical;* intr.ru *refers to intrusion (interference effect) in reflexive dependencies, ungrammatical;* intr.rg *stands for intrusion (interference effect) in reflexive dependencies, grammatical.*

| | Agreement | | | | Reflexives | | | |
| | Gram | | Ungram | | Gram | | Ungram | |
	No intr	Intr	No intr	Intr	No intr	Intr	No intr	Intr
dep	−0.5	−0.5	−0.5	−0.5	0.5	0.5	0.5	0.5
intr.au	0	0	−0.5	0.5	0	0	0	0
intr.ag	−0.5	0.5	0	0	0	0	0	0
intr.ru	0	0	0	0	0	0	−0.5	0.5
intr.rg	0	0	0	0	−0.5	0.5	0	0

reflexives with respect to the interference manipulation, an interaction must be demonstrated between dependency type and the interference manipulation. However, such an interaction was not present in the original data (Jäger et al., 2020).

Thus, although the experiment design had the potential to demonstrate that dependency type determines whether interference occurs, the data don't seem to provide a basis for a conclusion.

A major issue in the Dillon et al. study was that the sample size was quite small. A prospective power analysis of the Dillon et al. data – using their sample size and predicted effects from the cue-based retrieval model of Lewis and Vasishth – shows that prospective power is likely to have ranged from 20% to 40% for subject-verb agreement configurations and 5–25% for reflexives; see Jäger et al. (2020) for details on the power calculations.

We attempted to replicate the key results from total reading times with a larger sample size (181 participants). This work is reported in full in Jäger et al. (2020). Figure 2.9 shows the total reading times at the critical region (the auxiliary or reflexive). Figure 2.9 shows that both agreement and reflexives in ungrammatical conditions show very similar facilitatory interference patterns in total reading times. These similar estimates for the two dependencies are not consistent with the claims by Dillon and colleagues. However, an exploratory analysis of first-pass regressions did show some weak evidence consistent with the interaction pattern predicted by Sturt and Dillon and colleagues. If this

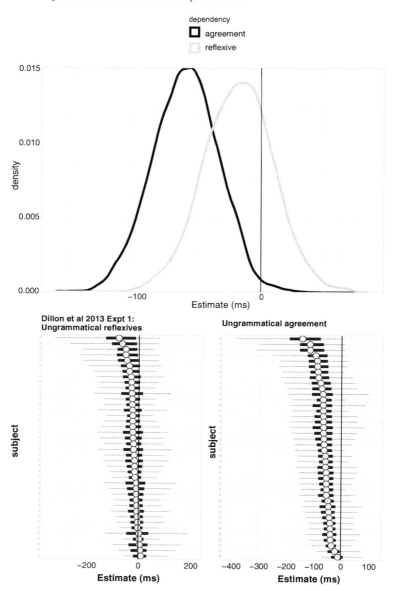

Figure 2.8 Summary for total reading time of the Dillon et al. (2013) comparisons for ungrammatical sentences involving agreement and reflexives. The sample size was 40 participants. The upper plot shows the posterior distributions of the facilitatory interference effect in agreement and reflexives, and the lower plots show the individual-level estimates of the effect, with 80% and 95% credible intervals.

2.5 Reflexives and Reciprocals 43

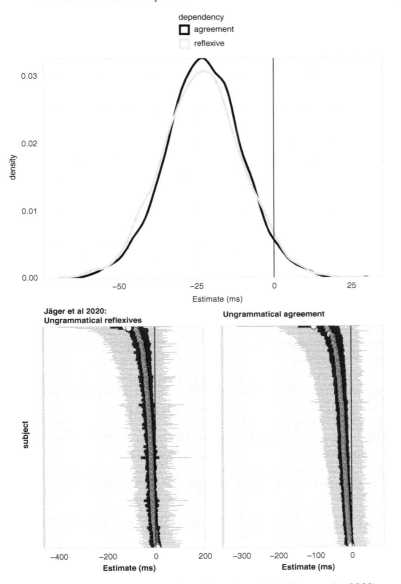

Figure 2.9 Summary for total reading time of the Jäger et al. (2020) comparisons for ungrammatical sentences involving agreement and reflexives. The sample size was 181 participants. The upper plot shows the posterior distributions of the facilitatory interference effect in agreement and reflexives, and the lower plots show the individual-level estimates of the effect, with 80% and 95% credible intervals.

44   Dependencies in Sentence Comprehension

pattern can be replicated in future work, it would suggest that Sturt's original proposal may have been correct, that only in the early moments of processing (expressed in first-pass regressions) is there immunity from interference; in later stages (expressed by total reading times), agreement and reflexive dependency types show similar interference profiles.

As an aside, it is worth noting here that if the Jäger et al. (2020) study's results for total reading times had been interpreted using the strict cut-off of 0.05 for the p-value practiced in psycholinguistics, we would be forced to conclude that there is no effect of agreement or reflexives! This kind of simplistic conclusion is a good example of why the p-value-based decision process that is standardly used in psycholinguistics is deeply flawed.

2.5.1 Individual-Level Effects in the Dillon et al. Design

Figures 2.8 and 2.9 show an interesting consistency across the original Dillon et al. study and the Jäger et al. replication attempt: essentially all the subjects show facilitatory interference effects in both agreement and reflexive constructions, in both the original experiment and the replication attempt. In both studies, the magnitude of the effect varies in the two dependencies from subject to subject, but the sign is consistently negative. This is a potentially interesting pattern that could have a theoretical explanation. For example, some subjects might show very large facilitatory interference effects because they are engaged in good-enough processing, or are not using syntactic constraints to complete dependencies to the same extent as other subjects, who show smaller facilitatory interference effects. This modulation of the effect size for individual subjects can be modelled in the Lewis and Vasishth (2005) architecture, as we show in Section 3.2.1, and in Yadav et al. (2020).

So, given the above data (the original Dillon et al. data and our replication data), what should we conclude about the processing of reflexives and subject-verb agreement? In psycholinguistics, researchers feel obliged to take one or the other position. This type of deterministic thinking is highly misleading. A more realistic approach is to simply lay out what we learnt from the data given different prior beliefs about the problem. We discuss this point next.

2.5.2 A Sensitivity Analysis on the Ungrammatical Agreement and Reflexives Conditions Using Informative Priors

In this chapter, we summarized the main evidence available from reading studies relating to interference effects in different dependency types. On the surface, one might think that empirical data are "objective" in the sense that they speak for themselves. However, in practice researchers always interpret data in the light of their prior beliefs, and sometimes these beliefs can be

2.5 Reflexives and Reciprocals

very strong. When these prior beliefs are strong, it makes intuitive sense that a single counterexample from one experimental result should not change our beliefs much. In the case of reflexives, in the course of informal discussions, researchers have expressed scepticism about the estimates of the facilitatory interference effect in English reflexives reported in Jäger et al. (2020). The argument here is that there is a lot of prior data that doesn't match the Jäger et al. findings. Essentially, the objection is that in the analysis of the Jäger et al. replication data, we do not use all available information from prior work. This kind of use of prior knowledge need not be invoked informally; one can simply take one's prior beliefs into account in the data analysis. This is not normally done in psycholinguistics, but with the increasing availability of Bayesian tools for data analysis, it is easy to formally incorporate prior beliefs into account.

In this section, we briefly demonstrate how prior beliefs can be taken into account in the specific case of the data from Jäger et al. Below, we illustrate how the expert can formally interpret available data in the light of either prior data or their own prior subjective beliefs. The reason we bring this point up here is that we feel that incorporating prior beliefs in the analysis is a very important tool for understanding "what the data tell us". The data never "speak for themselves"; they always speak through the filter of our beliefs. We show below how this subjectivity can be formally incorporated into the interpretation of data.

All the statistical models fit in Jäger et al. (2020) used mildly uninformative, regularizing priors, which effectively assume an agnostic starting point (Schad et al., 2020a). Bayesian methods allow us to quantitatively take into consideration prior knowledge or beliefs about the plausible values of a parameter, by using an informative prior.

Priors may arise from different sources, an obvious one being a body of empirical data on the specific issue in question. When empirical data are scarce, other sources can be expert opinion (Oakley and O'Hagan, 2010; O'Hagan et al., 2006), or via quantitative predictions of existing theories.

Speaking informally, the posterior mean can be seen as a weighted sum of the prior mean and the sample mean, weighted by the relative precision (inverse of the variance) of the prior and the data. If the prior has relatively higher precision, it will dominate in determining the posterior mean, and if the data has higher precision (this is a function of standard deviation and the sample size), then the data will dominate in determining the posterior mean. A consequence of this fact is that when we have a very strong prior belief, expressed through a distribution with a relatively small standard deviation, even large amounts of data may not shift the posterior mean away from the prior mean.

Hence, when investigating a controversial research question, it may be desirable to quantitatively take into account opposing theoretical views by using a representative spectrum of different priors. In this context, medical statisticians

46   Dependencies in Sentence Comprehension

like Spiegelhalter et al. (2004) have proposed the use of a "community of priors": opposing perspectives of researchers are incorporated in the data analysis by using different priors. In this way, one can use *agnostic priors* (mildly uninformative priors), *enthusiastic priors* that support a particular position, and *adversarial or sceptical priors* that represent alternative positions. The different posterior distributions from the data can then be examined in the light of these priors, and the researcher can draw their own conclusion.

In the reflexives replication data, we can examine next how agnostic, adversarial, and enthusiastic priors affect the posterior distributions of the effects of interest. The case of ungrammatical agreement constructions is relatively uncontroversial, and we will see below that a range of different priors have little effect on the estimates from the Jäger et al. data. More interesting is the effect of different prior specifications on the interference effects in ungrammatical reflexive conditions. We demonstrate here that the effect estimates here are quite sensitive to prior beliefs.

We carried out a sensitivity analysis on the estimates for the ungrammatical conditions, defining priors that represent three sources of beliefs. The different priors are summarized in Table 2.2.

(i) **Mildly uninformative priors (Agnostic prior)** As a baseline, we used a mildly uninformative prior for both the agreement and reflexive conditions. This prior represents an agnostic starting point where no information is incorporated from any prior knowledge.

(ii) **Meta-analysis priors (Adversarial prior for reflexives)** We derived posterior distributions of the interference effect in ungrammatical agreement and reflexive conditions using data from existing reading time studies (Jäger et al., 2017). These studies represent a synthesis of the evidence available from self-paced reading and eyetracking studies on agreement and reflexives. Because the dependent measure of interest in our studies is total fixation time, the estimates from the eyetracking studies are based on total fixation times. We refer to this prior as an adversarial prior because the estimate for ungrammatical reflexives is $N(9,10.75)$, which is a relatively tight prior for the reflexives interference effect in our replication study. A great deal of data would be needed to shift the posterior mean such that a facilitatory interference effect is seen.

(iii) **LV05 priors (Enthusiastic prior)** As a prior representing the equal cue-weighting retrieval proposal, we used a normal approximation of the range of predicted effects from the Engelmann et al. (2020) model.

The results of this sensitivity analysis are shown in Table 2.2. Agreement conditions show similar facilitatory interference effects regardless of the prior chosen. This confirms that the agreement interference effect is robust to the choice of prior. For reflexives, the situation is different. The reflexive conditions

2.6 Concluding Remarks

Table 2.2. *Summary of the sensitivity analysis investigating the effect of incorporating prior knowledge from mildly uninformative priors; a meta-analysis of existing reading data on ungrammatical agreement and reflexives; and the model predictions in Engelmann et al. (2020). The dependent measure in the analysis is total fixation time and the posterior estimates are back-transformed to the ms scale from log ms. The priors are shown in the ms scales.*

Sensitivity analysis			
Condition	Source for Prior	Prior (ms)	Posterior (ms)
Agreement	Mildly uninformative	$N(0,7600)$	−22 [−46,1]
(Ungram)	Meta-analysis	$N(−32,8.5)$	−25 [−36,−14]
	LV05 Model	$N(−26,13)$	−22 [−34,−7]
Reflexives	Mildly uninformative	$N(0,7600)$	−24 [−50,2]
(Ungram)	Meta-analysis	$N(9,10.75)$	−3 [−17,12]
	LV05 Model	$N(−26,13)$	−22 [−38,−6]

show facilitatory interference effects only when we use mildly uninformative priors and the LV05 predictions as priors. With the relatively tight meta-analysis prior $N(9,10.75)$, we see no indication of facilitatory interference effects in the replication data.

Thus, for reflexives, the conclusion that one can draw from these data is not as clear as for agreement; the conclusion depends quite a bit on the researcher's prior beliefs. Of course, future studies could now use the Jäger et al. reflexives estimates as priors. By incrementally incorporating prior knowledge in newer and newer studies, eventually it could become clear what the facts are about reflexives.

2.6 Concluding Remarks

The reading studies that have investigated these different types of dependency constructions show very limited evidence for inhibitory and facilitatory interference. Although subject-verb non-agreement dependencies seem to often show patterns consistent with inhibitory interference, grammatical subject-verb dependencies often do not. This is a puzzle for similarity-based interference researchers. Furthermore, it has been argued that reflexives (and perhaps also reciprocals) are immune to inhibitory or facilitatory interference because binding theory ensures that the antecedent is unerringly found in memory. If this claim turns out to be true, it would be an interesting and important exception to the general principles of interference that are claimed to apply in sentence processing. One important implication would be that linguistic

48   Dependencies in Sentence Comprehension

constraints, often subtle constraints, can play a greater role in online processing than general working memory constraints. This would show, inter alia, that sentence processing is at least partly subject to purely linguistic constraints.

One thing that stands out from reviewing the published evidence (Jäger et al., 2017) is the generally low statistical power of the published studies. If the meta-analytical estimates of inhibitory and facilitatory interference effects are accurate estimates of the true underlying effects, then none of the published reading studies so far can be considered properly powered for detecting the effects. The reason: the effects are too small to be capable of being detected accurately by the published studies.

The single biggest reason that low-power studies have proliferated in psycholinguistics is that fundamental misunderstandings exist in psycholinguists' minds about what a p-value can and cannot not tell us, given no other information. Null results are widely assumed to indicate that the true effect is 0, and statistically significant, exaggerated estimates, which never replicate, get published as big-news results. We discuss these points at length in Vasishth et al. (2018), Nicenboim et al. (2018, 2020), and Jäger et al. (2020).

This is a disappointing empirical starting point for evaluating the computational models considered in this book. As discussed in the previous chapter, one of the Roberts and Pashler (2000) criteria for a persuasive model fit – higher precision data – has not yet been met in the literature. But the situation is what it is. Given the data that are available today, it is possible to draw some initial conclusions about the models' performance. That is what the rest of this book tries to achieve. Our hope is that some day there will be higher-precision benchmark data for evaluating sentence processing models of the sort discussed here.

3 The Core ACT-R-Based Model of Retrieval Processes

Any comprehensive theory of sentence comprehension needs to explain the mechanisms behind the formation of dependencies between non-adjacent words such as a verb and its subject. This process necessarily involves storing and accessing information in working memory. There is a large body of evidence for a content-addressable memory architecture underlying human cognition in general (Anderson et al., 2004; Anderson and Lebiere, 1998; Ratcliff, 1978; Watkins and Watkins, 1975) and sentence processing in particular (Lewis and Vasishth, 2005; McElree, 2000; McElree et al., 2003; Van Dyke and Lewis, 2003; Van Dyke and McElree, 2011).

In a content-addressable memory, a cue-based retrieval mechanism can activate certain items in parallel on the basis of how well their properties, i.e., their *features*, agree with a set of requirements, i.e. *cues*, which are determined by the type of dependency. This stands in contrast to search mechanisms which assume that items in memory are checked based on, for example, their serial order position (Berwick and Weinberg, 1984; Sternberg, 1966, 1969) or their position in a syntactic tree (Sturt, 2003).

A cue-based model of sentence parsing has been described in Van Dyke and Lewis (2003), Lewis and Vasishth (2005), Lewis et al. (2006), and Vasishth and Lewis (2006). Lewis and Vasishth (2005) implemented the model in the cognitive architecture *Adaptive Control of Thought Rational* (ACT-R; Anderson et al., 2004; Anderson and Lebiere, 1998) with the objective of grounding the means of language processing in general cognitive mechanisms. The parser uses rapid associative memory retrievals to form inter-word dependencies, incrementally building a structural sentence representation. The success and latency of the retrieval process depends on the activation of syntactic representations, which is affected by time-based decay, and interference from similar items.

3.1 ACT-R

ACT-R (Adaptive Control of Thought–Rational) is a comprehensive, implemented theory which integrates processes of working memory access, rule-guided behaviour, learning, sensory input, and motor control. It is a constantly developing framework that incorporates findings from experimental work in various areas of cognitive psychology. ACT-R consists of a long-term memory of declarative and procedural knowledge and short-term buffers with limited capacity, representing a limited focus of attention (Cowan, 2001; McElree, 2006; Miller, 1956). Procedural knowledge is realized in the form of a production system (Newell, 1973, 1978) that consists of condition-action pairs that operate on short-term or working memory.

The contents of short-term memory buffers serve as conditions that trigger if-then production rules to fire. The action(s) carried out by a production rule – which usually manipulates buffer contents – lead to a new state of the buffers. This new state serves as a condition that triggers other production rules. Hence, the sequence of events is defined through if-else condition-action specifications that operate through the serial firing of production rules. At the same time, associated items are related by a mechanism of spreading activation that affects an individual item's activation dependent on the presence of related items. Memory items, so-called *chunks*, enter the buffers by being retrieved from declarative memory. Memory items are accessed by a cue-based retrieval mechanism on the basis of their activation, which is subject to decay, reactivation, similarity-based interference, and noise.

Next, the equations that underlie ACT-R content-addressable memory access will be explained in a (sometimes simplified) way, as they are relevant for the model of sentence comprehension described in Lewis and Vasishth (2005).

In ACT-R, the probability and latency of retrieving a memory item is determined by its activation value. An item's activation changes over time as the result of decay, reactivation, and noise. At the time of a retrieval request, a limited amount of activation spreads among all items in relation to their match with the retrieval specification, which is defined by a comparison of an item's *features* with the retrieval *cues*.

An item's final activation value is the sum of four components: a base-level B_i, which includes decay and frequency of use; the spreading activation S_i, which includes similarity-based interference; a penalty component P_i for mismatches with the retrieval specification; and a random noise component ε. The base-level activation B_i is computed from a *base-level constant* β_i and the item's history of use:

$$B_i = \log\left(\sum_{j=1}^{n} t_j^{-d}\right) + \beta_i, \qquad (3.1)$$

where n is the number of times the item was accessed in memory, t_j is the time since the jth access, and d is the *decay parameter*. An item's activation decreases over time, with a decay parameter of 0.5 by default, and receives a reactivation boost when it is accessed.

3.1 ACT-R

At the time of a retrieval request, activation is spread from each retrieval cue to all matching items. This activation, however, is limited for each cue and distributed among the items that share the requested feature, i.e., the *competitors*. The number of items competing for activation from a certain cue is called the *fan*. An item with a high fan will thus receive less spreading activation than one with no competitors, i.e., it is inhibited by similarity-based interference or the so-called *fan effect*.[1] The spreading activation component S_i of item i is summed over all cues $j \in J$ in the retrieval specification:

$$S_i = \sum_j W_j S_{ji}, \qquad (3.2)$$

where W_j is the amount of activation from the cue j and S_{ji} is the strength of association between cue j and item i. The term S_{ji} is a function of the fan of item i for cue j:

$$S_{ji} = S - \log(fan_{ji}), \qquad (3.3)$$

where S is the *maximum associative strength* (MAS). The fan of item i for cue j is defined by the number of competing items in memory that match the feature associated with j: $fan_{ji} = 1 + items_j$.[2] As a consequence, the spreading activation component S_i increases the item's activation by Eq. (3.2) for each matching retrieval cue and reduces its activation by Eq. (3.3) for each distractor item that also (partially) matches the retrieval cues. Note that (3.3) is the core equation of similarity-based interference in ACT-R as it defines the influence of competitors on an item's activation at the time of retrieval.

The final activation component assigns a penalty for mismatches. Some activation is subtracted for each retrieval cue j that is not matched:

$$P_i = \sum_j PM_{ji}. \qquad (3.4)$$

P is the *mismatch penalty parameter* (MP). M_{ji} is the similarity between cue value j and the value in the corresponding slot of item i. The similarity M_{ji} is a value between 0 (identity) and -1 (maximum difference). This way, the more dissimilar a feature value of an item is to the cue value, the more activation is subtracted for this item. If, for example, one defines some similarity between

---

[1] Note that the description of ACT-R for the present purpose is simplified to reflect the way that it was used in the model of Lewis and Vasishth (2005). In default ACT-R, spreading activation is not a property of retrieval cues per se. Rather, any buffer's content can spread activation to related items. Usually, the chunks in the goal buffer are the sources of spreading activation and, hence, of the fan effect. In the Lewis and Vasishth (2005) parser, the retrieval cues are always mirrored in the goal buffer, such that the model behaves as if spreading activation is specific to retrieval cues.

[2] In fact, all *slots* in all memory items containing the feature are counted. For simplicity, we assume here that a linguistically relevant item will have a certain feature in only one slot.

52 The Core ACT-R-Based Model of Retrieval Processes

the colour values *red* and *orange*, orange items would be less penalized than, e.g., blue items when cueing for something that has the feature RED.

The item i that is finally retrieved in a particular trial is the one that happens to have the highest activation A_i. The activation A_i is the sum of the base-level B_i and the spreading activation S_i, the mismatch penalty, plus Gaussian noise ϵ_i, where ϵ_i is sampled from a normal distribution with mean 0 and some standard deviation σ (Eq. 3.5):

$$A_i = B_i + S_i + P_i + \epsilon_i, \text{ where } \epsilon_i \sim Normal(0, \sigma). \tag{3.5}$$

The time to retrieve an item i is a function of its activation A_i, as determined by the following equation:

$$RT = Fe^{-(f \times A_i)}, \tag{3.6}$$

where F is the *latency factor* (LF) and f the *latency exponent*. If no item has an activation above a certain threshold τ, retrieval fails. The duration of a failed retrieval is calculated by the same Eq. (3.6) with A_i substituted with τ.

3.2 The Lewis and Vasishth (2005) Model

The computational model of parsing difficulty developed by Lewis and Vasishth (2005) adopts ACT-R's general principles, a limited focus of attention and cue-based retrieval of memory items subject to fluctuating activation as a function of decay and retrieval history and similarity-based retrieval interference. An essential property of cue-based retrieval in contrast to structural search is that serial order information is not used in the search mechanism (McElree, 2006; Ratcliff, 1978). Lewis and Vasishth (2005) argue that this partly explains the speed with which language processing unfolds; most dependencies can be established without serial order information, purely based on the items' features and recency in terms of activation decay over time. The lack of immediate serial order information in incremental sentence processing explains severe comprehension difficulty in cases where this information is needed. An example is double centre-embeddings such as Example (20):

(20) The book that the editor who the receptionist married admired ripped.

The model of Lewis and Vasishth (2005) implements knowledge of parsing in the form of production rules that incrementally build a structural representation in the fashion of a left-corner parser following X-bar syntax rules (Chomsky, 1986). Figure 3.1 from Lewis and Vasishth (2005) shows how sentence structure is represented in memory. Syntactic constituents are stored as single chunks being related to each other through feature slots for *specifier*, *complement*, and *head*. New structure is built at a new input word and then attached into previously built structure by retrieving a syntactic object that matches certain search

3.2 The Lewis and Vasishth (2005) Model

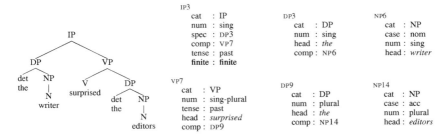

Figure 3.1 Figure 1 of Lewis and Vasishth (2005). The figure shows the representation of chunks (maximal projections of phrases) that constitute a syntactic tree. The figure is copyrighted by Wiley, and is reused with permission, license number 4782371233287.

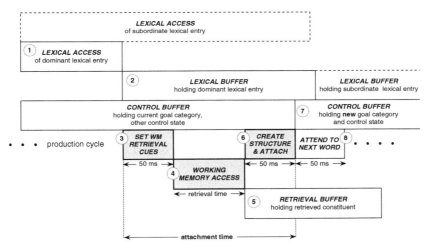

Figure 3.2 Figure 2 of Lewis and Vasishth (2005). The figure shows the processing cycle of the parsing algorithm. The figure is copyrighted by Wiley, and is reused with permission, license number 4782380063983.

cues like gender, number, syntactic category, and also information as to whether the relevant constituent is embedded or contains a gap waiting to be filled.

The productions essentially operate on four buffers, each holding one chunk: a control buffer (the goal buffer), a lexical buffer holding the lexicon entry corresponding to the current word, a retrieval buffer holding the syntactic chunk retrieved from memory, and a buffer for creating new structure. The goal buffer holds syntactic expectations in the form of a syntactic category that is necessary in order to complete the currently pursued structure. Figure 3.2 from

Lewis and Vasishth (2005) illustrates the cycle carried out at each input word. First, the corresponding lexical entry is accessed in the lexicon in declarative memory. Based on the lexical entry and on the current goal category, the cues for retrieving a matching constituent are specified and retrieval is initiated. Finally, a new syntactic node is created and attached to the one retrieved. Attention is then sent to the next word. The essential step is memory retrieval. Through ACT-R's independently motivated principles of cue-based working memory access, the simulations in Lewis and Vasishth (2005) provide quantitative predictions for effects of distance, structural interference, and embedding type in sentence comprehension.

The parsing architecture has been further used to model several different aspects of sentence comprehension such as antilocality (Vasishth and Lewis, 2006); intrusive interference in negative polarity constructions (Vasishth et al., 2008); interference effects in reflexive processing (Jäger et al., 2015; Parker and Phillips, 2014; Patil et al., 2012) and subject-verb processing (Dillon et al., 2013; Wagers et al., 2009); and impaired sentence comprehension in aphasia (Lissón et al., 2021; Mätzig et al., 2018; Patil et al., 2016a).

3.2.1 A Priori Predictions of the Model

In this section, we explain how two classes of effect – inhibitory interference and facilitatory interference – arise in the model. Inhibitory interference arises in target-match configurations, where the target for retrieval matches the retrieval cues perfectly, and the distractor partially matches the retrieval cues; and facilitatory interference arises in target-mismatch configurations, where both the target and distractor only partially match the retrieval cues.

Example 21 shows the two configurations, and Figure 3.3 presents a graphical representation of how the model's predictions arise. The oval boxes indicate matching (black or grey) or mismatching (white) features of an item with respect to the retrieval cues. The darker the boxes, the better the match of the item and the higher its activation level.

(21) a. *Target-match; distractor-mismatch*
   The surgeon$_{+CCOM}^{+MASC}$ who treated Jennifer$_{-CCOM}^{-MASC}$ had pricked himself$\{_{CCOM}^{MASC}\}$...

   b. *Target-match; distractor-match*
   The surgeon$_{+CCOM}^{+MASC}$ who treated Jonathan$_{-CCOM}^{+MASC}$ had pricked himself$\{_{CCOM}^{MASC}\}$...

   c. *Target-mismatch; distractor-mismatch*
   The surgeon$_{+CCOM}^{-FEM}$ who treated Jonathan$_{-CCOM}^{-FEM}$ had pricked herself$\{_{CCOM}^{FEM}\}$...

3.2 The Lewis and Vasishth (2005) Model

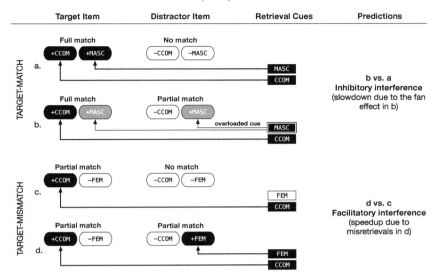

Figure 3.3 Spreading activation according to ACT-R/LV05 in the four conditions shown in Example 21. Line weights indicate the amount of spreading activation from a cue to an item. Black oval boxes represent a feature match. Grey oval boxes indicate features matching an "overloaded" cue (MASC in b), and white boxes indicate a mismatch. The figure is by Engelmann and Vasishth (2019); available at https://doi.org/10.6084/m9.figshare.9305456 under a CC-BY4.0 license.

d. *Target-mismatch; distractor-match*
   The surgeon$^{-\text{FEM}}_{+\text{CCOM}}$ who treated Jennifer$^{+\text{FEM}}_{-\text{CCOM}}$ had pricked herself{$^{\text{FEM}}_{\text{CCOM}}$}...

Inhibitory Interference through the Fan Effect The relative activation levels of memory items in ACT-R determine which item will be retrieved. All items available in memory enter into a race at the time of retrieval, such that the one which happens to have the highest activation is retrieved. Thus, only one "winning" item is ever retrieved in any one trial. The higher the activation of the "winning" item, the faster the retrieval time. Each item i has a **base-level activation** B_i that reflects past usage by accounting for all reactivation events (t_j represents the time elapsed since the j-th activation) and a time-based decay with rate d (this usually has the default value 0.5 in ACT-R):

$$B_i = \log\left(\sum_{j=1}^{n} t_j^{-d}\right) + \beta_i. \tag{3.7}$$

In this equation, β_i is the resting-state activation for item i, and n indexes the number of times that the item i has been retrieved in the past.

In addition to the base-level activation, spreading activation is added to every (partially) matching item at the time of retrieval. The spreading activation component is the main source of similarity-based interference effects in ACT-R. An item receives spreading activation from all matching cues j depending on the *associative strength* S_{ji} between cue j and item i and the cue's weight W_j; see Eq. (3.8) and Eq. (3.9). W_j is standardly set to $1/\textit{number of cues}$, meaning that all cues are weighted equally. We are adopting this standard assumption throughout this work. The implications of cue-weighting are discussed in (Jäger et al., 2020; Vasishth et al., 2019; Yadav et al., 2020).

$$S_i = \sum_j W_j S_{ji}. \tag{3.8}$$

The arrows in Figure 3.3 show how activation from the retrieval cues is distributed to the target and the distractor based on their features. The thickness of the lines with arrows indicates the amount of spreading activation that is added to an item due to that feature. In Figure 3.3a (cf. Example 21a), the target is a full match for the set of retrieval cues, MASC and CCOM. Both cues are also unambiguous because they are matched by the target only and not by the distractor. The target thus receives the maximal amount of spreading activation at retrieval. By contrast, in the interference condition b in Figure 3.3 and Example 21, the gender cue is matched by the distractor in addition to the target. Thus, the MASC cue is now ambiguous, or "overloaded" (Watkins and Watkins, 1975). This cue overload has the consequence that the activation from this cue is now split between the target and the distractor. This follows from Eq. (3.3), which is repeated below for convenience as Eq. (3.9). The associative strength between a cue and an item is reduced in relation to the fan – the number of items associated with the cue. (Recall that *MAS* is the value of the maximum associative strength.)

$$S_{ji} = MAS - \log(\textit{fan}_j). \tag{3.9}$$

Each cue distributes the *limited* available activation equally between all matching items (with the maximally available amount being $W_j \times MAS$). The more competitor items are present that match a cue j, the weaker the association S_{ji} of this cue with the item i. In other words, each competitor reduces the spreading activation to the target by some amount and thus makes it harder to be distinguished from the other items. This is the fan effect discussed earlier (Anderson, 1974). In our example (Figure 3.3 and Example 22), the fan effect causes a reduction of the spreading activation received by the target in b in comparison with a, thus reducing the target's total activation A_i (where i indexes the identity of the target chunk).

3.2 The Lewis and Vasishth (2005) Model

A decrease in activation A_i causes the retrieval time (also called *retrieval latency*) RT_i to increase. As shown in Eq. (3.10), the retrieval latency of an item is a negative exponential function of its activation at the time of retrieval, where F and f are two scaling parameters – the *latency factor* and the *latency exponent*, respectively.

$$RT_i = Fe^{-(f \times A_i)}. \tag{3.10}$$

Hence, the similarity in gender between target and distractor in target-match configurations shown in Figure 3.3a vs. 3.3b predicts a slower retrieval latency due to the fan effect, i.e., inhibitory interference. At any retrieval event, only the item with the highest activation at that moment is retrieved, and only when its activation is equal or above the retrieval threshold τ. Therefore, the processing time at the word where the retrieval is triggered is dependent only on the time it takes to retrieve the item that happens to have a higher activation, i.e., the winner. Due to the Gaussian noise component in Eq. (3.5), activation fluctuates, such that there is always the possibility – depending on the relative difference in activation between target and distractor – of a **misretrieval**, i.e., that the distractor is erroneously retrieved instead of the target. Therefore, because of the increased distractor activation in 3.3b, there is a higher probability of misretrievals in b compared to a.[3]

Facilitatory Interference through a Race Process In target-mismatch configurations (c and d of Figure 3.3 and Example 21), the predictions for retrieval latencies are different from those in target-match configurations. In c and d, the target is only a partial match, as it does not exhibit the correct gender feature +FEM. When the distractor matches the gender in d, there is, however, no reduction in the target's activation. The reason is that both cues FEM and CCOM are only matched by one item each and are thus not ambiguous. Hence, no fan effect and no inhibitory interference is predicted. However, since target and distractor now both receive the same amount of spreading activation – each matches exactly one cue – their activation levels are relatively close to each other. Because activation fluctuates due to the random noise component in Eq. (3.5), when two items receive the same amount of spreading activation from their match with the retrieval cues, the winning item at the time of retrieval is chosen randomly with a probability of around 0.5. Since the winner is always

---

[3] In an alternative model of cue-based retrieval proposed by McElree (2006), the direct-access model, interference is only reflected in a decreased retrieval probability of the target but not in retrieval time. Effects observed in reading times are then explained as a by-product of changes in the retrieval probabilities. The idea here is that misretrievals may trigger a reanalysis process that inflates reading times (McElree, 1993). For implementations and quantitative comparisons of the direct-access model (McElree, 2006) with the LV05 model, see Nicenboim and Vasishth (2018) and Lissón et al. (2021).

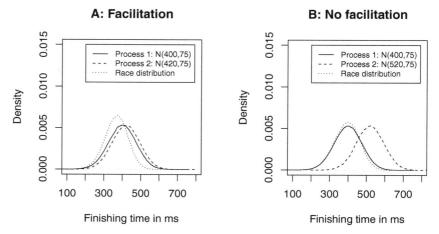

Figure 3.4 An illustration of a race process involving two distributions that represent retrieval time distributions of two items. When the two distributions have similar means (Figure A), the distribution of the retrieval times of the winner (which may differ from trial to trial) will have a distribution with a mean that is lower than the mean of the two distributions involved in the race (statistical facilitation). When one distribution has a much smaller mean than the other distribution's mean (Figure B), the distribution of the winner's retrieval times will have the same mean as that of the distribution of the item with the smaller mean.

the item with the highest activation (i.e., the shortest retrieval latency) at the time of retrieval, this fulfils the conditions of a *race process*. As shown in Figure 3.4, in a race process, when the finishing times of two items' retrieval times can be described by distributions that have similar means, the retrieval times of the winner (which can differ from trial to trial) will have a distribution that has a smaller mean than the means of the two items' retrieval time distributions. This is called statistical facilitation (Raab, 1962). A race process therefore has the effect that, *on average* over multiple trials, the retrieval latency is shorter when the two competing items have similar mean retrieval times than when there is a clear winner due to a bigger difference in retrieval latency as is the case in condition c (also see Logačev and Vasishth, 2015).

Because of this statistical facilitation, the prediction for target-mismatch configurations in Figure 3.3d vs. 3.3c is a speed-up on average over multiple trials, i.e., facilitatory interference.

Figure 3.5 shows the quantitative predictions of the model for target-match and mismatch conditions. Shown are the mean predicted retrieval times (an average of 6,000 simulations) for a range of parameter values. The parameter values are varied over a narrow band to show how they influence the retrieval

3.2 The Lewis and Vasishth (2005) Model

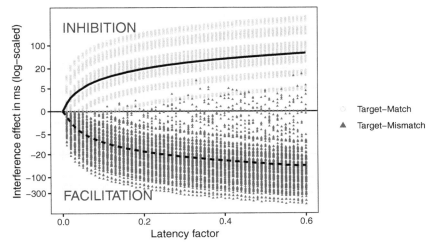

Figure 3.5 Prediction space for the interference effect in ACT-R in target-match (circles, solid line) and target-mismatch configurations (triangles, broken line). Interference is plotted in terms of the difference in mean retrieval latencies between the interference (labelled distractor-match) and the no-interference (labelled distractor-mismatch) condition, and as a function of the latency factor F. Positive values indicate longer mean retrieval latencies in the interference condition (*inhibitory interference*) due to cue-overload (fan effect) from a partially matching distractor; negative values indicate shorter mean retrieval latencies in the interference condition (*facilitatory interference*) due to retrievals of the partially matching distractor on trials where the distractor is highly activated and hence fast. Each individual data point represents the mean interference effect of 6,000 iterations with one out of 10,980 different parameter settings (each in target-match and target-mismatch configurations; i.e., there are 21,960 data points plotted in total). Each parameter setting is a combination of the following parameter values: latency factor $F \in \{0, 0.01, \ldots, 0.6\}$, noise parameter $ANS \in \{0.1, 0.2, 0.3\}$, maximum associative strength $MAS \in \{1, 2, 3, 4\}$, mismatch penalty $MP \in \{0, 1, 2\}$, retrieval threshold $\tau \in \{-2, -1.5, \ldots, 0\}$.

time. One important point to notice is that, depending on the numerical parameter settings in the model, the magnitude of the interference effects (inhibitory and facilitatory) can vary. This is an interesting observation because it shows that individual-level differences could in principle be modelled through systematic differences in the parameters. Figure 3.5 should also remind the reader of the Roberts and Pashler (2000) desiderata: it shows the range of predictions are relatively restricted. This is important for model validation; it shows that the model's predictions are in principle falsifiable. It is not the case that the model can predict any possible outcome.

60 The Core ACT-R-Based Model of Retrieval Processes

We turn next to a comparison of the model predictions for empirical data from the different dependency types discussed in Chapter 2.

3.2.2 Comparison of the LV05 Prediction Space with the Results of the Jäger et al. Meta-analysis

Methods All simulations reported here were run in R (R Core Team, 2016) using the ACT-R equations specified above or (for the extended model) specified in Chapter 4. All model parameters and their values (if not specified otherwise) are summarized in the appendix for Chapter 4. Simulations were run over a number of trials (and in some cases for a number of parameter values) such that results always represent the mean from multiple runs. Each iteration generated retrieval time predictions for the four conditions shown in Figure 3.3, which were simulated by specifying the respective match between cues and target and distractor respectively as follows: at retrieval, two memory items were available and two retrieval cues were specified. The first (structural) cue was matched by one memory item in all conditions, which distinguished this item as the target.[4] The second cue was matched by the target in conditions a and b (target-match) and by the distractor in conditions b and d (distractor-match). The predicted interference effect was determined for target-match and target-mismatch configurations separately by subtracting the retrieval latency in the distractor-mismatch condition (no interference) from that of the distractor-match condition (interference).

Results Figure 3.5 shows the range of possible predictions for the interference effect in target-match and target-mismatch configurations based on the four conditions shown in Figure 3.3. The simulations covered the range of values for the most relevant ACT-R parameters (see Figure 3.5 caption), which were chosen such that the simulated parameter space included all values commonly used in ACT-R simulations.

Values above zero indicate *inhibitory* interference (slowdown) and values below zero indicate *facilitatory* interference (speed-up). Along the x-axis of Figure 3.5, increasing values of the latency factor F are plotted, which is

---

[4] We acknowledge that the representation of the structural binding requirement as a single cue is a simplification. Theoretically, anaphor binding would require an item to be c-commanding and within the anaphor's binding domain. In some of the studies simulated here, the distractor mismatches both of the requirements and in some studies it mismatches only one of them. However, the number of overloaded cues that stay unchanged across conditions (i.e., match the same items in all conditions) does not affect the predictions because an interference effect arises in the model due to the difference in matched cues between conditions. In the case where the distractor mismatches two structural cues instead of one, the distractor would receive less spreading activation in all conditions. As a consequence, the predicted sizes of the effects would be smaller. Qualitatively, however, the results would not change.

3.2 The Lewis and Vasishth (2005) Model 61

usually the most freely varied parameter in ACT-R models and simply scales the retrieval latency. While there is variation in the mean interference effect along different parameter values, the figure clearly shows that the predictions of the LV05 model are restricted to *inhibitory interference* in *target-match* configurations (caused by the fan effect) and *facilitatory interference* in *target-mismatch* configurations (caused by the race process between target and distractor).[5]

How well do these predictions fare compared to the evidence published in the literature? It turns out that the answer is: not very well. A comprehensive systematic review and meta-analysis of reading studies on interference by Jäger et al. (2017) provides a basis for comparing model predictions with available data. This meta-analysis took into account 77 published experimental comparisons that investigated target-match and target-mismatch configurations for three dependency types. Table 3.1 summarizes the quantitative results of the meta-analysis. The table shows the mean effect estimates and 95% credible intervals, which mark the uncertainty of the estimates.[6]

In Jäger et al. (2017), subject-verb dependencies were divided into *agreement* dependencies (e.g., Pearlmutter et al., 1999; Wagers et al., 2009) and *non-agreement* dependencies (e.g., Van Dyke, 2007; Van Dyke and McElree, 2011), because these constitute two distinct lines of research and usually show different patterns. While agreement studies have focussed on effects of number attraction, non-agreement studies investigated interference effects involving other semantic and syntactic cues. Reflexive-antecedent and reciprocal-antecedent dependencies were treated as one category in the meta-analysis because both follow a similar syntactic constraint and the data of only two publications on reciprocals were available when the Jäger et al. (2017) article was published.

Clearly, the model cannot account for all the findings of the meta-analysis shown in Table 3.1. In *target-match* configurations, the predicted inhibitory effect was found only for non-agreement subject-verb dependencies. The other dependency types did not provide enough evidence for any effect in target-match configurations; however, these cases may not necessarily be problematic for the model because of the generally low power of the published studies (see Jäger et al., 2017, 2020; Nicenboim et al., 2018; Vasishth et al., 2018, for discussion). Most problematic for the model predictions in target-match configurations are individual studies that found a facilitatory effect. For

---

[5] Note that, in Figure 3.5, there are 334 out of 10,980 simulated data points in target-mismatch configurations that show *inhibitory* interference. These are associated with a specific parameter configuration, namely, with a high retrieval threshold (0) and a low maximum associative strength (1). These outcomes are therefore most likely related to retrieval failures. For this reason, and because the effects are small and make up only 3% of target-mismatch data points, we do not consider inhibitory target-mismatch effects a systematic prediction of LV05.

[6] The 95% credible intervals are computed within the Bayesian data analysis framework (Gelman et al., 2014). The range specified by a 95% credible interval contains the range of plausible values of the estimated parameter with 95% certainty, given the model and the data.

62 The Core ACT-R-Based Model of Retrieval Processes

Table 3.1. *Results of the Jäger et al. (2017) meta-analysis showing mean effect estimates $\bar{b}$ with Bayesian 95% credible intervals in the Estimates column. The range specified by a 95% credible interval contains the true value of the estimated parameter with 95% certainty, given the model and the data. A positive interference effect means inhibition, a negative one facilitation. Results are compared with the predictions of cue-based retrieval as implemented in the LV05 ACT-R model, and the additional contributions of the extensions* item prominence *(IP) and* multi-associative cues *(MAC), which are discussed in Chapter 4.*

Dependency	Target	Estimate ($\bar{b}$)		LV05	+IP	+MAC
Subject-verb non-agreement	Match			✓		
Subject-verb agreement	Match			✗	✓	
	Mismatch			✓		
Reflexives/ Reciprocals	Match			✗	✓	
	Mismatch			✗		✓
		-20 0 20 ms				

target-mismatch configurations, the prediction of a facilitatory effect is only supported by subject-verb agreement studies; reflexive-/reciprocal-antecedent dependencies show inhibition. For non-agreement subject-verb dependencies, no target-mismatch data were available at the time of the meta-analysis. However, two recent studies show evidence for the predicted facilitatory effect in target-mismatch configurations in reflexives (Parker and Phillips, 2017) and in non-agreement subject-verb dependencies (Cunnings and Sturt, 2018). Furthermore, we have recently established in a relatively large-sample (181 participants) eyetracking experiment (Jäger et al., 2020) that in total fixation time, target-mismatch configurations in English reflexives show facilitation effects, as predicted by the ACT-R model. Compare this to one of the studies (Dillon et al., 2013) in the meta-analysis, which had a relatively small sample size (40 participants) and found no evidence for facilitatory interference in the target-mismatch reflexive construction.

As discussed in Jäger et al. (2017), one important observation here is that in both target-match and target-mismatch configurations, the individual results of different studies show a considerable range of variability, ranging from

3.3 A More Principled Approach to Parameter Estimation

facilitatory to inhibitory interference. Later, in Chapter 4, we will explore to what extent an extension of LV05 with independently motivated assumptions can explain the observed variability. We will do this in two parts: we first look at the principal consequences of taking into account item prominence, i.e., the strength of the distractor's representation in memory relative to the target's, and then explore possible causes and consequences of multi-associative cues. In both sections, we compare empirical evidence with the prediction space of the revised model that we present. By accounting for item prominence and cue associations on the level of individual studies, the revised model is able to explain some of the facilitatory effects in subject-verb agreement target-match configurations and inhibitory effects in reflexive/reciprocal dependency target-mismatch configurations (as indicated in columns 6 and 7 in Table 3.1). The apparent absence of a clear effect in the results of the meta-analysis for reflexive/reciprocal dependency target-match configurations can be explained by a mixture of inhibitory and facilitatory effects predicted by the revised model in a principled way as a result of different levels of distractor prominence in individual studies. We then spell out how our revisions to the model are implemented and, finally, present quantitative simulations of the individual studies included in the Jäger et al. (2017) meta-analysis, comparing the estimates from the empirical data with the results of both LV05 and the revised model.

3.3 A More Principled Approach to Parameter Estimation

One drawback of the modelling results presented above is that we estimated the parameter values using a simple grid search: all possible combinations of parameters are used to generate predictions, and then these are compared to the data to find the combination that best matches the observed data. This is a very simple method for parameter estimation, but it has several disadvantages: it is inefficient and it doesn't necessarily yield a unique set of parameters as the optimal ones for a particular data-set. A more principled approach to parameter estimation is possible to implement.

In this section, we illustrate how model predictions can be derived by learning from data, using a parameter estimation approach called Approximate Bayesian Computation (ABC). The ABC approach is useful when the model cannot easily be expressed as a likelihood. Of course, one can always simplify an ACT-R model and express it as a likelihood, as was done in Nicenboim and Vasishth (2018) and Lissón et al. (2021). However, fully implemented models such as the original Lewis and Vasishth implementation are difficult to express as a likelihood, and it is for such complex process models that ABC is an appropriate tool.

In the following discussion, we illustrate how ABC can be used in future work to evaluate model predictions, for predicting both average effects and

64   The Core ACT-R-Based Model of Retrieval Processes

individual-level effects. For recent advances in this direction, see Yadav et al. (2020).

The following section reuses material from Vasishth (2020), which is copyrighted by Elsevier and published under a Creative Commons CC-BY license.

3.3.1   Bayesian Parameter Estimation

In ACT-R and other process models, numerical parameters determine the quantitative predictions of the model. For example, in ACT-R, we have the decay parameter d, the latency factor F, the noise parameter σ, and so on. These parameters can be thought of as a vector $\Theta = \langle d, F, \sigma, \dots \rangle$. When we want to derive predictions from a model, we have to assign some values to these parameters to obtain quantitative predictions. The goal usually is to figure out which combination of parameter values for Θ gives predictions closest to the observed effects from experimental data. That is, given a model $\mathcal{M}$ that takes parameters Θ, we want to minimize the discrepancy between the predicted retrieval time $\mathcal{M}(\Theta)$ and the observed difference in reading time between two experimental conditions (this difference is treated as a measure of the difference in retrieval time between the two conditions). The parameter values that provide the closest fit to the data are then considered to be the "best" or "optimal" parameters for explaining how the data arose, given the model's assumptions.

This goal of parameter estimation can be implemented very elegantly within the Bayesian paradigm. In the Bayesian parameter estimation framework, given a vector of data y and a vector of model parameters Θ, we begin by defining a so-called prior distribution $p(\Theta)$ on the parameters. For example, the noise parameter could be defined to have a plausible range of values going from 0.2 to 0.5, all of these being equally likely a priori. This prior belief about the noise parameter can be expressed by stating that the prior distribution of the noise parameter is a Uniform distribution with lower bound 0.2 and upper bound 0.5. We would write this as $\sigma \sim Uniform(0.2, 0.5)$. This is just an example of how a prior distribution can be assigned to a parameter. This seemingly simple step has major implications for us: what we are doing by defining a prior distribution on a parameter is expressing some uncertainty, before we see the data, as to what the plausible values of that parameter can be. As we show below, this uncertainty is propagated through into the model predictions, leading to more realistic model predictions.

Given such prior distributions on all the parameters in the vector Θ (which we can write compactly as $p(\Theta)$), consider next the data y from an experiment. When we carry out data analysis in the Bayesian paradigm, we define a likelihood function for the data $p(y \mid \Theta)$. As a very general example, in reading studies, when we compare the reading times from two conditions, the data can

3.3 A More Principled Approach to Parameter Estimation

be considered to come from a LogNormal likelihood, which has parameters μ and σ for the mean and the standard deviation – the likelihood is written as $LogNormal(y \mid \mu, \sigma)$, or treating the parameters as a vector $\Theta = \langle \mu, \sigma \rangle$, we can alternatively write $LogNormal(y \mid \Theta)$. The vertical bar indicates that we are talking about a conditional distribution. For more on conditional probability distributions, see Blitzstein and Hwang (2014).

The prior distribution $p(\Theta)$ and the likelihood $p(y \mid \Theta)$ together allow us to compute the so-called posterior distribution of the parameters given the data, $p(\Theta \mid y)$. This remarkable switch from $p(y \mid \Theta)$ to $p(\Theta \mid y)$ is possible because of Bayes' rule, which states that the posterior distribution of the parameters is proportional to the likelihood times the prior distribution on the parameters:

$$p(\Theta \mid y) \propto p(y \mid \Theta)p(\Theta). \tag{3.11}$$

For details on how this rule is derived from the conditional probability rule, see Blitzstein and Hwang (2014).

The posterior distributions of parameters are generally computed using Monte Carlo Markov Chain methods. Examples are Gibbs sampling, Metropolis-Hastings, and Hamiltonian Monte Carlo (Gelman et al., 2014; Lunn et al., 2012). What is remarkable here is that the result of this computation gives us not point values for each parameter in the vector Θ of parameters that we want to estimate, but a probability distribution for plausible values of the parameters, given the data, model, and the priors.

The likelihood and the priors together constitute the model, which we will call $\mathcal{M}$. As mentioned above, given a particular model $\mathcal{M}$, one important question we usually have is: what predictions does the model make? In the Bayesian framework, the model makes two kinds of predictions: a priori predictions, before any data have been taken into account; and a posteriori predictions, after the data have been taken into account. The distributions of these two kinds of predictions are called *prior predictive distributions*, and *posterior predictive distributions*, respectively.

The prior predictive distribution can be computed by drawing random samples of the parameters $\tilde{\Theta}$ from $p(\Theta)$, and then using these values to simulate data $\tilde{y}$ from the likelihood $p(y \mid \tilde{\Theta})$. The posterior predictive distribution $p(y_{pred} \mid y)$ can be computed once we have the posterior distribution of the parameters, $p(\Theta \mid y)$. Here, we assume that past and future observations are conditionally independent given θ:

$$p(y_{pred} \mid y) = \int p(y_{pred} \mid \Theta)p(\Theta \mid y) \, d\Theta. \tag{3.12}$$

In this equation, we are integrating out the parameters to produce the posterior predicted distributions. What this means is that we are taking a weighted sum of the likelihood, weighted by all possible values of the parameters. In other words, we are taking the uncertainty of the parameters into account in order to derive predictions from the model. This is superior to the conventional grid-search method we have used in the past because the latter only gives us predictions based on point values of the parameters – those predictions don't take the inherent uncertainty about the parameters into account.

Thus, this equation produces the posterior predicted distribution of the data y_{pred} given the observed data y, taking the uncertainty of the parameters Θ into account. For detailed discussion of the concept of integrating out a parameter, see Lunn et al. (2012) and Nicenboim et al. (2021).

With this (admittedly brief) discussion of how Bayesian parameter estimation works, we now consider how this approach can be used to estimate parameters from the ACT-R (or some other process) model. For such process models, Approximate Bayesian Computation is the appropriate method.

3.3.2 Approximate Bayesian Computation

Approximate Bayesian Computation (ABC) (Sisson et al., 2019) is a method for estimating posterior distributions of parameters given a model. ABC is useful when Bayes' rule cannot be employed to draw samples from the posterior distributions; this situation arises when the generative model cannot be easily expressed as a likelihood function. For extensive treatments of the theory and practical aspects of ABC, see Sisson et al. (2019) and Palestro et al. (2018). The algorithm used in the example below is rejection sampling; see Listing 1 for pseudo-code describing the algorithm.

Step 1: Define a Prior Distribution for the Parameter In this example, we will only try to estimate a single parameter, the latency factor. We begin by defining a prior distribution on the latency factor in the cue-based retrieval model. Several priors can be considered here: a Uniform prior or a Beta prior are examples. For illustration, we use the *Beta*(2, 6) prior. As shown in Figure 3.6, this is a relatively uninformative prior which downweights very small and very large values of the latency factor parameter.

The Estimates from Data for Ungrammatical Conditions In the ungrammatical conditions of the Dillon et al. (2013) data, the estimate of the interference effect in agreement conditions is -60 ms, Credible interval (CrI) $[-112, -5]$ ms. Taking a normal approximation, this implies an effect coming from the distribution $Normal(\mu = -60, \sigma = 33)$. Similarly, the estimate of the interference effect in reflexive conditions is -18 ms, CrI $[-72, 36]$ ms, which corresponds approximately to the distribution $Normal(\mu = -18, \sigma = 27)$.

3.3 A More Principled Approach to Parameter Estimation 67

Algorithm 1: ABC using rejection sampling. Shown is the case where we need to sample posterior values for a single parameter θ. Each iteration of the algorithm consists of drawing a single random sample from a prior distribution for the parameter (here, $Beta(2,6)$), and then generating the predicted mean effect from the model using that sampled parameter value. If the predicted mean effect is near the observed data (in our implementation, if the predicted effect lies within one standard error of the mean effect of interest), then accept the sampled parameter value; otherwise reject that sampled value. This process is repeated until we have sufficient samples from the posterior distribution of the parameter. These samples therefore constitute the posterior distribution of the parameter.

Input: Tolerance bounds *lower* and *upper* from data
begin
    for *i in 1:N_Simulations* **do**
        Take one sample from prior $\pi(\theta)$;
        Generate predicted mean effect $\tilde{\tilde{y}} \sim Model(\theta)$;
        if *lower* $\leq \tilde{\tilde{y}} \leq$ *upper* **then**
           | Save θ value as sample from posterior;
        end
        else
           | Discard θ sample;
        end
    end
end

These normal approximations of the differences in means in the agreement and reflexives conditions will be used to estimate parameters. The basic approach will be as follows. First, generate data from the model by sampling one value from the prior on the parameter or parameters of interest. If the generated data from the model lies "close" to the observed data's mean effect, then accept the parameter value(s) that generated the data. Otherwise, reject the parameter values, and repeat. In this way, one can obtain a vector of parameter values that produce predicted differences in means that are close to the observed difference in means. What constitutes "close"? This can be defined by the modeller; we will take one standard deviation above and below the observed difference in means as constituting a close-enough prediction (hence the name of the approach, *Approximate* Bayesian Computation).

We can use the normal approximations defined above to work out a lower and upper bound for the ABC algorithm. In our case, we choose one standard deviation about the observed mean.

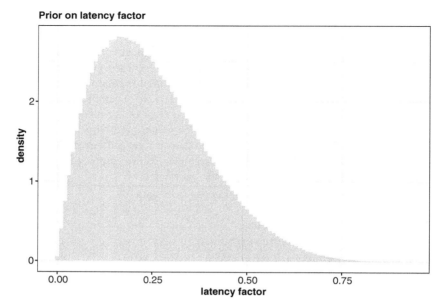

Figure 3.6 A *Beta*(2, 6) prior on the latency factor.

In the Jäger et al. (2020) data, the estimate of the interference effect in agreement conditions is −22[−46, 3], which can be approximated by the following normal distribution: *Normal*($\mu = -22, \sigma = 13$). The estimate in reflexive conditions is −23[−48, 2], which can be approximated as *Normal*($\mu = -23, \sigma = 13$).

Step 2: Compute Posterior Distributions of the Latency Factor Using ABC Rejection Sampling Here, we simply implement the ABC algorithm to derive a posterior distribution for the parameter of interest (here, the latency factor). Figure 3.7 shows the posterior distributions of the latency factor parameter for ungrammatical agreement and reflexive conditions in Dillon et al. (2013) and Jäger et al. (2020). The estimates for the Dillon et al. (2013) data-set have wider uncertainty than those for Jäger et al. (2020) because the uncertainty of the facilitatory interference effects in the data is relatively large.

Step 3: Generate Posterior Predicted Data Having estimated the posterior distributions of the latency factor for the two data-sets in the two conditions (agreement and reflexives), we can now generate posterior predicted data from the model. We use the posterior distributions of the latency factor to generate the posterior predictive distribution of the interference effect in these

3.4 Concluding Remarks

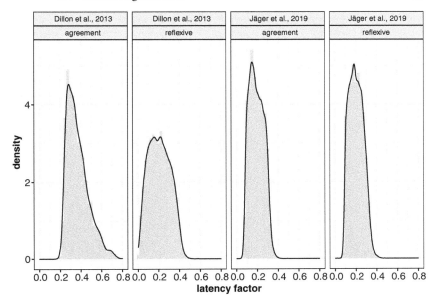

Figure 3.7 The posterior distributions of the latency factor parameters for agreement and reflexive conditions using the original Dillon et al. (2013) data (40 participants, 48 items) and our own Jäger et al. (2019) replication data (181 participants, 48 items).

experimental conditions. These posterior predictive distributions are shown in Figure 3.8.

The ABC method can be generalized using other, more effcient sampling approaches (e.g., Metropolis-Hastings) to sample the posterior from more than one parameter. The method can be computationally expensive, but the advantages afforded by taking parameter uncertainty into account in the predictions is very valuable. Here, we only demonstrate how ABC could be used to evaluate predictions for agreement and reflexive constructions, and we only estimated the latency factor. The broader point we intend to make here is that in future modelling work, ABC could be a very important and useful tool for evaluating model predictions, especially when working with complex process models like the Lewis and Vasishth model. In future work, we plan to use ABC for more extensive modelling of individual-level differences (Yadav et al., 2020).

3.4 Concluding Remarks

The source code for the model presented here is available in several different forms from the following website: https://vasishth.github.io/RetrievalModels/.

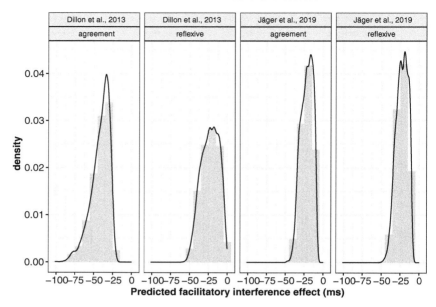

Figure 3.8 The posterior predictive distributions of the facilitatory interference in ungrammatical agreement and reflexive conditions, derived using the posterior distributions of the latency factor parameter.

Once the parameters are constrained to either their default values or through mildly informative prior distributions, as illustrated above, the model makes fairly constrained predictions. As discussed in Chapter 1, what is missing for evaluating this model is properly powered data (Roberts and Pashler, 2000). Once such data become available, it will become possible to test the a priori predictions of the model. Because the creation of such benchmark data has just begun (Jäger et al., 2020; Mertzen et al., 2020a; Vasishth et al., 2018), we must leave such an evaluation for future work.

4 An Extension of the Core Model

Modelling Prominence and Multi-associative Cues

The preceding chapter discussed the empirical coverage of the Lewis and Vasishth model against two broad classes of explanation: target-match and mismatch effects. The essential finding was that the model has only partial ability to explain the existing data. In this chapter, we discuss two important cases where the model makes incorrect predictions. One case arises when the target for retrieval is more/less prominent relative to the distractor. Modulating the prominence (e.g., through discourse prominence) seems to lead to empirically attested effects that the original Lewis and Vasishth model cannot explain. The second class of effect that the original model cannot explain is when a retrieval cue co-occurs with multiple features. For example, in the English reciprocal construction, the antecedent not only must c-command the reciprocal, but must also be plural. The collocation of the c-command and plurality features leads to one retrieval cue becoming linked to the co-occurring features, leading to cue-overload (fan effects).

In this chapter, we show how prominence and multiple association of cues and features can be implemented in the model, and the empirical consequences of these extensions of the original model. Because the proposed extensions presented here are post hoc (developed after seeing the data), it would be important in future work to test the predictions that now emerge from this extended model. We make some proposals below on how to test the predictions of these extensions of the model.

Interestingly, the "extensions" we propose are already present in the ACT-R architecture. Prominence is a function of the activation of an item in memory, but this activation is not taken into account in the fan effect computations. It is only natural that discourse and other kinds of linguistic prominence modulate the activation of items. Similarly, the association between a feature on an item and a retrieval cue is actually assumed in ACT-R to be a continuum, but the standard equations for spreading activation and the fan effect do not take this into account and instead effectively treat the match between features and cues as binary: either there is a match or there isn't. The same type of graded, continuous association is seen in language acquisition; there, it is well-established that in the course of learning associations statistically, one can associate one cue with multiply co-occurring features. It is this general property of statistical learning that we exploit when discussing the multi-associative cues discussed here.

These extensions are tentative proposals for expanding the relevance of the ACT-R framework for an application like language processing. After all, language comprehension does not simply involve processing unstructured lists of words like in a classical working memory experimental task in cognitive psychology. Linguistic strings have structure and statistical properties, and this should arguably be reflected in the model.

There is a danger here: it's possible to keep extending the model with newer and newer constructs to capture more and more facts that the core model cannot explain. Avoiding such post-hoc reverse engineering is however the responsibility of the modeller. The aim here is not to mindlessly capture more and more empirical facts, but to make principled and independently motivated extensions that reflect the nature of the linguistic input. Such extensions can only be taken seriously if they have empirical validity, something that only future empirical tests of the model will show.

4.1 Incorporating Prominence and Multi-associative Cues

Here, we introduce two new constructs that could in principle explain facilitatory interference in target-match conditions and inhibitory interference in target-mismatch conditions. These two constructs are prominence and cue-confusion.[1]

(22) a. *Target-match; distractor-mismatch*
The surgeon$^{+\text{MASC}}_{+\text{CCOM}}$ who treated Jennifer$^{-\text{MASC}}_{-\text{CCOM}}$ had pricked himself$\{^{\text{MASC}}_{\text{CCOM}}\}$...

b. *Target-match; distractor-match*
The surgeon$^{+\text{MASC}}_{+\text{CCOM}}$ who treated Jonathan$^{+\text{MASC}}_{-\text{CCOM}}$ had pricked himself$\{^{\text{MASC}}_{\text{CCOM}}\}$...

c. *Target-mismatch; distractor-mismatch*
The surgeon$^{-\text{FEM}}_{+\text{CCOM}}$ who treated Jonathan$^{-\text{FEM}}_{-\text{CCOM}}$ had pricked herself$\{^{\text{FEM}}_{\text{CCOM}}\}$...

d. *Target-mismatch; distractor-match*
The surgeon$^{-\text{FEM}}_{+\text{CCOM}}$ who treated Jennifer$^{+\text{FEM}}_{-\text{CCOM}}$ had pricked herself$\{^{\text{FEM}}_{\text{CCOM}}\}$...

---

[1] This chapter is reused (with minor changes in wording) with permission from Engelmann et al. (2020). Copyright (2019) Wiley; license numbers 4736530410746 (text) and 4736591287981 (figures and table).

4.1 Incorporating Prominence and Multi-associative Cues   73

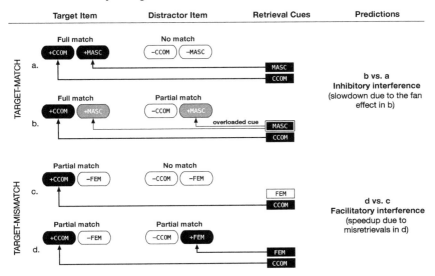

Figure 4.1 Predictions of ACT-R for the four conditions shown in Example (22). Line weights indicate the amount of spreading activation from a cue to an item. Black oval boxes represent a feature match. Grey oval boxes indicate features matching an "overloaded" cue (MASC in b), and white boxes indicate a mismatch.

We reconsider three assumptions in the ACT-R cue-based retrieval model that constitute the basis of the LV05 predictions. These are the following:

1. The base-level activation of items in memory is a function only of decay and reactivation through study-relevant retrieval events. Other influences (discussed in detail below) are usually ignored.
2. The fan effect (the inhibitory interference effect caused by cue overload) is a function of the number of items that match a specific retrieval cue, independent of their activation.
3. The associative strength between a retrieval cue and a memory item is based on a binary (match/mismatch) one-to-one mapping between the cue and a feature value.

These assumptions are, in fact, oversimplifications that do not accurately reflect general aspects of cognition. In particular, considering that the memory activation of an item represents its strength of representation or its accessibility, it should (a) affect the strength of interference and (b) take into account more aspects of the linguistic context than only the retrieval event that is relevant in a particular experiment. Furthermore, given that cognitive associations between

74   Modelling Prominence and Multi-associative Cues

contextual cues and certain representations are the result of associative learning through experience, one should account for the fact that these associations can be graded and multi-associative in nature and are not necessarily strictly categorical. Motivated by these considerations, the revised assumptions we propose are as follows:

1'. The base-level activation of items in memory (i.e., accessibility) is affected by – in addition to recency – their prominence in the current context, i.e., their relevance/salience in terms of syntactic relations in a sentence or information-structural and discourse properties.
2'. The strength of any interference effect – including the fan effect – is not simply a function of presence vs. absence of a distractor but changes as a function of the distractor's activation in memory relative to the target.
3'. The associative strength between a retrieval cue and a memory item can be the result of multiple cues being associated with multiple features at variable degrees. Cue-feature associations are based on associative learning through language experience.

In the following two sections, we show how the revised assumptions change the prediction space of LV05 and how this compares to the empirical evidence. We begin with an investigation of the way that different levels of distractor prominence can change the predictions (revised assumption 1'), assuming that relative activation affects the strength of the fan effect (revised assumption 2').

4.1.1   Item Prominence

The activation of a noun in memory prior to being retrieved (its base-level activation) is usually considered a function of the time since it is encountered in the sentence (cf. Eq. (3.7)). However, whether it was introduced as a subject or an object might change the way the noun is maintained in memory. Similarly, if a noun has been introduced in a context sentence previously may affect its memory representation. Indeed, independent evidence shows that the accessibility of a noun phrase is increased in prominent grammatical positions or through increased discourse saliency, such as being the discourse topic (Ariel, 1990; Arnold, 2007; Brennan, 1995; Chafe, 1976; Du Bois, 2003; Grosz et al., 1995; Keenan and Comrie, 1977). It is plausible that items which have a high prominence by virtue of their grammatical or discourse status are retrieved intermittently or maintained with high activation in memory. This implies that their base-level activation is higher than that of less prominent items due to reactivation boosts and reduced decay. More prominent items would thus have an elevated activation level prior to retrieval and will therefore – other things being equal – be retrieved with higher probability and lower latency than items with lower prominence. In the same way, prominence could include other factors that we do not consider here: for example, thematic role (Arnold, 2001), contrastive focus (Cowles et al., 2007), first mention (Gernsbacher and Hargreaves, 1988), and animacy (Fukumura and van Gompel, 2011) are known to affect discourse saliency and might thus influence an item's activation in memory. We focus here on the effects of grammatical position and discourse status, which have been discussed in the literature on memory interference in dependency resolution (Cunnings and Felser, 2013; Patil et al., 2016b; Sturt, 2003; Van Dyke and McElree, 2011).

In the model, instead of modelling each additional hypothesized retrieval or reactivation event, we simply add a term to the base-level activation that is a function of the grammatical role or discourse status of the memory item. Because of our revised assumption 2′, according to which the magnitude of the interference caused by a distractor in the model depends on its activation relative to the target, a sentence containing a high-prominence distractor should show a different interference effect than a sentence with a low-prominence distractor, even if the target and the retrieval cues are the same. Expressed in ACT-R terms, a high prominence status results in an increased base-level activation B_i, which is the activation of an item before spreading activation S_i is added as the result of the retrieval cues.

The full details on the implementation will be presented in the section beginning on page 89. Here, we already show the results of simulations with the extended model in order to illustrate the general predictions as a function of prominence.

Figure 4.2 shows the interference effect predicted by our model as a function of the prominence of the distractor p_{dstr} (in terms of its base-level activation) with respect to the prominence of the target, which stays constant at zero. The figure clearly shows a non-linear relationship between distractor prominence and the interference effects in target-match and target-mismatch configurations.

We explain the causes of the observed patterns in detail below by referring to Figures 4.3 and 4.4. We first look at the predictions for target-mismatch configurations (broken line), as these are less complex than the target-match predictions. The discussion surrounding Figures 4.3 and 4.4 is technically demanding, and can be skipped without loss of the main thread of this chapter. This discussion is only of interest to readers who want to understand the model's behaviour in its full details.

Predictions in Target-Mismatch Configurations Figure 4.2 shows a facilitatory interference effect that first increases then decreases with increasing distractor prominence. In order to understand the causes for the behaviour of the model, it is important to be clear about how Figure 4.2 was generated: (i) The interference effect shown in Figure 4.2 is the latency difference between the interference condition (when the distractor matches one of the retrieval

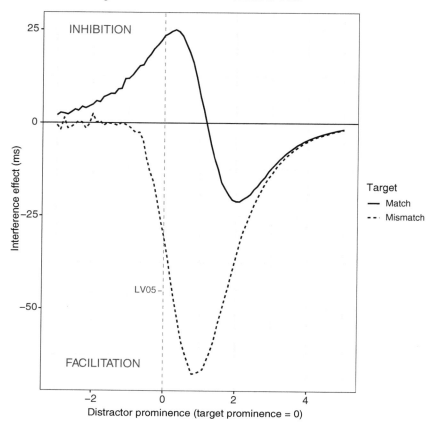

Figure 4.2 Predicted target-match and target-mismatch interference effects (distractor-match minus distractor-mismatch) as a function of distractor prominence (p_distr ranging from $\{-3,\ldots,5\}$ when target prominence is zero (mean of 10,000 iterations with parameters $F = 0.2, ANS = 0.2, MAS = 2, MP = 0$). Positive values indicate longer mean retrieval latencies (inhibition) in the interference condition due to cue overload (fan effect). Negative values indicate shorter mean retrieval latencies (facilitation) in the interference condition due to retrievals of the distractor on trials where the distractor is highly activated and hence fast. The points where the vertical line intersects with the curves represent standard LV05 predictions.

cues) and the no-interference condition (when the distractor does not match the retrieval cues). The interference effect therefore reflects how distractor prominence affects both these conditions. (ii) The effects shown are computed from mean retrieval latencies per condition across multiple trials. (iii) The

4.1 Incorporating Prominence and Multi-associative Cues 77

latency values in each trial are a function of the activation value of only the most activated (hence, retrieved) item, which can be either the target or the distractor. Hence, the mean latency in each condition reflects a mix of target and distractor activation values. (iv) The distractor in the no-interference condition is always less activated than the distractor in the interference condition, because the latter matches one of the retrieval cues and therefore receives spreading activation. (v) Without differences in base-level activation between target and distractor, the interference effect in target-mismatch configurations is caused solely by statistical facilitation due to a race process between two similarly activated items (Raab, 1962). This is the case for the predictions of the original LV05 model, which are equivalent to the situation of equal prominence between target and distractor, as represented by the vertical line in Figure 4.2. Note that, further to the right of the LV05 line, facilitatory effects are caused less by statistical facilitation and mainly by a difference in base-level activations due to distractor prominence. Figure 4.3 provides a graphical summary of the main observations and their underlying causes in target-mismatch configurations. The following is a summary of the mechanisms we explain in detail below (the enumeration corresponds to the markers in Figure 4.3):

(a) low interference due to low prominence
(b) equivalent to LV05 when distractor prominence is 0
(c) maximal facilitatory interference due to misretrievals at maximal latency difference between conditions
(d) low interference due to individual latencies being close to zero

At LV05 equivalence (vertical line in Figure 4.2 and point b in Figure 4.3), the activation level of target and distractor in the interference condition is equal (Figure 4.3.1). Therefore, both have equal retrieval probability (Figure 4.3.2), leading to a race situation with faster retrievals on average due to statistical facilitation (Figure 4.3.3) and, hence, a facilitatory interference effect (Figure 4.3.4). To the left of the LV05 equivalence, the distractor has lower activation than the target and is thus retrieved less often, hence (a) the statistical facilitation is smaller.[2] To the right of the LV05 equivalence, the distractor becomes more activated than the target and, similarly, the statistical facilitation becomes smaller because of different completion times between target and distractor. Despite this, however, the facilitation effect in target-mismatch keeps increasing. This is because the distractor is now much more activated and has a higher retrieval probability than the target in the interference condition, while the target is still more active and more likely to be retrieved in the no-interference condition because of its better match with the retrieval cues (Figure 4.3.2).

---

[2] As discussed in Logačev and Vasishth (2015), facilitation in a race process is largest when the two racing processes have similar completion times.

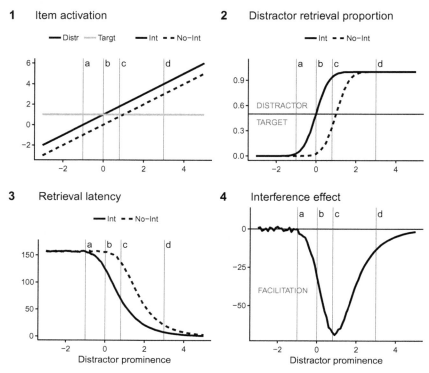

Figure 4.3 Mechanisms underlying the effect of distractor prominence in target-mismatch configurations. The x-axis in each panel shows increasing distractor prominence (with target prominence = 0). The panels from top left are: (1) Mean activation of target and distractor at retrieval event in interference (distractor-match) and no-interference (distractor-mismatch) condition (the sign of the activation value – negative or positive – has no special meaning in ACT-R). (2) Proportion of distractor retrievals over multiple iterations (retrieval probability). Values above 0.5 indicate higher retrieval probability for the distractor than the target (misretrievals). (3) Mean retrieval latencies (of most activated item at retrieval). (4) Mean interference effect as the difference in retrieval latencies between interference and no-interference condition. Positive values mean inhibitory interference (longer latencies when distractor matches); negative values mean facilitatory interference (short latencies due to misretrievals when distractor mismatches). The vertical lines mark locations of (a) low interference due to low prominence; (b) LV05 equivalence at prominence = 0 (equal activation of target and distractor in interference condition); (c) maximal facilitatory interference effect due to misretrievals; (d) low interference due to latencies close to zero.

Hence, the average retrieval latency is lower in the interference condition (Figure 4.3.3) due to more fast misretrievals of the highly activated distractor. At the maximal facilitatory interference effect around $p_{dstr} = 0.9$ (point c in Figure 4.3), the retrieval probability of the distractor in the interference condition approaches 100% while being just under 40% in the no-interference condition (Figure 4.3.2). This means that the mean latency in the interference condition is 100% caused by fast misretrievals of the highly activated distractor, while, in the no-interference condition, the mean latency is still mostly influenced by target (i.e., correct) retrievals. This maximizes the mean latency difference between the conditions (Figure 4.3.3) and therefore the interference effect (Figure 4.3.4). After point c, the retrieval probability of the distractor in the no-interference condition surpasses that of the target, giving the distractor more influence on the mean retrieval latencies, such that the retrieval latency receives a sharper decrease as a function of distractor prominence (broken line in Figure 4.3.3). Therefore, the retrieval speed in the no-interference condition starts catching up with that in the interference condition, where the latency decreases more slowly because the number of misretrievals – and therefore the influence of the highly activated distractor – in the interference condition stays constant (at 100%). Because the retrieval latency becomes more similar in both conditions, we see a decreasing interference effect. Above $p_{dstr} = 2$, the distractor is so highly activated that it is retrieved in every iteration in both the interference and no-interference conditions (d). At this point, the only difference between both conditions is the constant activation boost for the distractor due to the cue match in the interference condition (Figure 4.3.1). Further increasing distractor prominence affects both conditions in the same way. As activation goes to infinity with increasing prominence, retrieval latencies in both conditions asymptote to zero (see ACT-R latency Eq. (3.6)). Therefore, the facilitation effect also decreases further towards zero (see Figure 4.3.3).

Predictions in Target-Match Configurations We now turn to target-match configurations (the solid line in Figure 4.2), where we see a more complex pattern than in target-mismatch configurations: The inhibitory target-match interference effect increases with increasing distractor activation, and decreases when the distractor activation exceeds the target activation, eventually turning into a facilitatory interference effect, which later decreases again. In explaining this pattern, we refer to Figure 4.4, which highlights six points of interest along the curve:

(a) low interference due to low prominence
(b) maximal inhibitory interference effect due to increased fan
(c) equal activation of target and distractor in interference condition: lower fan effect due to statistical facilitation

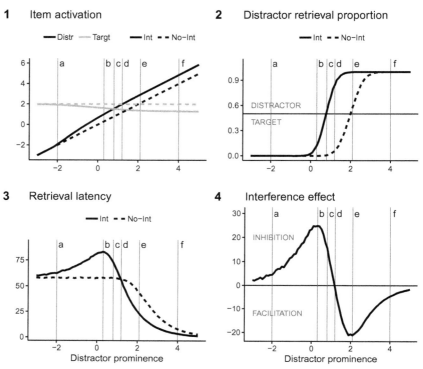

Figure 4.4 Mechanisms underlying the effect of distractor prominence in target-match configurations. The x-axis in each panel shows increasing distractor prominence (with target prominence = 0). The panels from top left are: (1) Mean activation of target and distractor at retrieval event in interference (distractor-match) and no-interference (distractor-mismatch) condition (the sign of the activation value – negative or positive – has no special meaning in ACT-R). (2) Proportion of distractor retrievals over multiple iterations (retrieval probability). Values above 0.5 indicate higher retrieval probability for the distractor than the target (misretrievals). (3) Mean retrieval latencies (of most activated item at retrieval). (4) Mean interference effect as the difference in retrieval latencies between interference and no-interference condition. Positive values mean inhibitory interference (longer latencies when distractor matches); negative values mean facilitatory interference (short latencies due to misretrievals when distractor mismatches). The vertical lines mark locations of (a) low interference due to low prominence; (b) maximal inhibitory interference effect due to increased fan; (c) equal activation of target and distractor in interference condition: lower fan effect due to statistical facilitation; (d) zero interference effect because of equal strength of fan effect and facilitation due to misretrievals of the highly activated distractor; (e) maximal facilitatory interference effect due to misretrievals; (f) low interference due to latencies close to zero.

4.1 Incorporating Prominence and Multi-associative Cues 81

(d) zero interference effect because of equal strength of fan effect and facilitation due to misretrievals of the highly activated distractor
(e) maximal facilitatory interference effect due to misretrievals
(f) low interference due to latencies being close to zero.

To the left of the LV05-equivalence line in Figure 4.2, the target-match interference effect increases with increasing prominence (a) because the new fan equation in the extended model (see Eq. (4.4) in the implementation below) takes into account the activation of each distractor item instead of only the number of distractors. The inhibitory interference effect is maximal at (b) just before the distractor activation value approaches that of the target (see Figure 4.4.1), when a statistical facilitation effect begins to arise due to a race between both items. The statistical facilitation is maximal when distractor activation and target activation are equal in the interference condition (c). At this point, the inhibitory effect is reduced because the statistical facilitation counteracts the fan effect. Beyond the point of equal activation between target and distractor, the statistical facilitation decreases again. However, the facilitatory effect continues to increase and counteract the fan effect because now the retrieval probability of the distractor is higher than that of the target (Figure 4.4.2) and, hence, the mean retrieval latency in the interference condition (Figure 4.4.3) reflects the increasingly activated distractor. When the strength of the facilitation equals that of the fan effect, the interference effect is zero (d). At this point, the activation of the distractor in the interference condition equals the activation of the target in the no-interference condition (Figure 4.4.1). Because the distractor is the most retrieved item in the interference condition while the target is still the most retrieved item in the no-interference condition, Figure 4.4.2, the mean retrieved latency, is the same in both conditions (Figure 4.4.3). As the activation and retrieval probability of the distractor in the interference condition keep increasing, the mean retrieval latency is now lower in the interference condition than in the no-interference condition (Figure 4.4.3), leading to a facilitatory interference effect (Figure 4.4.4). From here, the pattern and its explanation are the same as in target-mismatch configurations. The facilitatory effect reaches its maximum when the retrieval probability for the distractor in the interference condition is 100% and the distractor's activation and probability in the no-interference condition are also about to surpass the target's (point e in Figure 4.4.1–3). The latency difference between the conditions, and thereby the effect, keeps decreasing while the retrieval probabilities of the highly activated distractor become more similar in both conditions, and additionally, because the latencies approach zero with very high prominence values (f).

How do these predictions match up with the data? In the literature on target-match interference configurations with high-prominence distractors, there is some evidence for both (A) inhibitory effects as well as (B) facilitatory effects.

For the remainder of this section, we summarize this evidence in comparison with the predictions shown in Figure 4.2.

A: Target-match inhibition In an eyetracking and a speed-accuracy trade-off experiment with target-match configurations, Van Dyke and McElree (2011) found that a distractor noun phrase in the subject position of a subordinate clause, such as *the witness* (vs. *motion*) in (23a), causes inhibitory interference at the main verb *compromised*, while no such effect was present when the distractor *the witness* was in object position as in (23b).

(23)   a. The judge who had declared that **the witness/the motion** was inappropriate realized that the attorney in the case compromised.

          b. The judge who had rejected **the witness/the motion** realized that the attorney in the case compromised.

Patil et al. (2016b) found an interference effect at the reflexive in an eyetracking experiment using sentences as in 24 with the distractor *Fred* in subject position, which was a modification of Sturt (2003) (shown in 25) where the distractor was in object position.

(24)   The tough soldier that **Fred**/Katie treated in the military hospital introduced himself to all the nurses.

(25)   The surgeon who treated **Jonathan**/Jennifer had pricked himself with a used syringe needle.

In the manipulation of Van Dyke and McElree (2011), a prominent distractor (in subject position) in a target-match configuration caused inhibitory interference while a non-prominent distractor (in object position) did not. As shown in Figure 4.2, our prominence model predicts that the inhibitory effect in target-match configurations increases with higher distractor prominence as long as the distractor activation is still lower than the target activation (see region between points a and b in Figure 4.4.1).

In a reflexive-antecedent study in Mandarin Chinese, Jäger et al. (2015) found a similar difference in target-match configurations between their Experiment 1, where a distractor was present in the sentence, and their Experiment 2, where three distractors were presented as memory load. An inhibitory target-match interference effect was only found in Experiment 2. In addition to the higher number of distractors in Experiment 2, the need to rehearse the distractors while reading/comprehending the target sentence would make them more prominent in memory, i.e., increase their activation, which would amplify the interference effect, again as shown in Figure 4.2.

4.1 Incorporating Prominence and Multi-associative Cues

B: Target-match facilitation Experiment 1 by Sturt (2003) and Experiment 2 by Cunnings and Felser (2013) found facilitatory interference in target-match configurations when the distractor was in subject position *and* had been made the discourse topic using a context sentence. Cunnings and Felser used sentences such as Example (26) and the baseline condition shown in Example (27), where the distractor noun phrase was introduced in a context sentence and was co-referred to in the target sentence through the pronoun *he*. The authors hypothesized that the distractor was more prominently encoded due to reactivation at the anaphor, and that this may have increased the probability of observing an interference effect at the reflexive (pp. 212–213).

(26)   **James** has worked at the army hospital for years.
The soldier that **he** treated on the ward wounded himself while on duty in the Far East.

(27)   **Helen** has worked at the army hospital for years. The soldier that **she** treated on the ward wounded himself while on duty in the Far East.

A distractor that is a discourse topic and is also in subject position would arguably be more prominent than if it were just in subject position but not a discourse topic. The qualitative difference of the target-match effects described above is thus predicted by our model. As explained above, a distractor that is more activated than the target causes an increasing number of misretrievals of the highly activated distractor, which has a faster retrieval latency and therefore yields a facilitatory interference effect on average when the speed-up is strong enough to counteract the fan effect (right-hand side of point d in Figure 4.4).

In summary, the integration of prominence in the form of base-level activation (assumption $1'$) and the fan effect being a function of distractor activation (assumption $2'$) can explain inhibitory interference effects in target-match configurations with a prominent distractor that were not found with a non-prominent distractor (Jäger et al., 2015; Patil et al., 2016b; Van Dyke and McElree, 2011), and facilitatory interference effects in target-match configurations with a highly prominent distractor that was in subject position *and* the discourse topic (Cunnings and Felser, 2013; Sturt, 2003). The original LV05 model predicts neither facilitatory interference effects in target-match configurations nor the systematic absence of an effect under certain conditions. Earlier, in Table 3.1, we indicated the explanatory gaps of LV05 with respect to the outcomes of the Jäger et al. (2017) meta-analysis, specifically the facilitatory interference effect in target-match configurations in subject-verb agreement and the absence of an overall effect in reflexives and reciprocals. Taking into account item prominence as presented above, these unexplained effects are possible outcomes of low, medium, or high prominence values on the continuum shown in Figure 4.2.

84   Modelling Prominence and Multi-associative Cues

Next, we investigate the prediction space of LV05 under assumption 3′ that retrieval cues can be associated with multiple features to varying degrees.

4.1.2   Multi-associative Cues

The noun *surgeon* in the sentence "the surgeon who treated Jennifer had pricked herself" receives increased activation in memory when retrieval is triggered at *himself* because it matches the syntactic cue CCOM. The distractor *Jennifer* receives the same amount of activation through its match with the gender cue FEM. As depicted in Figure 4.1d, this leads to the situation with two similarly activated items, but no fan effect because their features do not overlap – each item is associated with a different cue. This leads to statistical facilitation in the way explained earlier.

In ACT-R models, a match between a cue and a feature is binary and categorical: a feature and a cue can only match or not match, there is no gradation; and a gender cue can only be matched by gender features (masc, fem, neut) and is not associated at all with features of a different category. Such categorical one-to-one relations are, of course, a simplification made for modelling, but they are not well motivated when we accept that language acquisition is essentially a gradual process of learning the mapping from form to meaning on the basis of contextual cues (see, e.g., Bybee, 2006; Langacker, 1987; Tomasello, 2003). The strength and distinctiveness of representational associations are thus dependent on similarities with other associations. In that sense, retrieval cues represent abstract knowledge about the features that successfully identify the correct retrieval target, as derived from experience with a certain dependency context. Hence, cue-feature associations evolve as graded associations between a retrieval context and any features of the correct target resulting from a process of learning relevant discriminations between features. As a result, it is possible that, in certain situations, a cue can be associated with multiple feature values to varying degrees.

Now, there is no specific reason why, in the sentence "the surgeon who treated Jennifer had pricked herself," the syntactic cue would be associated with gender features or vice versa. But consider, for example, the sentence "the nurse who cared for the children had pricked each other." The relevant retrieval cues for the reciprocal *each other* are CCOM and PLURAL. The cue CCOM is matched by the syntactically correct target *the nurse* and PLURAL is matched by the distractor *the children*. The difference between reciprocals, such as *each other*, and reflexives, such as *herself*, is that the correct target in a reciprocal context always exhibits the features +PLUR and +CCOM, while there are several possible forms in a reflexive context, e.g., *himself, herself, itself*, and *themselves*, which all trigger different combinations of the syntactic cue with gender and number cues, as listed in Table 4.1.

4.1 Incorporating Prominence and Multi-associative Cues

Table 4.1. *Possible feature combinations exhibited by correct antecedents of English reflexives, reciprocals, and Chinese* ziji.

Context	Target features	Form
EN reflexive	$\{{}^{+MASC}_{+CCOM}\}$	himself
	$\{{}^{+FEM}_{+CCOM}\}$	herself
	$\{{}^{+NEUT}_{+CCOM}\}$	itself
	$\{{}^{+PLUR}_{+CCOM}\}$	themselves
EN reciprocal	$\{{}^{+PLUR}_{+CCOM}\}$	each other
CN reflexive	$\{{}^{+ANIM}_{+CCOM}\}$	ziji

The CCOM cue in reflexive contexts would therefore not be strongly associated with, e.g., the +FEM feature because this would activate the wrong items whenever the form of the reflexive is not *herself* but *himself* or *themselves*, etc. Therefore, the reflexive context requires syntactic, gender and number features to be discriminated. In reciprocal contexts, however, the correct target has to be plural. In this case, if the CCOM cue were to be associated with the +PLURAL feature, it would always activate the correct target. Because +CCOM and +PLURAL co-occur frequently in similar contexts for reciprocal-antecedent dependencies, a strong discrimination is less necessary than in reflexive contexts. Instead, it might even be more efficient to also activate plural items with the CCOM cue and vice versa. This reasoning builds on the ideas of classical conditioning (Rescorla and Wagner, 1972), where two stimuli that require similar responses in similar contexts become less discriminated than when they elicit different responses. As a consequence, the cues CCOM and PLURAL in reciprocal-antecedent dependencies would be less discriminative than the cues in reflexive-antecedent dependencies and would therefore both be associated to some degree with both the features +CCOM and +PLUR. We will say that, in this situation, two cues are cross-associated due to feature co-occurrence. A similar situation arises for the Chinese reflexive *ziji* (also shown in Table 4.1), which requires an animate and c-commanding target. Thus, in the case of *ziji*, CCOM would be cross-associated with ANIM.

For an illustration of the predictions that would arise from cross-associated cues, consider Figure 4.5. The figure shows the no-interference (c) and interference (d) conditions in target-mismatch configurations when cues are cross-associated in contrast to Figure 4.1, where no cross association was present.

Because the CCOM and PLUR cues are cross-associated, both cues behave here as a kind of amalgamated cue that is associated with both the +CCOM

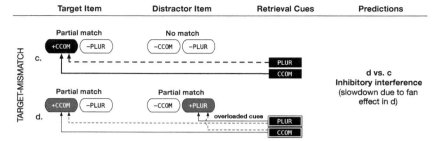

Figure 4.5 Spreading activation in conditions labelled distractor-match (c) and distractor-mismatch (d) conditions in target-mismatch configurations when cues are cross-associated. Line weight and box shading indicate the amount of spreading activation added to an item due to a feature match. Dashed lines represent spreading activation to a cross-associated feature.

and the +PLUR feature. In the target-mismatch/distractor-mismatch condition c, the target therefore receives activation from both cues although it only carries the +CCOM feature. In the target-mismatch/distractor-match condition d, the target carries +CCOM and the distractor carries +PLUR. As a consequence, both cues now share their activation between target and distractor, i.e., they are overloaded. This leads to a similar situation as in target-match configurations shown earlier in condition b of Figure 4.1: as spreading activation is shared between target and distractor, inhibitory interference, i.e., the fan effect, arises. This is because both items are less activated in d than the target is in c and will be retrieved slower in d vs. c.[3]

In order to explore the quantitative consequences for the predicted interference effect, we implemented cross-associated cues in an extension of LV05 and ran simulations with a range of values for the cross-association level. As the results in Figure 4.6 clearly show, an increasing cross-association level causes an inhibitory fan effect in target-mismatch configurations that eliminates the facilitatory effect.

The cross-association level c takes values between 0 and 1, where $c = 0$ means that two features are maximally discriminated (distinct cues activate

---

[3] The reader may wonder why a facilitatory race effect does not emerge in target-mismatch when cross-associated cues induce a fan effect: after all, both the target and distractor again have similar activations. A similar activation of target and distractor is a prerequisite for a race-based statistical facilitation. For a race-induced facilitation, however, the target would have to be similarly activated in both conditions c and d, as is the case without cross association (Figure 4.1). With cross association, the target has higher activation in c, whereas in d, the activation is shared with the distractor and therefore reduced. Therefore, the target's activation in c is much higher relative to the activations in condition d of the two racing items (i.e., the target and the distractor). Hence, the target in c will be retrieved faster on average than the winner of the race in condition d, and consequently no facilitation effect will be observed in d vs. c.

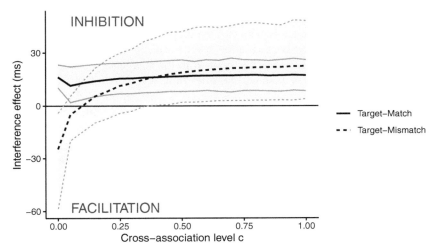

Figure 4.6 Predicted target-match and target-mismatch interference effects (distractor-match minus distractor-mismatch) as a function of the cross-association level c. Lines and shaded area show mean and range of the effect, respectively, for parameter values of the latency factor F ranging from 0.2 to 0.4, and distractor prominence ranging from $-0.5, 0, 0.5$, running 5,000 iterations each; other parameters were fixed as $ANS = 0.2, MAS = 2, MP = 0$. Positive values indicate longer mean retrieval latencies (inhibition) in the interference condition due to cue-overload (fan effect). Negative values indicate shorter mean retrieval latencies (facilitation) in the interference condition due to misretrievals of the distractor.

distinct features) and $c = 1$ means that their corresponding features are treated as functionally identical, i.e., each cue activates both features.

More formally, $c_{kl}(Context)$ is the cross-association level c with respect to features k and l in a particular retrieval context (e.g., English reciprocals), and is equal to the strength with which each feature is associated with the corresponding cue of the other feature. For example, if the cross-association level of +CCOM and +PLURAL in reciprocals equals 0.5, it means that the CCOM cue is associated with the +PLURAL feature with strength 0.5 and the PLURAL cue is associated with the +CCOM feature with strength 0.5. This means that, in the absence of the plural cue, a plural item would still receive activation from the cue CCOM, but the plural item would not receive as much activation as a c-commanding item would. Thus, at $c = 0.5$, there is still some discrimination between the features in question. If, however, $c = 1.0$, plural and c-command would not be discriminated at all as distinct information. Any item with one of the two features would be activated by any of the two cues in the same way.

This effectively means that we would not think of two cues in this case but only one that is associated equally with two features.

Theoretically, the cross-association level c reflects the relative frequency of co-occurrence of both features, relative to the frequency of occurrence of either of the features. For example, consider Table 4.1, which shows several co-occurring features. We could say that the cross-association level $c_{kl}(Context)$ is the ratio of all feature combinations with both k and l with respect to all combinations with at least k or l, given a particular context:

$$c_{kl}(Context) = \frac{\sum [k \wedge l | Context]}{\sum [k \vee l | Context]} \tag{4.1}$$

where the square brackets represent an Iverson bracket which denotes 1 if the enclosed condition is satisfied and 0 if not. This way, we can say, e.g., that the cross-association levels for the examples in Table 4.1 are for reflexives $c_{CCOM,MASC}(refl\text{-}EN) = 1/4 = 0.25$, for reciprocals $c_{CCOM,PLUR}(reci\text{-}EN) = 1/1 = 1.0$, and for $ziji$ $c_{CCOM,PLUR}(ziji) = 1/1 = 1.0$.

The absolute values of these parameters are not of importance here; this example only serves as an illustration of the difference between English reflexives on the one hand and English reciprocals or $ziji$ on the other. What this calculation suggests is that, when processing English reflexives, more distinct cue representations are used due to a greater variety of feature combinations than for reciprocals or $ziji$.

In summary, the theory of multi-associative cues predicts that a cue could in some situations share its spreading activation between what would otherwise be categorically distinct features. In these situations, a fan effect can arise even in target-mismatch configurations. Table 3.1 shows inhibitory instead of facilitatory interference in target-mismatch configurations. This has been found, for instance, in some studies on reflexives and reciprocals and can be explained neither by LV05 nor by item prominence. According to ACT-R, inhibitory interference simply cannot arise in target-mismatch configurations because the necessary condition for a fan effect – an overloaded cue due to multiple matches – is not met. Our approach of using multi-associative cues predicts a higher cross-association level for both reciprocals and the Chinese reflexive $ziji$ compared to English reflexives. This could explain the result of Kush and Phillips (2014), who found inhibitory interference in target-mismatch conditions in Hindi reciprocals,[4] as well as our finding of an inhibitory target-mismatch effect for Chinese $ziji$ in Experiment 1 of Jäger et al. (2015).

The following section explains the implementation of both multi-associative cues and item prominence in our extended ACT-R model.

---

[4] As discussed in Kush and Phillips (2014), Hindi reciprocals have properties identical to English reciprocals: the antecedent must c-command the reciprocal and also match the reciprocal in morphological features (plural), and the antecedent must be in the same clause as the reciprocal.

4.1.3 Implementation of Item Prominence and Multi-associative Cues

The ACT-R architecture already has the basic theoretical constructs needed for implementing prominence and multi-associative cues. For example, in ACT-R, any two memory items can be assigned a numerical value that signifies how similar they are to each other. Thus, the colours orange and red can be treated as more similar to each other than orange and green. Because feature values are also treated as items in memory, similarities can be assigned to pairs of features as well. In ACT-R, similarities are used, for example, in the equation for a component called mismatch penalty that enables the model to retrieve items that do not match the retrieval cues but might nevertheless be similar. Thus, an orange item can be retrieved even though the retrieval cue specifies a red one. We extend the ACT-R framework such that the similarity between features is also used in the computation of the fan effect.

The general idea of our extension is that each item's prominence as well as specific cue-feature associations are reflected in the associative strength S_{ji} between a cue j and an item i, which in turn affects the activation A_i of that item. In other words, the associative strength that a memory item has with a specific cue reflects the prominence status of all memory items and the relative associations of that cue with all features of all memory items. Therefore, the two mechanisms, item prominence and multi-associative cues, are merely two aspects of one broader mechanism, namely the association of the available retrieval cues with specific memory items. In order to incorporate prominence and multi-associative cues, we redefine the associative strength S_{ji}. Recall from Eq. (3.5) that, given a set of retrieval cues ($Cues = \{q1, \dots, qJ\}$), the activation A_i of an item i is a function of spreading activation S_i:

$$A_i \propto S_i \text{ where } S_i = \sum_{j \in Cues} W_j S_{ji}. \tag{4.2}$$

For each cue j, the standard ACT-R calculation of S_{ji} is based on its fan, which is defined as the number of items that match this cue. Instead of this simplified definition, we base our implementation on the more general definition of S_{ji} (Schneider and Anderson, 2012, p. 129). This general definition states that the association between cue j and item i reflects the probability of the item being needed (i.e., is the target of the retrieval) given cue j:[5]

$$S_{ji} = \text{MAS} + \log[P(i|j)]. \tag{4.3}$$

The standard equation (which is usually used in ACT-R implementations) that calculates the fan as the number of matching items makes the simplifying assumption that all items associated with cue j are equally likely (i.e., useful in

---

[5] We thank Klaus Oberauer for his helpful comments, which led to the present implementation.

the context of cue j), such that $P(i|j) = 1/fan_j$. It is important to note here that the probability $P(i|j)$ for item i is only defined when it is associated with cue j.

In order to reflect differences in encoding strength between items (prominence) and cross associations between cues, we define $P(i|j)$ here as the match quality Q_{ji} (which will be defined further below) of item i with cue j in proportion to the match quality Q_{jv} of all active memory items v with j:

$$P(i|j) = \frac{Q_{ji}}{\sum_{v \in Items} Q_{jv}}. \quad (4.4)$$

The next two subsections will explain how this leads to multi-associative cues and the influence of item prominence on the fan effect.

4.1.4 Multi-associative Cues

We assume that a cue can have variable discrimination, i.e., it can be associated with multiple features to different degrees. The associative strength between a cue j and a feature k is given by M_{jk}, which takes values between 0 (not associated) and 1 (maximally associated). The individual match quality Q_{ji} of cue j with a specific item i then depends on the associative strength between j and all features K_i of i:

$$Q_{ji} = \sum_{k \in K_i} M_{jk}. \quad (4.5)$$

As shown in Figure 4.6, cross association predicts a fan effect also for items that do not share any of their features, as long as the same cue is associated with features from both items. We work through some examples next.

For the worked-out examples below, assume that an item i has feature f1 but not feature f2, and a distractor item i' has feature f2 but not f1 (see Figure 4.7). Assume also that the retrieval cue q1 matches f1, and cue q2 matches f2. Retrieval is triggered using the two cues q1 and q2. This is the typical target-mismatch/distractor-match scenario discussed earlier.

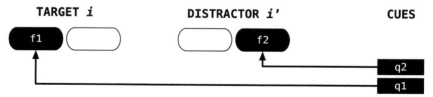

Figure 4.7 Standard target-mismatch/distractor-match condition without cross-associated cues.

4.1 Incorporating Prominence and Multi-associative Cues 91

(i) **No cross association of features (standard ACT-R case)**: In the case that there is no cross association, the spreading activation to item i from cue q1 depends on the probability of item i given cue q1:

$$P(i|q1) = \frac{Q_{q1,i}}{\sum\limits_{v \in Items} Q_{q1,v}} \tag{4.6}$$

The numerator is computed as follows. Since only feature f1 matches cue q1 in item i, we have

$$Q_{q1,i} = \sum_{k \in K_i} M_{q1,k} = M_{q1,f1} = 1. \tag{4.7}$$

The denominator, $\sum\limits_{v \in Items} Q_{q1,v}$, also has value 1 because it is the sum of the match of cue q1 to item i (which is 1) and to item i' (which is 0):

$$\sum_{v \in Items} Q_{q1,v} = Q_{q1,i} + Q_{q1,i'} = 1 + 0. \tag{4.8}$$

The calculation of $P(i|j)$ is therefore

$$P(i|j) = P(i|q1) = \frac{Q_{q1,i}}{\sum\limits_{v \in Items} Q_{q1,v}} = \frac{1}{1} = 1. \tag{4.9}$$

This implies that the spreading activation from cue q1 to item i is

$$\begin{aligned} S_{q1,i} &= MAS + \log[P(i|q1)] \\ &= MAS + \log[1] = MAS. \end{aligned} \tag{4.10}$$

As no other cue matches item i, $S_{q1,i}$ equals the total amount of spreading activation S_i that item i receives:

$$S_i = S_{q1,i} = MAS. \tag{4.11}$$

Thus, there is no penalty to the activation of item i caused by spreading activation (fan effect) in target-mismatch/distractor-match configurations when there is no cross association.

(ii) **Cross association of 0.5**: Now consider the activation spread to item i when the cross-association level of the cues is 0.5. Under this scenario, item i receives not only 100% activation from the fully matching cue q1, but also from q2 which spreads 50% of its activation to feature f1. The distractor i' similarly gets activation not only from q2, which fully matches f2, but also from q1 which spreads 50% of its activation to feature f2. Graphically, this corresponds to the following scenario (Figure 4.8):

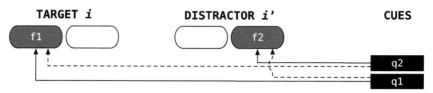

Figure 4.8 Target-mismatch/distractor-match condition when cues are cross-associated.

Now, $P(i|q1)$ is not 1 but $1/1.5$ or $2/3$.

$$P(i|q1) = \frac{Q_{q1,i}}{\sum_{v \in Items} Q_{q1,v}} = \frac{1}{1.5} = \frac{2}{3}. \qquad (4.12)$$

This is because $Q_{q1,i} = 1$ as before, but the denominator is the sum of the match of cue q1 to item i (a match of 1) as well as the match of cue q1 to item i' (a match of 0.5).

$$\sum_{v \in Items} Q_{q1,v} = Q_{q1,i} + Q_{q1,i'} = 1 + 0.5 = 1.5. \qquad (4.13)$$

We then use $P(i|q1)$ to calculate the spreading activation $S_{q1,i}$ from cue q1 to item i. In contrast to the scenario above without cross association, the amount of activation spread $S_{q1,i}$ is now smaller than MAS:

$$S_{q1,i} = MAS + \log\left[\frac{2}{3}\right] = MAS + [-0.41] = MAS - 0.41. \qquad (4.14)$$

Next, the calculation for item i and cue q2 is

$$P(i|q2) = \frac{Q_{q2,i}}{\sum_{v \in Items} Q_{q2,v}} = \frac{0.5}{1.5} = \frac{1}{3}. \qquad (4.15)$$

Here, $Q_{q2,i} = 0.5$ because of the cross association of 0.5 of cue q2 with the feature f1. The denominator is the sum of the match of cue q2 to item i (a match of 0.5) as well as the match of cue q2 to item i' (a match of 1).

$$\sum_{v \in Items} Q_{q2,v} = Q_{q2,i} + Q_{q2,i'} = 0.5 + 1 = 1.5. \qquad (4.16)$$

We now use $P(i|q2)$ to calculate the spreading activation $S_{q2,i}$ that item i receives from cue $q2$. Similar to $S_{q1,i}$, $S_{q2,i}$ will also be smaller than MAS:

$$S_{q2,i} = MAS + \log\left[\frac{1}{3}\right] = MAS + [-1.1] = MAS - 1.1. \qquad (4.17)$$

4.1 Incorporating Prominence and Multi-associative Cues

Having computed $S_{q1,i}$ and $S_{q2,i}$, the total amount of spreading activation S_i that item i receives can be calculated (W_j is 0.5 as we have two equally weighted cues):

$$
\begin{aligned}
S_i &= \sum_{j \in Cues} W_j S_{ji} \\
&= \frac{1}{2} S_{q1,i} + \frac{1}{2} S_{q2,i} \\
&= \frac{1}{2} \left(MAS + \log \left[\frac{2}{3} \right] \right) + \frac{1}{2} \left(MAS + \log \left[\frac{1}{3} \right] \right) \\
&= MAS + \frac{1}{2} \left(\log \left[\frac{2}{3} \right] + \log \left[\frac{1}{3} \right] \right) \\
&= MAS - 0.75.
\end{aligned}
\tag{4.18}
$$

Because the spreading activation S_i received by item i will have a value less than MAS, activation of item i will go down due to the presence of the matching distractor, leading to inhibitory interference even in a target-mismatch configuration, when the cross-association level is sufficiently high.[6]

4.1.5 Prominence

We assume that the prominence of an item is reflected in its base-level activation, which also reflects how recently the item has been retrieved or created. For this purpose, we simply introduce a prominence component p_i as a constant added to the base-level activation B_i, such that Eq. (3.7) for B_i is changed to

$$
B_i = \log \left(\sum_{j=1}^{n} t_j^{-d} \right) + \beta_i + p_i.
\tag{4.19}
$$

Thus, more prominent items are more highly activated and are therefore more likely to be retrieved. In addition, the base-level activation including prominence should affect how strongly an item interferes with the retrieval of other items: a highly activated and thus very salient item will have a stronger fan effect than an item that is less active in memory. We therefore introduce a saliency component as a weighting of the individual match quality Q_{ji}, changing Eq. (4.5) in the following way:

$$
Q_{ji} = \sum_{k \in K_i} M_{jk} \times \frac{1}{1 + qe^{-(B_i - \tau)}}.
\tag{4.20}
$$

---

[6] The actual level that leads to detectable inhibitory interference depends on the specific situation being simulated and the values of other ACT-R parameters.

The saliency component (the second factor) is a logistic function that bounds the base-level activation value between 0 and 1, such that it functions as a scaling factor for Q_{ji}. In the denominator, τ is the retrieval threshold, and q is a scaling constant that scales how strongly the match quality Q_{ji} is affected by an item's saliency. It can be used to switch the quality correction on and off and thus make our model identical to standard ACT-R: when $q = 0$, the item's base-level activation including prominence is not reflected in $P(i|j)$. Furthermore, when $q = 0$ and all cues are maximally discriminative (i.e., exactly one feature matches one cue), $P(i|j) = 1/fan_j$, in which case the model behaviour is identical to standard ACT-R. If, however, $q > 0$, the base-level activation of an item–and with it the item's prominence – affects the associative strength between the retrieval cues and the item.

Figure 4.2 shown earlier illustrates the relationship between distractor prominence and the interference effect as predicted by the extended model, assuming that target prominence is a fixed value. In addition to the facilitatory effect of highly activated distractors in target-match predicted also by standard ACT-R, the extended model additionally predicts that the fan effect only arises for sufficiently activated distractors (cf. the rising inhibition in target-match configurations in the figure).

In sum, we define the probability of a memory item i being needed given cue j, $P(i|j)$, with respect to the item's base-level activation, which in turn depends on its prominence, and its association with cue j, M_{ji}. The equations ensure that cues can be of variable discrimination (i.e., can be associated with one or more features), and that more prominent items are more strongly associated with the cues and, hence, receive more spreading activation. Since $P(i|j)$ is a probability that takes into account all memory items, both the discrimination of cues and the prominence of the item itself and of all of its competitors affect the fan effect, i.e., the strength of inhibitory interference. The equations for the total spreading activation for item i (Eq. (3.2)) and the retrieval latency (Eq. (3.6)) remain the same as in the original implementation.

4.2   A Simulation of the Meta-analysis Studies

In this section, we compare the specific predictions of LV05 and an extended model with item prominence and multi-associative cues for the experiments in the Jäger et al. (2017) meta-analysis. We make the following assumptions with regard to the relation between a specific experiment and the extended model settings for prominence and cue-feature associations:

- Being a sentential subject and being mentioned in a context sentence (discourse topic) both increase the prominence – and hence the base-level activation – of a target or distractor compared to being an object and not the

4.2 A Simulation of the Meta-analysis Studies 95

discourse topic. The combination of both (subject and topic) has the highest prominence status.

- The cue-feature cross-association level is raised only for dependency contexts where the cues can be assumed to have low discrimination due to feature co-occurrence. These contexts are experiments involving reciprocals and those involving the Chinese reflexive *ziji*.

The simulations presented here can be reproduced using the accompanying web application at https://engelmann.shinyapps.io/inter-act/. The model code is available on GitHub at https://github.com/felixengelmann/inter-act.

4.2.1 Data

We included all studies that were part of the meta-analysis in Jäger et al. (2017). Table 4.6 in the Appendix lists all included studies with their dependency types and distractor prominence levels. Figure 4.9 shows the number of target-match and target-mismatch comparisons for each dependency type and prominence category. At the time of the meta-analysis, no data were available for target-mismatch configurations in non-agreement subject-verb dependencies. A recent study by Cunnings and Sturt (2018) fills this gap but was not included in the simulations. However, we summarize the findings from this study in the Discussion. We categorized the experiments into three different prominence relations for the distractor: *subject position*, *discourse topic*, and *other*. Subject position and discourse topic are considered high prominence levels, although we do not make any a priori assumptions about which of the two is more prominent than the other. The third category, *other*, stands for all relations considered low prominence, which mainly consisted of the distractor being in object position or in a prepositional phrase. As a fourth category, the figure shows the studies where the distractor was both in subject position and a discourse topic. We expect the prominence in this case – and thus the distractor activation – to be particularly high. As the figure shows, distractors that are a discourse topic, and the combination of discourse topic and subject position have so far only been tested in reflexives.

4.2.2 Method

The extended model as described above was implemented in R. Prominence and multi-associative cues could be switched off such that the model behaviour is then equivalent to LV05. The model was set up as described on page 60 in order to simulate the four conditions shown in Figure 4.1, representing retrieval processes in sentences similar to Example (22). Different from the simulations

96   Modelling Prominence and Multi-associative Cues

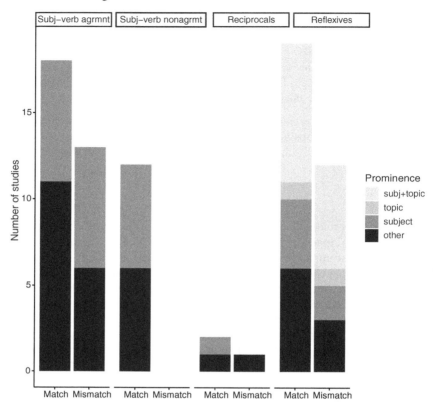

Figure 4.9 Number of studies included in the Jäger et al. (2017) meta-analysis and in the simulations, grouped by dependency type and distractor prominence status (studies are listed in Table 4.6 in the Appendix).

above, multiple distractors were specified for some of the studies that were part of the present simulation.

The model was run for 5,000 iterations on each experiment and yielded the mean effect sizes for target-match and target-mismatch configurations, which in each case were determined by subtracting the retrieval latency in the distractor-mismatch condition from that of the distractor-match condition.

Parameter estimation In order to ensure common parameter settings within experiments, the 77 data points used in the meta-analysis were modelled in 51 experimental sets, such that parameters were held constant between target-match and target-mismatch conditions of the same experiment. Certain

4.2 A Simulation of the Meta-analysis Studies

Table 4.2. *Root-mean-square deviation between modelling results and observed data, averaged within dependency type and model (best values in bold). The superscript* no dec *means that the decay parameter is set to 0.*

Dependency	LV05	LV05$^{no\ dec}$	LV05+IP+MAC	LV05+IP+MAC$^{no\ dec}$
Subj-verb agreement	18.06	15.54	14.47	**13.03**
Subj-verb non-agreement	7.04	7.85	**5.04**	7.96
Reflexives/ Reciprocal	12.40	11.68	7.46	**6.3**

parameters were estimated by running the model iteratively while changing the parameter value within a pre-specified range (details are discussed below). The best value was determined by finding the lowest mean-squared error between the simulated and experimental effects using grid search.

As is common practice in ACT-R modelling, we estimated the latency factor $F \in \{0.1, 0.125, \ldots, 0.25\}$ (see Eq. (3.6)) for each experiment in both models to scale the numerical results into a range that is comparable with the data. In the extended model, the distractor prominence parameter p_{dstr} was estimated across experiments for each of three prominence categories within dependency types: *low* (neither subject nor topic), *medium* (subject *or* topic), and *high* (subject *and* topic). For each of these categories, p_{dstr} was restricted to a certain range that was determined according to the pattern in Figure 4.2 as follows: Medium prominence was constrained to be close to the target prominence ($p_{trgt} = 0$) in the area where the distractor has an influence on the fan effect of the target ($p_{dstr} \in \{-1, -0.9, \ldots, 2\}$); low prominence was constrained to be smaller than the target prominence ($\{-2.5, -2.4, \ldots, 0\}$); and high prominence was bound to values higher than the target prominence and above the point where in Figure 4.2 the target-match fan effect begins to disappear ($\{1, 1.1, \ldots, 4\}$).

Thus, the full range of predictions shown in Figure 4.2 can be generated theoretically, but the generating process is restricted to specific properties of the distractor. Without restricting the prominence parameter in this way, the model cannot be fit in a meaningful way because some predictions can result from multiple prominence values. This can be seen in Figure 4.2 (e.g., the absence of a target-match effect is predicted at very low, very high and at a medium prominence just over 1). The value ranges were allowed to overlap, however, in order not to pre-impose any assumptions about specific effect sizes on the model. The target, which was a subject in all experiments, was assumed to have equal prominence across experiments. Its prominence value was therefore set to 0.

98 Modelling Prominence and Multi-associative Cues

The cross-association level c was estimated only for the two cases we have motivated above: reciprocals and the Chinese reflexive *ziji*. It was estimated in these cases within $\{0.1, 0.2, \ldots, 1\}$ and set to 0 otherwise.

Interference type (retroactive vs. proactive interference) was reflected in the model by manipulating the order of target and distractor. For retroactive interference designs, the target was more distant from the retrieval site than the distractor, and vice versa for proactive interference designs. Hence, interference type affects the model through the memory decay component, which reduces the activation of an item as a function of time.

4.2.3 Results

We ran simulations both with the original LV05 model and with the extended model that included item prominence and multi-associative cues (this is abbreviated as LV05+IP+MAC). Because Lewis and Vasishth (2005) speculated that model fit might improve without the decay component of ACT-R,[7] we also ran variants of both models without the decay component.

Table 4.2 summarizes the fit for all four model configurations in terms of the root-mean-square deviation, averaged within dependency types. Overall, the extended model with IP and MAC fit the available data better than the original model of LV05. Except for non-agreement subject-verb dependencies, the use of decay did not improve the fit with the data. With respect to the extended model, decay only improved the fit for non-agreement subject-verb dependencies but, for the other dependency types, produced a worse fit compared to the model without decay. Since decay generally does not improve the fit, this suggests that the information about the linear order of target and distractor (pro- vs. retroactive interference) may not be useful as a predictor in the models and data considered here. We revisit this point in the Discussion section.

More important than the numerical fit of a computational model with the data, however, is that the model correctly reproduces observed patterns in a principled way. As we saw in Table 3.1 earlier, certain observed patterns were incompatible with LV05, specifically, facilitatory interference in subject-verb agreement target-match configurations, inhibitory interference in reflexive/reciprocal target-mismatch, and the absence of an effect in reflexive or reciprocal target-match. The content of Table 3.1 is repeated here graphically in Figure 4.10. The figure shows the estimates for the mean effect along with 95% credible intervals, as well as the average simulated effects of both

---

[7] Lewis and Vasishth (2005) write on p. 408: "Any structural or quantitative change to the model that moves in the direction of decreased emphasis on decay and increased emphasis on interference would likely yield better fits."

4.2 A Simulation of the Meta-analysis Studies

Table 4.3. *Estimated values for prominence parameter in the LV05+IP+MAC model with decay for three prominence levels.*

Dependency	Low	Medium	High
agreement	0.00	1.70	
nonagreement	−0.20	−0.30	
reflexives	−1.40	−1.00	4.00
reciprocals	−1.90	0.70	

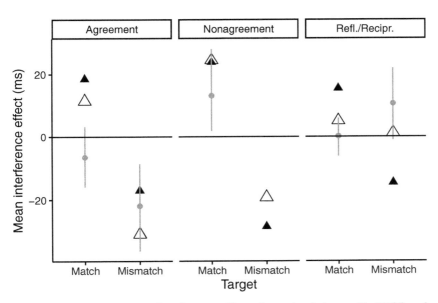

Figure 4.10 Mean interference effects from simulations with LV05 and the extended model, labelled LV05+IP+MAC, for target-match and target-mismatch configurations of the meta-analysis, grouped by dependency type (studies are listed in Table 4.6 in the Appendix). The behavioural data is shown as mean effect estimates with 95% credible intervals as reported in Jäger et al. (2017).

models for the same three dependency categories as in Table 3.1. A qualitative improvement can be seen in reflexive/reciprocal dependencies. The extended model's results are within the 95% credible intervals of the data estimates, showing that LV05+IP+MAC can potentially explain why no effect was found in target-match and inhibition was found in target-mismatch. In terms of the facilitatory effect in subject-verb agreement target-match configurations, the extended model does not show a qualitative difference to LV05, but merely shows a smaller effect that is closer to the mean estimated from the data.

A key difference between the two models is that LV05 cannot explain the data that show facilitation in target-match or inhibition in target-mismatch configurations. The extended model, however, can account for these patterns when they can be explained by distractor prominence and cross-associated cues.

This becomes more apparent when presenting the means by distractor prominence levels as in Figure 4.11. Here, the simulated means are compared to the *sample means* estimated from the *individual* studies' data, which are classified by dependency type and prominence category (see Table 4.6). Such a display of

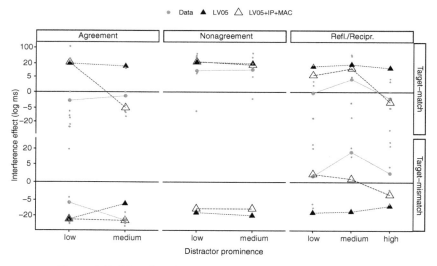

Figure 4.11 Mean interference effects from simulations with LV05 and the extended model, labelled LV05+IP+MAC, for target-match (top panel) and target-mismatch configurations (bottom panel) in the Jäger et al. (2017) meta-analysis, grouped by distractor prominence level within dependency types (studies are listed in Table 4.6 in the Appendix). The behavioural data is shown as raw means with additional smaller points representing individual studies. The target-mismatch plot in non-agreement subject-verb dependencies does not contain data because no data were available at the time of the meta-analysis. However, Cunnings and Sturt (2018) have recently found evidence consistent with the predictions of the model; in two experiments, they obtained an estimated mean of -22 ms with a 95% credible interval of $[-4, -42]$, and in a second experiment, a mean of -19 ms, $[-40, 1]$.

4.2 A Simulation of the Meta-analysis Studies

the studies' sample means is very different from the estimates from the meta-analysis of Jäger et al. (2017), which summarize what we have learnt from the collection of studies on each dependency type. The reason that we are not using the estimates in this figure is that, due to the sparsity of the data, these were not available by prominence level and dependency type in the meta-analysis.

Although the extended model does not show a facilitatory effect in subject-verb agreement target-match configurations on average (collapsing over all prominence levels in Figure 4.10), Figure 4.11 shows that it produces the correct result for those studies that are categorized as having higher distractor prominence. This result of facilitatory interference arises because the prominence parameter p_{dstr} in the LV05+IP+MAC model was estimated to be higher on average for medium prominence experiments compared to low prominence experiments, as summarized in Table 4.3.

For non-agreement subject-verb dependencies, the fit did not improve in the LV05+IP+MAC model, because the data only contain target-match configurations, for which the results – mainly inhibitory interference – are perfectly compatible with LV05. There are also no differences between prominence categories in the data. Consequently, the prominence parameter was not estimated to be different between low and medium prominent distractors.

The most interesting results are observed in reflexive and reciprocal dependencies. Looking at the means separately for each prominence category shows that the extended model offers an explanation for why the target-match and target-mismatch effects on average seem to deviate from the predictions of LV05. As can be seen in Figure 4.11, the average effects in reflexive/reciprocal target-match configurations show increasing inhibition from low to medium prominence and facilitatory interference in high prominence. This is exactly the pattern that our prominence model predicts (see Figure 4.2 shown earlier). Consequently, the extended model matches this pattern while LV05 does not. LV05+IP+MAC produces a mixture of inhibitory and facilitatory effects in target-match as a consequence of distractor prominence, which would explain why no effect could be found in the data on average. In target-mismatch configurations, the data shows inhibitory effects on average in all three prominence categories. This is incompatible with LV05. However, with multi-associative cues, LV05+IP+MAC produces means with a positive sign for low and medium distractor prominence of reflexives and reciprocals. These are driven by the model fitting the inhibitory target-mismatch effects of Kush and Phillips (2014) and Jäger et al. (2015) with an increased estimate of the cross-association parameter for both studies. Thus, the explanation for the inhibitory effect seen on average in reflexive/reciprocal target-mismatch effects in the data would be that some of the studies on reflexive/reciprocal dependencies contained in the meta-analysis qualify for high cue-feature cross-association levels.

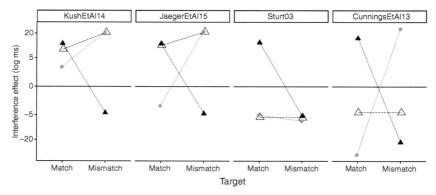

Figure 4.12 Reading time data and simulation results of LV05 and the extended model, labelled LV05+IP+MAC, for interference effects in target-match and target-mismatch configurations of four individual studies: Kush and Phillips (2014), (Jäger et al., 2015, Exp. 1), (Sturt, 2003, Exp. 1), and (Cunnings and Felser, 2013, Exp. 2, participants with low working memory).

Finally, for a better understanding of what drives the differences between the two models, we show four exemplary cases in Figure 4.12, where the data qualitatively deviates from the predictions of the original LV05 model. The studies by Kush and Phillips (2014) on reciprocals and by Jäger et al. (2015) on Chinese reflexives are two cases of low feature discrimination as explained in the section on multi-associative cues. As a result of the cue-feature cross association, LV05+IP+MAC shows inhibitory interference effects in target-mismatch configurations, whereas LV05 shows facilitation. The model parameter for the cross-association level was estimated at 0.7 for both reciprocals (Kush and Phillips, 2014) and *ziji* (Jäger et al., 2015). Cunnings and Felser (2013) and Sturt (2003) are examples of facilitatory effects in target-match configurations, which only the extended model accounts for as a consequence of high distractor prominence values.

However, Cunnings and Felser (2013) is also an example of a pattern that is not compatible with either of the two tested models. The inhibitory target-mismatch effect is not fit by LV05+IP+MAC because no increased cross association is assumed in English reflexives. And even if the cross-association level was assumed to be elevated in this case, it would be impossible to simulate an inhibitory target-mismatch effect and a facilitatory target-match effect at the same time. Hence, under the assumptions of the two cue-based retrieval models tested here, the data of Cunnings and Felser (2013) are not compatible with any model. We return to this point in the Discussion section.

4.3 Discussion

The aims of this chapter were to investigate the quantitative predictions of the Lewis and Vasishth (2005) model and to investigate the consequences of memory accessibility and context-dependent cue-feature associations in the light of the available evidence from reading studies on interference effects in dependency resolution. We have presented an implemented model of prominence and multi-associative cues as an extension to the cue-based retrieval model of LV05. The extension consisted of three revisions of previously simplifying assumptions of ACT-R/LV05 modelling:

1'. The base-level activation of items in memory (i.e., accessibility) is affected by – in addition to recency – their prominence in the current context, i.e., their relevance/salience in terms of syntactic relations in a sentence or information-structural and discourse properties.
2'. The strength of any interference effect, i.e., also the fan effect, is not simply determined by the presence vs. absence of a distractor but also changes as a function of the distractor's activation in memory relative to the target.
3'. The associative strength between a retrieval cue and a memory item can be the result of multiple cues being associated with multiple features at variable degrees. Cue-feature associations are based on associative learning through language experience.

For the reader's convenience, we have summarized the key technical terms used in this chapter (Tables 4.4 and 4.5 in the Appendix) and the data-sets modelled (Tables 4.6 and 4.7).

Our simulations show that prominence and multi-associative cues can account for a range of data points that were not predicted by the original model. In particular, while the prediction space of LV05 allows only two qualitatively different outcomes (inhibition in target-match and facilitation in target-mismatch configurations), the prediction space of the extended model allows, under certain specific circumstances, all four qualitative outcomes seen in the data (inhibition and facilitation in both target-match and target-mismatch configurations). This shows that well-motivated assumptions are of crucial importance when specifying a model, as slight alterations can have consequences not only quantitatively but also qualitatively. In the current case, accounting for individual study design and integrating independently motivated assumptions about memory accessibility and context-based feature discrimination considerably changed the model's prediction space. We therefore believe that these independently motivated extensions help to more precisely interpret individual empirical results as being evidence in favour of or against the model. The simulations presented here thus provide new insights into the cognitive mechanisms behind interference effects.

It is important to note that the model does not predict just any possible outcome; if that were the case, the model would not be very meaningful or useful (Roberts and Pashler, 2000). First of all, the predictions of prominence and cross-associated cues are restricted to very specific circumstances regarding the grammatical and discourse role of the distractor in the individual experiment and the type of dependency used (e.g., reflexive or reciprocal). The second constraint is that, while some parameters were estimated for best fit with the data in the simulations, parameters were fixed across all conditions of an individual experiment. This restricts the predictions of the model considerably; for example, the model cannot predict, for the same experiment, an inhibitory effect in target-mismatch as well as a facilitatory effect in target-match configurations, which was found in gaze durations of readers with low working memory capacity in Exp. 2 of Cunnings and Felser (2013), as shown in Figure 4.12. This is because a facilitatory target-match effect is caused by a high distractor activation that overrides the fan effect. Consequently, the fan effect must be eliminated in both the target-match *and* target-mismatch configurations in the presence of a highly prominent distractor even if we assumed a high cross-association level. Hence, the model makes the strong prediction that the pattern observed by Cunnings and Felser (2013) should not occur. An important line of future work would be to attempt to replicate the Cunnings and Felser result; the model predicts that it should not replicate. If the model simulations had involved separate parameter fits for target-match and mismatch within the same experiment, the model would have been able to predict this and other patterns that are implausible under the model's cognitive assumptions. Thus, our simulation methodology considerably restricts the model's prediction space and are based on independently motivated assumptions.

The model comparisons also suggest that decay could play a smaller role than generally assumed. Indeed, independent work in psychology argues that interference rather than decay is the more important construct (Berman et al., 2009; Oberauer and Lewandowsky, 2013, 2014). However, we cannot conclusively say whether decay has no impact or is only disguised by a counteracting effect of prominence. This is because interference type (pro- vs. retroactive interference) and distractor prominence are confounded in the literature: Studies with prominent distractors more often used a proactive rather than a retroactive interference design, whereas studies with non-prominent distractors more often used a retroactive interference design (see Table 4.6 in the Appendix). Hence, the two factors prominence and interference type, which both influence the distractor activation in memory, might tend to cancel each other out in particular experimental designs. The role of decay could be investigated in future work by designing an experiment that crosses pro- and retroactive distractor position with the prominence of the distractor.

4.3 Discussion

Some caution is also needed as regards the interpretation of the available data. As discussed in Chapter 1, low power and publication bias could be important factors that weaken the empirical claims. Appendix B of Jäger et al. (2017) shows that power for many of the published studies on interference could be as low as 10–20%. As Gelman and Carlin (2014) and many others before them have pointed out, low-power studies will not only fail to detect an effect under repeated sampling, but when an effect is found to be significant, it will be exaggerated in magnitude (Type M error) and can have the wrong sign (Type S error). It would therefore be worthwhile to re-evaluate the predictions of this extended LV05 model with larger-sample studies. For example, how do LV05's predictions fare in target-mismatch reflexives/reciprocals? In English reflexives, if we assume that gender marking on the reflexive *himself/herself* is used as a retrieval cue to seek out an antecedent, the LV05 model predicts facilitatory interference effects in target-mismatch configurations. Dillon et al. (2013) argued that the parser was immune to facilitatory interference based on an eyetracking study with 40 participants. As discussed earlier, a Bayesian reanalysis of their total fixation data in the critical region (Jäger et al., 2020) shows a mean estimate of -18 ms, and Bayesian 95% credible interval $[-72, 36]$. This was a fairly low-powered study; as discussed in Appendix A of Jäger et al. (2020), if the true effect size were to be -23 ms (the median effect predicted by LV05), then prospective power for a replication of their study would be about 13%. This means that there is an approximately 87% chance of obtaining a non-significant result even though the null hypothesis is false with this particular value for the effect size. The larger-sample replication attempt by Jäger et al. (2020), which had 181 subjects), had a power for the same effect size of -23 ms at about 42%. Jäger and colleagues' larger sample study found a facilitatory interference effect of -23 ms, 95% credible interval $[-48, 2]$. This estimate turns out to be consistent with the LV05 model's predictions (under the assumption that gender is used as a retrieval cue in English reflexives). This example illustrates the need for obtaining more precise estimates of the effects of interest than we currently have. In Vasishth et al. (2018), we provide further discussions of this general point about the adverse consequences of low power on developing an empirical base for theory testing, and provide constructive suggestions on how the situation could be improved.

The data on non-agreement subject-verb dependencies agree overall with the general LV05 predictions – inhibition in target-match configurations – and thus had a good fit in both models. The picture is, however, incomplete since no data on target-mismatch configurations for this dependency type were available at the time of the Jäger et al. (2017) meta-analysis and are thus not included in our simulations. However, a recent study by Cunnings and Sturt (2018) showed evidence for a facilitatory effect in target-mismatch configurations in non-agreement subject-verb dependencies, which is predicted by LV05. They conducted two eyetracking while reading studies in which they manipulated the plausibility of the correct dependent of the verb, and the plausibility of the distractor noun. They showed that when the correct dependent is implausible, the distractor's plausibility influences reading time at the verb, such that a facilitation is observed. For example, faster total reading times were observed at the verb *shattered* in (28a) compared to (28b).

(28) a. Sue remembered the letter that the butler with the cup accidentally shattered today in the dining room.

   b. Sue remembered the letter that the butler with the tie accidentally shattered today in the dining room.

Our own Bayesian estimate of their effect size in their Experiment 1 is -22 ms with a credible interval of $[-4, -42]$; for their Experiment 2, the estimate is -19 ms $[-40, 1]$. Using the region of practical equivalence (ROPE) approach, these are consistent with both the original and extended LV05 model's predictions.

To summarize, Table 3.1 suggested that the LV05 model makes the incorrect predictions for target-mismatch in reflexives and reciprocals, but the Jäger et al. (2020) replication attempt indicates that the LV05 predictions may be correct. Furthermore, the Cunnings and Sturt (2018) data are consistent with the LV05 predictions for target-mismatch configurations in non-agreement subject-verb dependencies.

A major contribution of the present chapter is that it spells out the predictions of the LV05 model with reference to all the evidence that was available from reading studies at the time of writing. The modelling presented here is highly constrained: (i) the presented model is built on independently motivated – and, in terms of ACT-R, domain-independently validated – assumptions about memory retrieval, item prominence, and multi-associative cues, which are sensitive to experimental design choices; (ii) the model predictions are restricted by interactions between variables such as prominence, recency, and cue-feature cross association; and (iii) the parameters are fixed within a given experiment, thus ruling out certain patterns of target-match and target-mismatch effects. An important prediction of the model in this respect is that the previously unexplained observations of facilitation in target-match or inhibition in target-mismatch can be explained under certain conditions, but, as explained above, seeing both *in the same experiment* is impossible according to the model's predictions. Constrained predictions such as these are important because they make the theory falsifiable in principle.

As we have discussed above, the conclusions to be drawn about prominence and cue associations are preliminary because (i) the available data are sparse with respect to the levels of distractor prominence studied within dependency types and different levels of feature discrimination, (ii) there may be confounds

4.3 Discussion

between prominence and other factors, and (iii) there may be different cognitive processes involved in certain dependency types that the model does not account for. In the following, we further discuss the implications of our approach for distractor prominence and cue-feature associations and potential alternatives.

4.3.1 Distractor Prominence

In the model we have presented, the prominence of a distractor is a function of its syntactic position and discourse status. An alternative account of how distractor position could affect the magnitude of interference has been discussed in Van Dyke and McElree (2011). By way of a weighting mechanism, a mismatching syntactic feature would lower the consideration of a distractor as a retrieval candidate – or, with gating rather than weighting, even rule it out completely, irrespective of any matching semantic or pragmatic features. This account predicts that interference effects are very small or absent if a distractor does not match the syntactic requirement, e.g., of being a grammatical subject. The predictions of syntactic weighting are consistent with our prominence account and are also compatible with ACT-R in general and LV05 in particular. Because of its reduced activation, a distractor that mismatches the subject cue would have a very low probability of being retrieved instead of the target, and, thus, no facilitatory interference is expected in target-mismatch configurations. The fan effect in target-match configurations would not be directly affected, because the fan effect in ACT-R is a consequence only of the feature that is manipulated between two conditions: the difference in the target activation between the distractor-match and the distractor-mismatch conditions is the same no matter how many additional cues the distractor matches across conditions. However, an effect of syntactic match in target-match configurations would nevertheless be predicted on the basis of a generally lower activated target: Because the relation between activation and latency in ACT-R is a negative exponential function (cf. Eq. (3.6)), differences in activation have less impact on the retrieval speed for items with a higher activation than for items with a lower activation. In case distractor and target both match the subject cue, the fan effect reduces the activation of both across conditions compared to the case when only the target matches the subject cue. As a consequence, when the distractor matches the subject cue, the retrieval latency of the target is more affected by the fan effect of a feature manipulation, i.e., a greater inhibitory interference effect is predicted in target-match configurations.

Hence, the predictions of the syntactic weighting account regarding syntactic position are similar to the predictions of our prominence account: a distractor in subject position compared to object position increases the inhibitory interference effect in target-match configurations and the facilitatory effect in target-mismatch configurations. However, the predictions of syntactic weighting are only valid when it can be assumed that grammatical position is part of the retrieval cues. In contrast, the predictions of our prominence account are independent of cue combinatorics and the match quality of the distractor at retrieval. Instead, the predictions rest on the assumption that items in subject position have a higher relevance for interpreting a sentence and are, thus, maintained more actively in memory (Brennan, 1995; Chafe, 1976; Grosz et al., 1995; Keenan and Comrie, 1977). In the same way, this account of prominence can be extended to discourse status or other contributing factors that we have not considered here: for example, thematic role (Arnold, 2001), contrastive focus (Cowles et al., 2007), first mention (Gernsbacher and Hargreaves, 1988), and animacy (Fukumura and van Gompel, 2011) are known to affect discourse saliency and might thus influence distractor prominence. Importantly, our account predicts a facilitatory effect in target-match configurations as a consequence of high distractor prominence. This cannot be explained in terms of cue combinatorics.

4.3.2 Multi-associative Cues

The principle of multi-associative cues states that cues can be associated with multiple features to different degrees depending on experience with the linguistic context. Crossed cue-feature associations between two cues predict inhibitory interference in target-mismatch conditions for dependency environments with high feature co-occurrence in comparison to environments with low feature co-occurrence. This is based on the assumption that cue-feature associations are the result of associative learning through exposure to different dependency types and their grammatical antecedents. One way of describing the learning process could be along the lines of the naive discriminative learning model developed by Baayen et al. (2011). Their model is an implementation of the Rescorla and Wagner (1972) equations for classical conditioning based on the presence and absence of cues and outcomes and has been applied to a range of effects in the context of language acquisition.

A possible way to test the multi-associative cues hypothesis for English in a controlled experiment would be to directly compare reflexives and reciprocals, manipulating the number cue in both. An example design we have also suggested in Jäger et al. (2015) is shown in Example (29).

(29) a. *Reflexive; distractor-match*
          The *nurse* who cared for the *children* had pricked *themselves* …

      b. *Reflexive; distractor-mismatch*
          The *nurse* who cared for the *child* had pricked *themselves* …

      c. *Reciprocal; distractor-match*
          The *nurse* who cared for the *children* had pricked *each other* …

4.3 Discussion

d. *Reciprocal; distractor-mismatch*
   The *nurse* who cared for the *child* had pricked *each other* ...

Under the multi-associative cues hypothesis, a reduced facilitatory effect or an inhibitory effect is predicted for the reciprocal *each other* compared to the reflexive *themselves*. In order to derive a finer-grained metric that predicts differences in cue-feature cross-association levels between different dependency environments, co-occurrence frequencies could be computed from a corpus in which sufficient dependency information is available.

Our theory of multi-associative cues predicts a higher cross-association level for both reciprocals and the Chinese reflexive *ziji* compared to English reflexives. This could explain the result of Kush and Phillips (2014), who found inhibitory interference in target-mismatch conditions in Hindi reciprocals, as well as our finding of an inhibitory target-mismatch effect for *ziji* in Experiment 1 of Jäger et al. (2015). The modelling results (Figure 4.11) showed that these two studies were sufficient to cause the average target-mismatch effect to be inhibitory in low and medium prominence reflexive/reciprocal studies. According to the meta-analysis in Jäger et al. (2017), the overall interference effect in target-mismatch configurations studies of reflexive- and reciprocal-antecedent dependencies is inhibitory (see Table 3.1). Importantly, this overall inhibitory effect was found even when excluding the Chinese reflexives study of Jäger et al. (2015), which had a larger-than-usual sample size and could therefore have unduly influenced the meta-analysis. Due to the two studies with cross-associated cues, the extended model predicted a tendency for an inhibitory effect on average in target-mismatch configurations, but not one as strong as the meta-analysis found. A less conservative simulation with a freely varying cross-association parameter would, however, result in an overall increased cross-association level for reflexives compared to subject-verb agreement dependencies (subject-verb agreement showed an overall facilitatory effect in target-mismatch configurations). In support for a theory of higher feature co-occurrence and, thus, a higher cross-association level in reflexive-antecedent than in subject-verb dependencies in general, one could argue that reflexive-antecedent dependencies have a rather restrictive set of cues that define the target, whereas subject-verb dependencies occur in a wide range of contexts in which various semantic cues in addition to morpho-syntactic ones might be used (cf. Van Dyke and McElree, 2006).

Under a theory of multi-associative cues, an interesting question is whether categorically distinguishing two cues requires cognitive effort. If so, one would expect an additional variation of the cross-association level that depends on task demands and individual differences. There is evidence that the depth of linguistic processing is influenced by task-specification (Logačev and Vasishth,

2015; Swets et al., 2008) and individual differences (Nicenboim et al., 2016; Traxler, 2007; von der Malsburg and Vasishth, 2013), resulting in underspecification of sentence representations or "good-enough processing" (Ferreira et al., 2002). In the same way, multiple cue-feature associations could be part of a dynamically adapted resource-preserving strategy. This assumption predicts elevated cross-association levels for readers with less cognitive resources in order to compensate for slower processing. It also predicts increased cross association for experiments with little task demand, like easy comprehension questions, because the effort of a precise cue specification would not be necessary. There is one experiment on reflexives that controlled for participants' working memory capacity: Cunnings and Felser (2013) found in their Experiment 2 on English reflexives an inhibitory effect on the critical region in target-mismatch conditions only for low-capacity readers. The effect has a very large standard error (mean 22 ms, *SE* 26 ms) but the sign of the estimated mean is consistent with the assumption of an individual-level variation of cue-feature associations due to adaptive processes. Note, however, that, even if it was the case that low-capacity readers experience higher cross association, for reasons explained above, the current model could not predict an *inhibitory* target-mismatch effect at the same time as a *facilitatory* target-match effect as is the case in Cunnings and Felser (2013). Since there is only one experiment testing low-capacity readers on target-mismatch configurations, a hypothesis of cue-feature associations being adaptive to individual capacity limits is currently speculative, and high-powered planned experiments should be carried out in order to test this hypothesis.

Other factors besides feature co-occurrence that affect the strength of cue associations have not been considered here. Most prominently, it has been claimed that syntactic cues are weighted more strongly than semantic cues (e.g., Nicol, 1988; Sturt, 2003; Van Dyke, 2007; Van Dyke and McElree, 2011). A stronger weighting for syntactic cues might actually be subsumed by co-occurrence, assuming that syntactic cues are more reliable (i.e., have a higher co-occurrence) in a certain construction than semantic cues.

Other associations may, however, go beyond pure co-occurrence. For example, an experiment conducted by Van Dyke and McElree (2006) showed interference effects based on similarities between nouns that tap into world knowledge, such as the property of being *fixable*. Some cues may be stronger than others based on their semantics and pragmatics: Carminati (2005) has proposed a hierarchy between features, such that *person* > *number* > *gender*. Additionally, in English, *number* has a regular, general affixal realization on nouns and verbs whereas *animacy* and *gender* don't. The effects of semantically, pragmatically, or morphologically motivated differences between retrieval cues remain to be investigated.

4.A Key Terms and Concepts

Table 4.4. *Shown here is the terminology used in the present chapter in relation to cue-based retrieval and interference in dependency resolution.*

Term	Definition
Feature	Any property of an item represented in memory. Example: the representation of the lexical item *girl* has features *animate* and *female*.
Retrieval cue	A feature used to seek out an item in memory for retrieval. Example: the retrieval cue *animate* is used to seek out the subject of *laughed*.
Relevant cues	The retrieval cues that are part of the experimental manipulation.
Target	The item that is the correct target for retrieval.
Distractor	An item that is not the correct target for retrieval.
Match	A match occurs when a retrieval cue and a feature on an item have the same value.
Mismatch	A mismatch occurs when a retrieval cue and a feature on an item do not have the same value.
Full match	All relevant retrieval cues (usually two) are matched by the features of an item.
Partial match	Some but not all (usually one of two) retrieval cues are matched by the features of an item.
Target-match	Target-match configurations are sentences where the target matches all relevant retrieval cues.
Target-mismatch	Target-mismatch configurations are sentences where the target does not fully match the relevant retrieval cue(s).
Interference	The effect of a (partially) matching distractor on the retrieval of the target.
Interference condition	(*distractor-match*) Manipulation of a target-match or target-mismatch sentence such that a distractor matches at least one of the retrieval cues.
No-interference condition	(*distractor-mismatch*) Manipulation of a target-match or target-mismatch sentence such that no distractor matches any relevant retrieval cues.
Inhibitory effect	A slowdown in processing during retrieval of the target due to interference from a distractor.
Facilitatory effect	A speedup in processing during retrieval of the target due to interference from a distractor.
Activation	The strength with which an item is represented in memory. More highly activated items are easier to access, resulting in more accurate and/or faster retrieval (depending on the theory).
Base-level activation	A function of an item's time of creation, its intermittent reactivations and time-based decay.
Spreading activation	The activation boost that a memory item receives as the result of a match with one or more retrieval cues.
Cue overload	This occurs when a retrieval cue matches the features of two or more items. The cue is ambiguous.

Table 4.5. *Shown here is the terminology used in the extension of the cue-based retrieval model (continued from previous page).*

Term	Definition
Misretrieval	The retrieval of a distractor rather than the target.
Fan effect	Reduction in activation of items in memory as a result of other items matching the same retrieval cue.
Statistical facilitation	A speed-up in average processing time caused by random noise in a race between two similarly activated items.
Interference effect	The difference in processing time (retrieval latency) between the interference and the no-interference condition (distractor-match − distractor-mismatch). The effect is positive (i.e., slowdown or inhibition) when processing in the interference condition is slower than in the no-interfere condition, and negative (i.e., speed-up or facilitation) when processing is faster.
Prominence	Elevated activation of an item in memory, caused by factors unrelated to the retrieval cues, e.g., grammatical position or discourse marking.
Cue-feature association	Assuming that the feature value of an item does not have to be identical with the retrieval cue in order to produce a match, the cue-feature association level determines how strong the match between a retrieval cue and a feature is.
Feature co-occurrence	Two features are called co-occurring in a certain retrieval context when the combination of both features identifies the correct target more often than other feature combinations.
Cross association	As the result of feature co-occurrence, two retrieval cues can become cross-associated in the sense that both cues are associated with – and therefore produce a match with – the same features to a certain degree.
Feature discrimination	A retrieval cue is highly discriminative if it is associated with only one (or very few) features. A retrieval cue is less discriminative if it is associated with multiple features. Low feature discrimination is the result of feature co-occurrence and can lead to cross association.

4.B List of Experiments Included in the Simulations

Table 4.6. *List of experiments included in the simulations.*

Dependency	Prominence	ID	Publication	Int. type	Lang.	Distr. pos.
S-V agreement	low	1	Franck et al. (2015, E1, Compl)	pro	FR	obj
		2	Franck et al. (2015, E1, RC)	pro	FR	obj
		3	Dillon et al. (2013, E1)	retro	EN	obj
		4	Pearlmutter et al. (1999, E1)	retro	EN	PP
		5	Pearlmutter et al. (1999, E2)	retro	EN	PP
		6	Pearlmutter et al. (1999, E3, plur)	retro	EN	PP
		7	Pearlmutter et al. (1999, E3, sing)	retro	EN	PP
		8	Tucker et al. (2015)	retro	AR	obj
		9	Wagers et al. (2009, E4, PP)	retro	EN	PP
		10	Wagers et al. (2009, E5)	retro	EN	PP
		11	Wagers et al. (2009, E6)	retro	EN	PP
	medium	12	Lago et al. (2015, E1)	pro	SP	subj
		13	Lago et al. (2015, E2)	pro	EN	subj
		14	Lago et al. (2015, E3a)	pro	SP	subj
		15	Lago et al. (2015, E3b)	pro	SP	subj
		16	Wagers et al. (2009, E2)	pro	EN	subj
		17	Wagers et al. (2009, E3, RN, plur)	pro	EN	subj
		18	Wagers et al. (2009, E3, RN, sing)	pro	EN	subj
S-V non-agrmnt	low	19	VanDyke et al. (2006)	pro	EN	3x memory
		20	VanDyke et al. (2011,E2b)	pro	EN	obj
		21	VanDyke (2007, E1, LoSyn)	retro	EN	PP
		22	VanDyke (2007, E3, LoSyn)	retro	EN	PP
		23	VanDyke (2007, E2, LoSyn)	retro	EN	PP
		24	VanDyke et al. (2011, E2b)	retro	EN	obj
	medium	25	VanDyke et al. (11E1bpro)	pro	EN	subj
		26	VanDyke et al. (11E1bretro)	pro	EN	subj
		27	VanDyke (2007, E1, LoSem)	retro	EN	PP, subj
		28	VanDyke (2007, E2, LoSem)	retro	EN	PP, subj
		29	VanDyke (2007, E3, LoSem)	retro	EN	PP, subj
		30	VanDyke et al. (2003, E4)	retro	EN	PP, subj
Reciprocals	low	31	Kush et al. (2014)	retro	HI	prepobj
	medium	32	Badecker et al. (2002, E4)	pro	EN	subj

Note: The experiments are ordered by dependency type, prominence level, and interference type. The experiments are further classified by language (AR = Arabic, CN = Mandarin Chinese, EN = English, FR = French, HI = Hindi, SP = Spanish) and by syntactic position of the distractor (subject, object, genitive attribute, prepositional phrase, sentence external memory load, discourse topic).

114 Modelling Prominence and Multi-associative Cues

Table 4.7. *List of experiments included in the simulations (continued from previous page).*

Reflexives	low	33	Badecker et al. (2002, E5)	pro	EN	gen
		34	Badecker et al. (2002, E6)	pro	EN	prepobj
		35	Jäger et al. (2015, E2)	pro	CN	3x memory
		36	Dillon et al. (2013, E1)	retro	EN	obj
		37	Dillon et al. (2013, E2a)	retro	EN	obj
		38	Dillon et al. (2013, E2b)	retro	EN	obj
	medium	39	Badecker et al. (2002, E3)	pro	EN	subj
		40	Chen et al. (2012, local)	retro	CN	subj
		41	Jäger et al. (2015, E1)	retro	CN	subj
		42	Patil et al. (2016)	retro	EN	subj
		43	Sturt (2003, E2)	retro	EN	obj, topic
	high	44	Cunnings et al. (2013, E1, HiWMC)	pro	EN	subj, topic
		45	Cunnings et al. (2013, E1, LoWMC)	pro	EN	subj, topic
		46	Cunnings et al. (2014, E1)	pro	EN	subj, topic
		47	Felser et al. (2009, inaccMism)	pro	EN	subj, topic
		48	Felser et al. (2009, noCcom)	pro	EN	subj, topic
		49	Sturt (2003, E1)	pro	EN	subj, topic
		50	Cunnings et al. (2013, E2, HiWMC)	retro	EN	subj, topic
		51	Cunnings et al. (2013, E2, LoWMC)	retro	EN	subj, topic

Note: The experiments are ordered by dependency type, prominence level, and interference type. The experiments are further classified by language (AR = Arabic, CN = Mandarin Chinese, EN = English, FR = French, HI = Hindi, SP = Spanish) and by syntactic position of the distractor (subject, object, genitive attribute, prepositional phrase, sentence external memory load, discourse topic).

4.C   Model Specifications

Table 4.8 lists all model parameters with their default values and the values used in the simulation of the studies in the meta-analysis.

Equations (4.21) to (4.25) specify model components that were not defined in the text or were represented in a simplified way. The noise component (Eq. 4.21) that is part of the activation function in Eq. (3.5) is a normally distributed random variable scaled by the noise parameter ANS. The mismatch penalty component (Eq. 4.22), which is usually part of the base-level activation function (here in its complete form in Eq. 4.23), assigns a penalty for every cue j that item i does not match. The complete equation for the retrieval time of item i (Eq. 4.24) is a function of that item's activation A_i if A_i is equal to or above the retrieval threshold τ, and is a function of τ otherwise. Noise is then added (Eq. 4.25) by transforming the retrieval time RT into a uniformly distributed random variable $\widehat{RT}$ within the range of $\pm\frac{1}{3}RT$.

4.C Model Specifications 115

Table 4.8. *Model parameters, their default values, and the
values used in the simulation of the studies in the meta-analysis.*

Parameter	Name	Default	Simulation
F	latency factor	0.2	$[0.1, 0.25]$
f	latency exponent	1	1
τ	retrieval threshold	-1.5	-1.5
d	decay constant	0.5	0.5
ANS	activation noise	0.2	0.2
MAS	maximum associative strength	1	1.5
MP	mismatch penalty	1	0.25
β	base-level constant	0	0
t_{trgt}	time since since last target presentation	$1,000$	$\{700, 1, 300\}$
t_{dstr}	time since last distractor presentation	$1,000$	$\{700, 1, 300\}$
Extended parameters			
q	match quality correction factor	10	0, 10
c	cross-association level	0	$[0, 1]$
p_{trgt}	target prominence	0	0
p_{dstr}	distractor prominence	0	$[-2.5, 4]$

$$\epsilon_i \sim \mathcal{N}(\mu = 0, \sigma = \sqrt{\frac{\pi^2}{3}ANS^2}) \quad \text{noise} \tag{4.21}$$

$$Penalty_i = MP \times \sum_{j=1}^{n}(P(i|j) - 1) \quad \text{mismatch penalty} \tag{4.22}$$

$$B_i = \log(\sum_{j=1}^{n} t_j^{-d}) + \beta_i + Penalty_i + p_i \quad \text{base-level} \tag{4.23}$$

$$RT_i = \begin{cases} Fe^{-fA_i}, & \text{if } A_i \geq \tau \\ Fe^{-f\tau}, & \text{otherwise} \end{cases} \quad \text{retrieval time} \tag{4.24}$$

$$\widehat{RT_i} = \mathcal{U}(a = \frac{2}{3}RT_i, b = \frac{4}{3}RT_i) \quad \text{noisy retrieval time} \tag{4.25}$$

5 An Extension of the Core Model

Modelling the Interaction of Eye-Movement Control and Parsing

Eye movements in reading have played an important role in uncovering the cognitive processes involved in sentence comprehension. As the reader's eyes move through a sentence, the sequence of fixations and their durations reflect the reader's allocation of attention and the processing effort necessary to combine the words incrementally into a coherent structure. The specific linking between fixation patterns and the underlying cognitive processes is, however, not trivial: fixations are determined not only by immediate low-level processes like word recognition but also by more complex operations such as structural parsing decisions, contextual integration, and non-linguistic oculomotor constraints. In recent years, a number of computational models have emerged that help understanding the reading process in detail (Bicknell and Levy, 2010; Engbert et al., 2002, 2005; Legge et al., 2002; Nilsson and Nivre, 2010; Reichle et al., 1998, 2006; Reilly and Radach, 2006). The two most developed models of this kind are E-Z Reader (Reichle et al., 2006) and SWIFT (Engbert et al., 2005). These generate predictions based on lexical variables like word frequency, word length, and cloze predictability. Although they differ fundamentally in their core assumptions about the nature of the reading process (E-Z Reader shifts attention serially while SWIFT allows for parallel word processing guided by an attentional gradient), both models make very accurate predictions about when and where the eyes move. However, since these models rely on word-level information, their predictions are limited to rather simple sentences that do not induce severe interruptions of the reading process.[1]

Postlexical processes like structural and semantic integration operate on a higher level and can only be uncovered by studying more complex sentences that contain long-range dependencies, ambiguities, or contextual inconsistencies. Challenging the sentence processor in this way reveals memory operations, structural and semantic predictions, and repair processes. In particular, there has been an abiding interest in identifying spatio-temporal distributions of short- and long-range regressions (backward saccades) in the psycholinguistic

---

[1] This chapter is reused with permission from Engelmann et al. (2013), Copyright (2013) Wiley; license number 4740811363588.

literature (Frazier and Rayner, 1982; Meseguer et al., 2002; Mitchell et al., 2008; Van Dyke and Lewis, 2003; von der Malsburg and Vasishth, 2011; von der Malsburg and Vasishth, 2013; Weger and Inhoff, 2007). In most established eye movement models, however, inter-word regressions are caused either by incomplete lexical processing (e.g., SWIFT) or motor error (e.g., older versions of E-Z Reader). An exception is the model of Bicknell and Levy (2010), which explains regressions as the result of a rational strategy guided by Bayesian inference on the sentence level. The postlexical level of sentence processing has been captured by a range of computational models (Binder et al., 2001; Budiu and Anderson, 2004; Elman et al., 2004; Hale, 2011; Just and Carpenter, 1992; Konieczny and Döring, 2003; Lewis and Vasishth, 2005; MacDonald and Christiansen, 2002; Spivey and Tanenhaus, 1998; Vasishth et al., 2008). These models predict word-by-word difficulty, which can be correlated with aggregated eyetracking measures but abstracts away from individual fixations.

In order to understand how postlexical difficulty and eye movements interact, it is necessary to combine both classes of computational models and investigate the link between high-level language processes and oculomotor control. In a recent approach, Reichle et al. (2009) introduced a postlexical integration stage into E-Z Reader 10 that interacts with eye movement control through regressions. Whenever the integration stage takes too long, a regression is triggered in order to buy time for the integration process to finish. Although Reichle and colleagues did not integrate a computational account of postlexical processing, they showed a suitable way towards studying the link between parsing and eye movements.

In the work presented here, we combine an eye movement control model with the Lewis and Vasishth parser in a similar way as Reichle et al. (2009) incorporated an integration stage in their eye-movement control model. We go beyond the Reichle et al. work by incorporating two well-tested computational accounts of parsing difficulty that capture memory retrieval and structural prediction, respectively: (1) the syntactic retrieval account of Lewis and Vasishth (2005); and (2) surprisal (Hale, 2001; Levy, 2008), which defines difficulty in terms of disconfirmed structural predictions. The combination of both metrics in one model is motivated by empirical evidence and statistical modelling: experimental results suggest a complementary relation between expectation-based and working-memory-based accounts (Demberg and Keller, 2008; Konieczny, 2000; Staub, 2010; Vasishth and Drenhaus, 2011), and corpus studies show that surprisal and retrieval are independent predictors of processing difficulty (Boston et al., 2008, 2011; Patil et al., 2009; Vasishth and Lewis, 2006). As an eye-movement control model, we use the ACT-R-integrated EMMA ("eye movements and movement of attention") developed by Salvucci (2001), which is in principle a simplified and domain-independent version of E-Z Reader.

118 Modelling the Interaction of Eye-Movement Control and Parsing

The goal of this chapter is to demonstrate the feasibility of extending the Lewis and Vasishth computational account of postlexical parsing difficulty with an eye movement control model. In order to provide a general assessment which is comparable to earlier studies (Reichle et al., 1998, 2009; Salvucci, 2001), we perform a qualitative examination of the framework on a suitable eyetracking corpus. Although E-Z Reader and EMMA were evaluated on the Schilling Corpus (Schilling et al., 1998), we used the German Potsdam Sentence Corpus (Kliegl et al., 2004) because measures of parsing difficulty are readily available for the latter. Section 5.1 introduces EMMA in detail. In Section 5.2, we present a replication of Salvucci (2001) on the English Schilling Corpus, which is necessary because ACT-R has developed further since Salvucci's evaluation of EMMA in 2001, and EMMA itself has been re-implemented. The successful replication provides the basis for an extension of the model with parsing theory which will be described in Section 5.3. Finally, Section 5.4 presents six simulations on the German Potsdam Sentence Corpus that assess a range of model configurations that integrate EMMA with surprisal and retrieval.

5.1 The EMMA/ACT-R Reading Model

EMMA's basic assumptions were inspired mainly by E-Z Reader. The main characteristics of the model are a dynamic calculation of word encoding time and a distinction between overt eye movements and covert shifts of attention. Attention is allocated serially and proceeds usually ahead of the eye movement. This enables the model to produce skipping and refixations. The programming of saccades consists of a labile stage, i.e., a stage that can be cancelled by upcoming attention shifts, and a non-labile state, after which the saccade preparation has passed a point of no return, leading to an inevitable eye movement. Below, we describe the version of EMMA that we used for our simulations in the environment of ACT-R 6.0.

The core function of EMMA calculates the encoding time of an object based on its frequency of occurrence and its eccentricity from the current viewing location. The resulting duration represents attention shift and word identification in one step. The encoding time T_{enc} is calculated in the following way:

$$T_{enc} = K(-\log f_i)e^{k\epsilon_i}, \tag{5.1}$$

where K (visual encoding factor) and k (encoding exponent) are scaling constants; k was kept at the default value of 0.4. ϵ_i is the eccentricity (degrees of visual angle; this value must have a positive sign) of the object (i) to be encoded, and f_i is the object's corpus frequency normalized to a range between 0 and 1 (word occurrence per one million words divided by one million). The saccade preparation time T_{prep} has been estimated in Salvucci's simulations

5.2 Replication of Salvucci (2001)

to be 135 ms.[2] The non-cancellable stage T_{exec} consists of 50 ms for saccade programming, 20 ms for saccade execution and additional 2 ms per degree of visual angle of the saccade length. The model introduces variability to T_{enc}, T_{prep}, and T_{exec} by randomly drawing from a uniform distribution[3] with a standard deviation of one-third of the actual value of the duration (T_{enc}, T_{prep}, or T_{exec}; see Section 4.C). Also, landing point variability of a saccade is determined by a Gaussian distribution with a standard deviation of 0.1 times the intended saccade distance. For empirical motivations for the choice of distributions, see Salvucci (2001).

Salvucci presented three evaluations of his EMMA/ACT-R model on empirical data from equation-solving, visual search, and reading. In the case of reading, which is the application of interest here, EMMA was interfaced with a simple ACT-R model that worked in the following way: each cycle begins with the initiation of an attention shift to the nearest object to the right. EMMA then initiates the encoding of the target object using the provided frequency values and, at the same time, starts the preparation of the corresponding eye movement. Once the visual encoding has finished, the model performs a lexical retrieval of the input word and starts the next cycle by shifting attention to the next word. The lexical retrieval had a fixed duration and, thus, did not contribute to the predictions in a relevant way. Salvucci tested EMMA on the 48 sentences of the Schilling Corpus (Schilling et al., 1998) and showed that the model reproduced well-known empirical effects of word-frequency on a range of eyetracking measures.

5.2 Replication of Salvucci (2001)

5.2.1 Data

The Schilling Corpus (SC) contains fixation data of 48 American English sentences with 8–14 words each, read by 48 students. For evaluating the model performance, Salvucci (2001) used data compiled by Reichle et al. (1998). They had calculated the means of six eyetracking measures for five logarithmic frequency classes (see Table 5.1). The frequency values available in the SC were obtained from Francis and Kucera (1982). In order to avoid confounds, the first and the last word of each corpus sentence was removed. Since the model did not produce regressions, trials that contained inter-word regressions (64%) were excluded from the analysis.

---

[2] In ACT-R 6.0, the planning time for motor processes amounts to 0, 50, 100, or 150 ms depending on feature-based similarity with the previous movement. However, for our simulations we used Salvucci's original definition of a fixed preparation time.

[3] A uniform distribution is the ACT-R 6.0 default for random time generation. In Salvucci's original model a Gamma distribution was used.

120 Modelling the Interaction of Eye-Movement Control and Parsing

Table 5.1. *Frequency classes used in the analyses of the Schilling Corpus (SC) and Potsdam Sentence Corpus (PSC).*

Class	Freq. in 1M	SC		PSC	
		Words	Mean	Words	Mean
1	1–10	77	3	186	3
2	11–100	87	50	173	41
3	101–1,000	71	333	200	335
4	1,001–10,000	92	5,067	207	5,020
5	>10,000	112	41,976	84	2,399

5.2.2 Model

Our ACT-R model consisted of four productions: `find-next-word` (search for the nearest object to the right), `attend-word` (initiate an attention shift and encoding by EMMA), `integrate-word` (start memory retrieval), and `stop-reading` (when the sentence is finished). The `integrate-word` rule did not do anything in this model apart from adding 50 ms to the processing time. It was used in later simulations, however, to initiate the parsing process. All simulations presented here were carried out in ACT-R 6.0. We used EMMA version 4.0a1 (with some minor adjustments by us) as it has been re-implemented by Mike Byrne and Dan Bothell in order to be fully integrated in ACT-R 6.0. All parameters except for those shown in Table 5.2 were kept at their default values. This is particularly important for the *default action time*, which is the firing duration assigned to each ACT-R production rule. Salvucci (2001) set it to 10 ms, but in ACT-R 6.0 it defaults to 50 ms.

5.2.3 Analysis

One simulation consisted of 10 complete model runs through the 48 sentences of the Schilling Corpus. Fixation times were recorded for each word. The analysis was carried out in the R statistics software R Core Team (2012). Following the analysis of Reichle et al. (1998) and Salvucci (2001), we excluded first and last words from the sentences and all trials that contained inter-word regressions. Then we divided the corpus words into five logarithmic frequency classes (see Table 5.1) and calculated the means for each class for six fixation measures: gaze duration (the time spent on a word during first pass, including immediate refixations); first fixation duration (FFD, duration of the first fixation on a word during first pass); single fixation duration (SFD, fixation duration on a word if it is fixated only once during first pass); the skipping rate of a word (skip); the probability of fixating a word exactly once (onefix); and

Table 5.2. *Fit and parameter estimates for all simulations. The interpretation of the data are discussed in the Results and Discussion sections.*

			Parameters				Fit			
			K	T_{prep}	F	P	R_{early}	R_{late}	$RMSD$	%reg
no regr.		Salvucci (2001)	0.006	0.135			0.97		0.362	0
	1	SC replication	0.002	0.135			0.96		0.303	0
	2a	PSC	0.003	0.120			0.86		0.326	0
PSC all	2b	EMMA	0.003	0.120			0.91	0.38	0.638	0
	3	$+s_1$	0.002	0.115		0.0030	0.93	0.39	0.645	0
	4	$+r$	0.002	0.110	0.2		0.90	0.86	0.201	18
	5	$+s_2$	0.003	0.115		0.0200	0.92	0.87	0.229	15
	6	$+rs_1$	0.003	0.115	0.2	0.0005	0.92	0.88	0.257	12
	7	$+rs_2$	0.003	0.115	0.1	0.0150	0.90	0.91	0.206	23

Notes: K = EMMA encoding factor, T_{prep} = EMMA saccade preparation time, F = ACT-R retrieval latency factor, P = scaling factor for surprisal. The fit was calculated for means of 5 frequency classes for each eyetracking measure. R_{early} = correlation coefficient between observed and predicted values for early measures (gaze, FFD, SFD, skip, onefix, and refix). R_{late} = correlation coefficient for late measures (RPD, TFT, RRT, FPREG, and reread). The last two columns show the total normalized root-mean-square deviation and the percentage of simulated trials that contained regressions. The labels $+s_1$ and $+s_2$ refer to the two surprisal models (low- and high-level surprisal) added to EMMA, $+r$ to the retrieval model, and rs_1 and rs_2 to models with both retrieval and surprisal.

122   Modelling the Interaction of Eye-Movement Control and Parsing

the probability of fixating a word more than once (refix). This analysis was done with both the experimental data and the model output. We quantified the goodness of fit between the model predictions and the data using the Pearson product-moment correlation coefficient R, and the root-mean-square deviation (*RMSD*). *RMSD*s were normalized by the standard deviation of the observed data in the same way as it was done in Reichle et al. (1998) and Salvucci (2001). A precise definition is given in the Appendix. The parameter optimization procedure was carried out by first identifying a number of parameter configurations with R values near the maximum and then, among these, choosing the one with the smallest *RMSD*. In this way, the optimization represented a priority for the quality of effects while also taking quantity into account.

5.2.4   Results

We re-estimated the encoding factor K and the saccade preparation time T_{prep} in order to compensate for the changes in the ACT-R environment. See Table 5.2 for a summary of the simulation results including estimated parameter values. The parameter fitting resulted in a decrease of K, which should mainly be due to the increased default action time of 50 ms in ACT-R 6.0. Figure 5.1 shows the predictions of the model (dashed lines) for six fixation measures as a function of frequency class. Besides the corpus data (grey solid lines), we also plotted the results of the original study (dotted lines) as reported in Salvucci (2001) for comparison. The main trends in the data are that high-frequency words are read faster and skipped more often than low-frequency words. These trends and the overall pattern of the data were reproduced by the model with a close fit to the original predictions. The mean correlation R with the data was 0.96 and the mean *RMSD* was 0.303.

5.2.5   Discussion

The EMMA/ACT-R model, as re-implemented in ACT-R 6.0, reproduces frequency effects on fixation durations and probabilities in the Schilling Corpus with a performance comparable to that of the original simulation of Salvucci (2001). Despite the different environment, a small adjustment to the encoding time was sufficient to replicate the results. The successful re-evaluation of EMMA in its current version is essential for the next steps that will extend the model with accounts of parsing theory.

5.3   The Extended EMMA/ACT-R Model

In order to augment the EMMA/ACT-R model with postlexical processing, we take a similar approach as Reichle et al. (2009). The integration stage of

5.3 The Extended EMMA/ACT-R Model

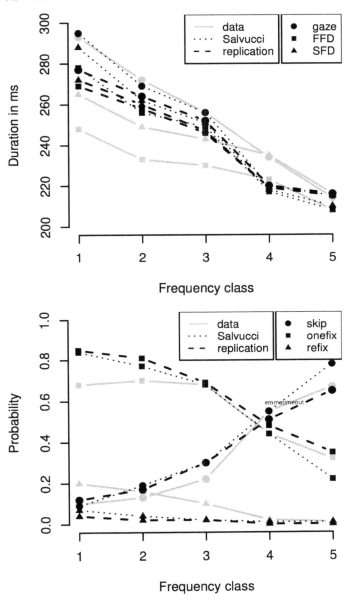

Figure 5.1 Replication of Salvucci (2001) on the Schilling Corpus. Effects of word frequency on gaze, first, and single fixation duration, and on the rate of skipping a word, fixating it once, and fixating it more than once. Grey solid lines represent experimental data, black dotted lines show Salvucci's simulation results, and black dashed lines show the replication results. Lexical frequency is divided into classes 1 (lowest) to 5 (highest).

124 Modelling the Interaction of Eye-Movement Control and Parsing

E-Z Reader 10 operates in parallel to eye movement control but can interrupt the reading process for two reasons: either integration of a word w_n just fails ("rapid integration failure") or the integration process takes too long ("slow integration failure"), which means that the integration of word w_n does not finish before the identification of word w_{n+1} is completed. In either case, the eyes are directed back to word w_n or w_{n-1} with a certain probability. Reichle and colleagues demonstrated the applicability of their model by re-configuring the model parameters for three cases of parsing difficulty: clause wrap-up, semantic violations, and garden paths.

Our goal is to evaluate a model which works in a similar way but uses a computational implementation of sentence comprehension to generate its predictions. Since in ACT-R only one retrieval request can be handled at a time, it follows naturally that retrieval of word w_n has to be completed before the integration of word w_{n+1} can start. Once initiated, retrieval operates in parallel to cognition and eye movement planning. As long as the difficulty is low and retrieval completes fast, the reading process is uninterrupted. The possibility that retrieval fails completely (rapid integration failure) is not included in the model for now. Similar to E-Z Reader 10, when identification of word w_{n+1} finishes before the complete integration of word w_n, our model initiates a regression back towards the previous word. Once word integration is complete, the model continues with normal reading. This type of regressions has been proposed by Mitchell et al. (2008). They called them "Time Out regressions" because their assumed function is to provide additional time for the sentence processor before taking up new input.

The above described concept of interrupting the "normal" reading process by Time Outs should not be misunderstood to mean that making regressions is not normal. We assume that these interruptions by the parser belong to normal reading as they happen quite regularly and are not under conscious cognitive control. A quite different case is an active reanalysis mechanism where the reader is aware of an inconsistency (syntactic or semantic) and has to make long-range regressions. However, although the presented framework can be used to study this kind of behaviour, we restrict our study to the simplest case for now.

For simulating postlexical processing, we use two complementary explanations of parsing difficulty: cue-based retrieval (Lewis and Vasishth, 2005) and syntactic surprisal (Hale, 2001; Levy, 2008). Because the Lewis and Vasishth sentence processing model has already been explained, we focus only on the surprisal metric.

5.3.1 Surprisal

Surprisal (Hale, 2001; Levy, 2008) formalizes the idea that unexpected structures cause processing difficulty (Konieczny, 2000). Hale (2001) defined the surprisal of a word as a function of the probability mass of all derivational options that have to be disconfirmed at that point in the sentence. The surprisal of a word w_i is the negative logarithm of the transition probability from word w_{i-1} to w_i. The lower the probability of a word given its preceding context, the higher its surprisal. While Hale assumed a complete knowledge of the grammar to define the surprisal value, there are also different accounts of calculating surprisal, e.g., using a neural network (Frank, 2009) or using a rationally bounded parallel dependency parser (Boston et al., 2011).

Although the difficulty associated with surprisal stems from building low-probability structures, it is not clear that the cause of the difficulty must be located in postlexical processing. Given the conceptual distinctness of surprisal and retrieval together with experimental evidence locating expectation effects earlier than memory effects (Staub, 2010; Vasishth and Drenhaus, 2011), we hypothesize that the source of these two types of difficulty may lie at different points in the processing time course. Theoretically, it is legitimate to assume that the contextually pre-activated high-probability structures (or parsing steps) would also pre-activate lexical items belonging to the corresponding categories. In that case, at every point in the sentence the activation of specific lexical items receives a boost by its structural context. This would directly affect the speed of the word identification process. Thus, although the source of surprisal difficulty is undoubtedly a "high-level" postlexical process, the actual realization of that difficulty could happen "low-level" at the stage of word identification.

The following simulations test both assumptions, surprisal affecting the high-level and affecting the low-level stages. The high-level variant is implemented by additively modulating the duration of the integration stage by a scaled surprisal value. For simulating surprisal affecting the low-level we include the surprisal values in EMMA's core equation of word encoding time. The resulting equation for T_{enc} will be shown in the next section.

5.4 Simulations on the Potsdam Sentence Corpus

In this section, we present six simulations that were carried out on the Potsdam Sentence Corpus (PSC) developed by Kliegl et al. (2004). The PSC was used because Boston et al. (2008) and Boston et al. (2011) provide retrieval and surprisal values for all corpus words. Simulation 2 evaluated EMMA on the PSC in order to compare the results with the model performance on the Schilling corpus. Besides assessing how well the model can be generalized to another corpus in a different language, this study pursued the goal to establish the basis for augmenting the EMMA/ACT-R model with postlexical processing. The other five simulations tested EMMA in different configurations that include and combine retrieval (r), low-level surprisal (s_1), and high-level surprisal (s_2):

126   Modelling the Interaction of Eye-Movement Control and Parsing

EMMA+s$_1$, EMMA+r, EMMA+s$_2$, EMMA+rs$_1$, and EMMA+rs$_2$ (see Table 5.2 for an overview).

5.4.1   Data

Potsdam Sentence Corpus   The Potsdam Sentence Corpus contains eyetracking data from 144 simple German sentences (1,138 words) with 5–11 words per sentence, read by 229 readers. The corpus contains values of printed word frequency obtained from the CELEX database, a corpus of about 5.4 million words (Baayen et al., 1993). Kliegl et al. (2004) report effects of frequency on reading times and probabilities using the same logarithmic frequency classes that were used in Salvucci (2001) (see Table 5.1). The trends are comparable to those in the Schilling Corpus: higher frequency correlates with shorter reading times and higher skipping rates, although the trend is not as strong in first and single fixation durations.

We integrated retrieval and surprisal information in the corpus data that provided the input for the EMMA/ACT-R model.

Retrieval   There are handcrafted ACT-R parsing rules available for a number of psycholinguistically interesting sentence constructions; however, there are not enough rules to cover the whole PSC. For the corpus-based benchmarking evaluation carried out here, we therefore used pre-calculated values from Boston et al. (2011). These retrieval values were calculated using a parallel dependency parser and approximately represent the duration a retrieve-and-attach cycle would require in the ACT-R parser. Each step of the dependency parser (SHIFT, REDUCE, LEFT, RIGHT) was assigned a duration of 50 ms – the *default action time* in ACT-R that it takes one production to fire. The duration of retrieving an item from memory was calculated using ACT-R equations, including a simplified version of similarity-based interference. The parser was assessed at different levels of parallelism, i.e., the number of alternative derivations to be pursued at the same time. The retrieval values obtained at the highest level of parallelism (100 parallel analyses) were the most significant predictors in Boston et al. (2011). These values ($M = 357.8$ ms, $SD = 122.16$ ms) were used in our model to imitate the parsing process. The values were scaled with the ACT-R-internal retrieval latency factor F.

Surprisal   For the present purposes, we used surprisal values ($M = 2.9$ bits, $SD = 2.06$ bits) from Boston et al. (2008), which were generated with a modified version of the probabilistic context-free phrase-structure parser[4] from Levy (2008).

---

[4]   The parser is publicly available at http://nlp.stanford.edu/$\sim$rog/prefixparser.tgz.

5.4 Simulations on the Potsdam Sentence Corpus

5.4.2 Model

For the following simulations, the model used in the replication of Salvucci (2001) was modified in the way described in the previous section. After encoding word w_n, the `integrate-word` rule starts the parsing actions and attention is shifted to the next word to the right. For the current study, the parsing duration was imitated by a timer set to the corresponding retrieval value from Boston et al. (2008) scaled by F. As long as the timer is running, no other word can be integrated.

In order to establish a link between cognition and eye movement control, two ACT-R production rules were added to the model: these are called `time-out` and `exit-time-out`. Their function is as follows: when integration of word w_n is still in progress while the encoding of word w_{n+1} has already completed, `time-out` initiates an attention shift to the word to the left of the currently fixated one (Time Out regression). Once the integration of word w_n has finished, the `exit-time-out` rule returns the model into the state of normal reading. For reasons of simplicity, no special assumptions are made about the reading process just after a Time Out regression, except for the fact that word w_n will not need to be integrated again. However, words w_n and w_{n+1} will go through the identification process again after leaving Time Out mode because word encoding is part of every attention shift carried out by EMMA. A more realistic model would probably not fully re-encode a word already identified. Figure 5.2 illustrates how Time Out regressions are triggered in structures like object relative clauses.

Note that a Time Out regression can be initiated from word w_n or w_{n+1} depending on how fast the encoding process of word w_{n+1} is in relation to the saccade execution to that word. The regression always targets the word to the left of the current fixation. This means the regression target can either be word w_n or w_{n-1}. However, the preparation of a regression can be cancelled before its execution in the case when the integration process completes before the non-cancellable state of motor preparation. In this case, the Time Out would show itself in the form of a refixation on w_n or w_{n+1}. In case this refixation is also cancelled because encoding was fast, a saccade to the next word is planned, and the Time Out only causes an increased fixation duration.

Finally, we included the two versions of surprisal described above. ACT-R was equipped with a surprisal scaling constant P. For simulating surprisal at the high level, the values scaled by P were added to the duration of the integration stage in milliseconds. In order to modulate the low-level word encoding process directly by surprisal, we added surprisal in EMMA's word encoding time equation as shown in Eq. 5.2:

$$T_{enc} = (K[-\log f] + Ps)e^{k\epsilon}. \tag{5.2}$$

SR: The reporter who **sent** the photographer to the editor hoped for a story.

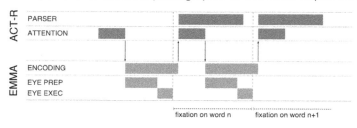

OR: The reporter who the photographer **sent** to the editor hoped for a story.

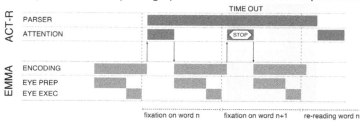

Figure 5.2 A schematic figure illustrating the Time Out mechanism in the case of object vs. subject relatives. In an object relative, if the integration of the relative clause verb is still in progress while the encoding of the word following it has already completed, time out initiates an attention shift to the word to the left of the currently fixated one (Time Out regression). Once the integration of the relative clause verb has finished, the `exit-time-out` rule returns the model into the state of continuing fixating in the reading direction.

where s is the surprisal value of the corresponding word and P is the surprisal scaling constant.

5.4.3 Results

Simulation results are summarized in Table 5.2. Each model was evaluated on the prediction of frequency effects similar to the evaluation of the previous simulation (see Table 5.1 for the frequency classes used in the PSC simulations). However, in addition to the six fixation measures, we also evaluated the models on the following so-called late measures: regression path duration (RPD, also called go-past duration, the sum of all fixations including previous locations beginning from the first fixation on a word until leaving it to the right), total fixation time (TFT, sum of all fixation on a word), re-reading time (RRT, time spent on a word after leaving it and returning to it), first-pass regression probability (FPREG, the probability of regressing from a word in first pass),

5.4 Simulations on the Potsdam Sentence Corpus

and the probability of re-reading a word after leaving it to the right (reread). Note that first-pass regression probability is not considered to be a late measure in reading research. However, we call it late here because in our model all regressions are caused by late (higher-level cognitive) processes. Except for Simulation 2a, all models were fit and evaluated on the full data-set that contained trials with regressions. Like in Simulation 1, the first and the last word of each sentence were excluded from the analysis. Following the corpus study in Kliegl et al. (2004), we removed words with first fixation durations longer than 1,000 ms and words with gaze and total fixation durations greater than 1,500 ms from the empirical data-set. This reduced the corpus by 79 words. The results shown in the table were obtained by running 100 iterations on the PSC with the respective parameter sets. For each model the best fit was determined in the way described in Simulation 1.

PSC vs. SC Simulation 2 was carried out on the PSC using the pure EMMA model without retrieval or surprisal information. For comparing the model performance on the PSC versus the Schilling Corpus, row 2a in Table 5.2 shows the model performance when trials containing inter-word regressions (40%) were not considered in the analysis. For this case, only early measures were compared. Encoding factor K and T_{prep} were re-estimated. The predictions have a good correlation with the observed frequency effects ($R_{early} = 0.86$). Numerically, the predictions deviate more from the data than for the Schilling Corpus, but the $RMSD$ is still reasonable with a value of 0.326. Note that $RMSD$s are not directly comparable between corpora. $RMSD$s for the PSC are generally a bit lower because the standard deviations used for normalization are higher than in the Schilling Corpus.

Influence of Parsing Difficulty In Table 5.2 the PSC simulations are sorted by goodness of fit as defined by the total correlation R, which is the mean of R_{early} (correlation for the early measures) and R_{late} (correlation for the late measures). It shows that the model performance on predicting frequency effects gradually improves through the extension with measures of surprisal and retrieval. In order to provide a baseline for the EMMA+ models, Simulation 2 was analyzed again on the complete data-set including trials that contained regressions (see row 2b). The results of 2b show that the fit for late measures (R_{late}) is very low, which results in a total R of 0.67. That is expected because three of the late measures (RRT, FPREG and reread) are not predicted at all by the model due to the lack of regressions. Note that although Model 2 did not produce Time Out regressions, some backward saccades happened due to motor error. However, these did not produce enough data to report mean RRTs over frequency classes: only six words out of 85,000 (850 analyzed corpus words times 100 simulations) were re-read.

130   Modelling the Interaction of Eye-Movement Control and Parsing

For the following simulations, the parameters F and P were estimated if the model used retrieval or surprisal, respectively. In Simulation 3 (EMMA+s_1), the fit for the early measures improves ($R_{early} = 0.93$), but here still no Time Outs were produced, as s_1 is only modulating word encoding time. In contrast, in Model 4 (EMMA+r), Time Out regressions were produced as a consequence of retrieval difficulty in 18% of the trials. That, of course, improved the prediction of late measures considerably, resulting in an R_{late} of 0.86. Note, however, that R_{early} (0.90) is not as good as with EMMA+s_1. Simulation 5 (EMMA+s_2) used high-level surprisal that interacts with the model through Time Outs just like retrieval. Interestingly, it produced a slightly better fit than EMMA+r, especially in early measures ($R_{early} = 0.92$). Combining retrieval and low-level surprisal in Simulation 6 (EMMA+rs_1) results in about the same fit as Simulation 5. However, the combination of retrieval and high-level surprisal in Simulation 7 (EMMA+rs_2) improves R_{late} even more and results in a total R of 0.91, with a fairly good $RMSD$ of 0.206.

Figure 5.3 compares the performance of pure EMMA (Simulation 2) with that of the best model, EMMA+rs_2 (Simulation 7). In the early probability measures (upper right panel), one can see that EMMA+rs_2 produces more refixations, which is also the reason for the prediction that gaze durations are generally longer than first and single fixation durations (upper left panel), which was not quite captured in pure EMMA. The predictions for late duration measures (lower left) show a good fit of TFT and RPD in the complex model up to frequency class 4 with a disproportionate drop in class 5. Also the RRT means are well correlated with the data, whereas the simple model did not predict RRT values at all. The situation is similar for late probabilities (lower right): while pure EMMA does not predict any regressions, EMMA+rs_2 shows a nearly perfect fit for reading proportions up to frequency class 4 and a little low but well correlated mean proportions of first-pass regressions.

As an additional assessment of surprisal and retrieval effects, we did a linear regression analysis for selected eyetracking measures using the predictors log frequency, length, log retrieval, and surprisal. This was done to see which of the six EMMA models produce variance that is explainable by surprisal and retrieval values. In order to ensure that the incorporation of surprisal and retrieval information does not just add random or redundant variance to the simulation results, the linear regression models should have sensible estimates for both predictors. This means that, ideally, surprisal effects should be significant in the output of simulations that included surprisal (EMMA+s_1, EMMA+s_2, EMMA+rs_1, and EMMA+rs_2), retrieval effects should be significant for EMMA+r, EMMA+rs_1, and EMMA+rs_2, and none of the two predictors should be significant for the pure EMMA simulation. Overall, the regression analysis confirmed these expectations. More details about the analysis can be found in the Appendix.

5.4 Simulations on the Potsdam Sentence Corpus 131

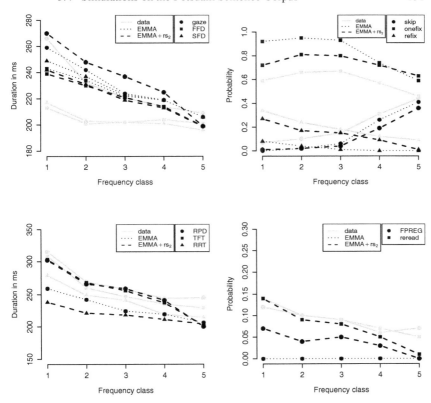

Figure 5.3 Shown are the predictions of Model 2 (EMMA, dotted lines) vs. Model 7 (EMMA+rs$_2$, dashed lines) vs. experimental data (grey solid lines) for the Potsdam Sentence Corpus. The figure shows means of early (first row) and late measures (second row) as a function of frequency class. Each row shows reading time durations on the left and probabilities on the right side.

5.4.4 Discussion

The results show that the extension with surprisal and retrieval information considerably improves EMMA's predictions for fixation measures. The interaction of postlexical processing with EMMA through Time Out regressions enables the model to predict regression-related measures. The best model was EMMA+rs$_2$, which combines retrieval with high-level surprisal, both interacting with EMMA through Time Outs. Compared to low-level surprisal, the high-level version improves the model much more. The main improvement, however, is due to the possibility of making regressions, which is not possible in EMMA+s$_1$. A fairer comparison between both surprisal versions is between

132   Modelling the Interaction of Eye-Movement Control and Parsing

EMMA+rs_1 and EMMA+rs_2, which both have the ability for Time Out regressions. When we compare each of these two models with EMMA+r, it shows that s_1 improves the prediction of both early and late measures a bit and that s_2 improves only the prediction of late measures but more than s_1 does. This means that both surprisal versions might be complementary and could be combined in one model. In any case, surprisal, whether high-level or low-level, seems to have more of an effect on early measures than retrieval when we compare EMMA+s_1 and EMMA+s_2 with EMMA+r. This is interesting because it is consistent with the results of experimental and corpus studies reported above.

5.5   General Discussion

The primary goal of the current work was to make two contributions: First, we replicated the EMMA reading simulation of Salvucci (2001) in a more recent ACT-R environment and extended it with simulations on the German Potsdam Sentence Corpus, thus evaluating EMMA on two different languages. Second, we presented an approach of augmenting EMMA with computational measures of post-lexical processing. The results showed that a combination of retrieval and surprisal substantially improves EMMA's predictions of fixation measures. The implementation of Time Out regressions (Mitchell et al., 2008) in a way similar to E-Z Reader 10 enabled the model to predict regression rates and re-reading time. The simulation results also corroborate the assumption that retrieval and surprisal are complementary in their influence on eye movements. This can be concluded from the fact that a combination of both predictors results in a better model than using just one of them, and that surprisal has more effect on early measures than retrieval has. The framework's components (ACT-R, EMMA, parser) were chosen with the aim for flexibility and expandability. The simulations presented here were intended as a general demonstration and should serve as a step towards a more detailed investigation of the interaction between eye movements and language comprehension. The use of the general modelling architecture ACT-R allows for an easy integration of the model with other sorts of linguistic or psychological factors. Also, all existing simulations that used the cue-based retrieval parsing architecture (e.g., Lewis and Vasishth, 2005; Vasishth et al., 2008; Vasishth and Lewis, 2006) can be further investigated by using the published parsing rules seamlessly with the eye movement control model.

5.5.1   *Comparison with E-Z Reader*

The EMMA/ACT-R model makes some simplifying assumptions with respect to eye movement control and its interaction with parsing. EMMA is a simplified eye movement model, designed for application in various cognitive domains. However, reading is undoubtedly a very specialized and highly trained task that involves enormous complexity. An example of the training aspect is that in E-Z Reader a forward saccade is automatically programmed after a first stage of lexical identification and before the attention shift. In EMMA, saccade programming always starts at the same time as the attention shift and word recognition. As a consequence, most of the word recognition in EMMA happens through preview and often finishes before the eyes have moved to the respective word. For that reason, most Time Out regressions are already initiated when the eyes are still fixating on word w_n (the word with postlexical difficulty) and therefore target word w_{n-1}. In contrast, regressions triggered by slow integration failure in E-Z Reader would be initiated most of the time from w_{n+1}, at least that seems to be suggested in Reichle et al. (2009). However, this difference might not be a problem for the EMMA model, at least as far as qualitative predictions are concerned. In fact, in the three experiments that are modelled in Reichle et al. (2009) the most relevant regression-related predictions are regressions *out* of the target region. In the following, these three experiments shall be briefly described including a short discussion of EMMA's capabilities with respect to according predictions.

The first experiment simulated clause wrap-up effects (Rayner et al., 2000). The critical observations and model predictions for clause-final words were an increased number of refixations and an increased regression probability from these words towards the previous region. In order to predict clause wrap-up effects in EMMA, further assumptions would have to be incorporated into the parsing model, because it does not contain specific processes related to the end of a clause. But, assuming that wrap-up operations increase the length of the integration stage, EMMA would be expected to make the correct predictions. The second experiment was about the effects of plausibility and possibility violations (Warren and McConnell, 2007). Possibility violations are detected early, observed as increased first fixation durations. The effect of implausibility appears later, increasing gaze durations and the probability of regressing out of the target word. As our extension of EMMA concerned only syntactic processing, the model does not predict semantic effects. A hypothetical version of EMMA could include a model of world knowledge similar to Budiu and Anderson (2004) that processes the result of syntactic integration, adding extra time to the integration stage. However, for a process model to account for the time-course difference between plausibility and possibility, the detection of both has to occur in distinct stages. An explanation for the earlier detection of possibility violations might be that such words are highly unexpected (and unfrequent) in the respective context so that predictability or a lexicalized version of surprisal could account for the effect. Assuming surprisal affects word recognition (as in the model EMMA+rs$_1$), it would produce an early effect

134 Modelling the Interaction of Eye-Movement Control and Parsing

for possibility violations. Finally, the third experiment discussed in Reichle et al. (2009) can be modelled by EMMA straightforwardly. This experiment examined the effects on disambiguating words in constructions that violate the principles of late closure and minimal attachment (Frazier and Rayner, 1982), so-called garden path sentences. In these sentences, on encountering the disambiguating word, the reader realizes that the syntactic structure built up to that point has to be revised. This again shows up as increased fixation durations and regressions out towards an earlier region. On the disambiguating word, the retrieval parser by Lewis and Vasishth (2005) would perform additional retrievals in order to reattach the ambiguous word to the correct node. This would lengthen the integration stage with the consequence of inflated fixation times and first-pass regressions. However, garden paths that lead to reanalysis are detected very early (effects show up in first fixation duration), which is not predicted by Time Out regressions or slow integration failure. Other than normal retrieval processes, a reanalysis is the consequence of a detection of an integration failure. This motivates the assumption that ongoing integration processes are cancelled as soon as the error is detected. Hence, the case of reanalysis is a good candidate for the application of what Reichle et al. (1998) call *rapid integration failure*, which cancels postlexical processing and initiates a regression. This would predict early effects and first-pass regressions in the disambiguating region in a garden path.

5.5.2 Future Prospects

The restriction of the current framework to syntactic processing is obviously a simplification. It is undeniable that higher cognitive levels like semantics and context play an important role in sentence processing. A relevant cognitive model in this context is the work of Budiu and Anderson (2004), who modelled contextual effects on sentence processing in ACT-R using a compositional semantic representation of propositions. In principle, the EMMA/ACT-R model could be augmented in a similar way. The tree structure built by the Lewis and Vasishth (2005) parser encodes basic relations necessary to understand a proposition, which in principle makes it possible to derive semantics from the tree. For the moment, however, we concentrate on syntactic effects. The next step would be to investigate the modelling of concrete examples of parsing difficulty. For the corpus study presented here, we used pre-calculated values for retrieval and surprisal. In future studies, the actual parsing architecture of Lewis and Vasishth (2005) could be used in runtime. As exemplified above, simulating explicit parsing processes at runtime enables the modelling of rapid integration failure in, e.g., garden paths. Furthermore, it makes it possible to use linguistic information to define saccade targets. Short, one-word regressions like the Time Outs modelled here are very frequent and explain some of the variance

5.5 General Discussion

in eye movement data. However, more complex regression patterns triggered by reanalysis have also been found (e.g., Frazier and Rayner, 1982; Meseguer et al., 2002; von der Malsburg and Vasishth, 2011, 2013). Readers sometimes make long-range regressions in order to find the ambiguous region where the wrong attachment decision was made. Important questions regarding the eye-parser connection are to what degree are these long-range regressions guided by linguistic information and what is their exact function (e.g., Booth and Weger, 2013; Inhoff and Weger, 2005; Mitchell et al., 2008; Weger and Inhoff, 2007). In combination with the explicit ACT-R parsing model, EMMA can be used for studying these questions. Ultimately, expectation should also be modelled as a runtime process instead of being pre-calculated like surprisal. This will help to understand the nature of expectation-related effects. A possible translation of surprisal in terms of an ACT-R parser would be that rare combinations of parsing rules are executed slower than more common sequences. Such an approach would ground surprisal in procedural preferences trained by reading experience.

To conclude, the presented simulations are a first step towards more advanced models that specify a concrete link between high-level cognitive processes and eye movements. The simulations show that predictions of parsing models contribute to the explanation of variance in an eyetracking corpus not only statistically but also in an explicit computational model of eye movement control. With the presented framework, it would be useful to examine the individual contributions of surprisal and retrieval to the behaviour at certain points of difficulty and the factors that guide long-range regressions.

In the next chapter, we investigate two consequences of the extended EMMA-based architecture developed here. The first interesting phenomenon is reanalysis processes in English relative clauses. In English, there is a temporary ambiguity when the relative clause marker *that* is encountered: is the sentence a subject or object relative?

(30)　The employees that...

The parsing system has expectations about how the sentence is likely to continue; in particular, the expectation is for the more frequent subject relative clause. However, if an object relative appears (i.e., if the relative clause marker *that* is followed by a noun phrase), some surprise is experienced as the parser engages in reanalysis, and this affects the subsequent eye movements. In the next chapter, we model this reanalysis process.

The second phenomenon we model in the next chapter using the architecture developed here is underspecification. It has been noticed in the literature that the human parsing system sometimes builds less structure incrementally than it is theoretically expected to. An example would be when there is an attachment ambiguity, as in a relative clause attachment:

136   Modelling the Interaction of Eye-Movement Control and Parsing

(31)   The son of the driver who had a moustache left the room.

In the above example, it is ambiguous as to who had the moustache, the son or the driver. In psycholinguistics it is traditionally assumed that the parser makes some commitment as to which noun the relative clause modifies, usually following some parsimony principle like local attachment. However, research has shown that in some cases readers might not be making any commitment at all. This kind of underspecification may be due to factors such as reduced processing capacity or reduced attention due to task demands. In the next chapter, we show how the extended eye-movement control and parsing architecture can capture some of the effects observed in the eye-movement record as a consequence of underspecification.

5.A   Root-Mean-Square Deviation

The root-mean-square deviation ($RMSD$) is used to estimate the relative goodness of fit between predicted and observed data. Reichle et al. (1998) and Salvucci (2001) normalized the $RMSD$ to be comparable between different scales (milliseconds and probabilities) by dividing the difference between observed and predicted values by the standard deviation of the observed values. In their Appendix, Reichle et al. (1998) state that this normalization was done after squaring the difference. However, the actual $RMSD$ values in Reichle et al. (1998) and Salvucci (2001) were obtained by first dividing the difference by the standard deviation and then squaring it.[5] For the reason of comparability, we also used the latter definition. For each model, we calculated the $RMSD$ for the frequency statistic over all fixation measures and frequency classes as defined below:

$$RMSD = \sqrt{\frac{1}{N} \sum_{k=1}^{N} \left(\frac{data_k - model_k}{SD_k} \right)^2}, \qquad (5.3)$$

where $data_k$, $model_k$, and SD_k range over all fixation measures and frequency classes.

5.B   Linear Regression Analysis

In order to assess the contributions of surprisal and retrieval in the model, we performed a linear regression analysis. Simply reporting means in the same way as it was done for frequency effects would not be informative for surprisal and retrieval, as their effects exhibit much interaction with other

---

[5] This was determined by a recalculation of their values and through personal communication from Dario Salvucci.

5.B Linear Regression Analysis

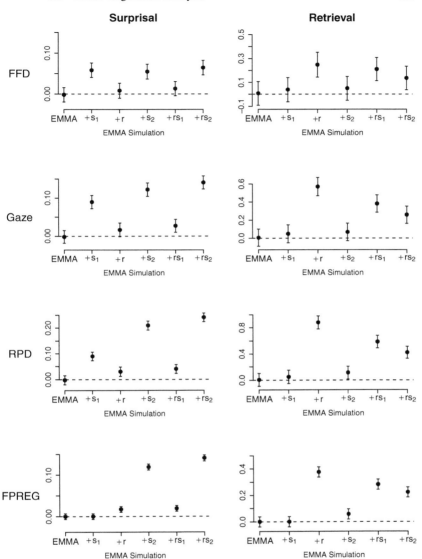

Figure 5.4 Coefficients and 95% confidence intervals for predictors surprisal and retrieval estimated by linear regression. Predictors were log frequency, length, log retrieval, and surprisal. Coefficients are plotted along the y-axis for surprisal on the left side and retrieval on the right side. Regressions were carried out on the simulated data of all six EMMA models (shown on the x-axis); 95% confidence intervals that do not cross 0 indicate statistical significance at $\alpha = 0.05$.

138   Modelling the Interaction of Eye-Movement Control and Parsing

factors. We fit linear models on the output of all six EMMA simulations for four selected dependent measures in the statistics software R (R Core Team, 2012). The models contained the predictors log frequency, length, log retrieval, and surprisal. See Eq. 5.4 for an example.

$$FFD_i = \beta_0 + \beta_1 log(freq_i) + \beta_2 len_i + \beta_3 s_i + \beta_4 log(r_i) + \epsilon_i. \tag{5.4}$$

For each predictor, β is the coefficient to be estimated. Each of the predictors was additionally centred around zero. Figure 5.4 plots estimates and 95% confidence intervals for surprisal and retrieval. It shows that surprisal and retrieval are significant predictors in almost all EMMA models that incorporate them but not in others, with some exceptions: surprisal is not significant for FFD in model EMMA+rs$_1$ but is significant in model EMMA+r for RPD and FPREG. It seems that retrieval here subsumes some of the variance that would also be caused by surprisal. Indeed, both predictors are slightly correlated with $r = 0.15$. The fact that surprisal is not significant in model EMMA+s$_1$ for first-pass regressions, on the other hand, is expected, because this model did not produce any regressions. Retrieval estimates are always significant where it would be expected. They are, however, also significant in model EMMA+s$_2$ for RPD and FPREG which, again, points towards a certain correlation with surprisal. The linear modelling results are consistent with the results on human data reported in Boston et al. (2011). Boston and colleagues fit linear mixed

Table 5.3. *Linear regression results for predictors retrieval and surprisal*

Measure	Predictor	Model EMMA+rs$_2$			Data (Boston et al., 2011)		
		Coef.	SE	t / z	Coef.	SE	t / z
SFD	Retrieval	0.102	0.056	1.8	0.00015	0.00001	18.2
	Surprisal	0.034	0.013	2.7	0.04384	0.00200	21.9
FFD	Retrieval	0.136	0.051	2.7	0.00016	0.00001	21.1
	Surprisal	0.065	0.009	7.1	0.05209	0.00179	29.0
Gaze	Retrieval	0.258	0.049	5.3			
	Surprisal	0.141	0.009	16.0			
TFT	Retrieval	0.439	0.047	9.4	0.00008	0.00001	8.0
	Surprisal	0.202	0.008	23.8	0.04588	0.00239	19.2
RPD	Retrieval	0.422	0.048	8.9	0.00010	0.00001	9.3
	Surprisal	0.241	0.009	28.0	0.05530	0.00253	21.8
FPREG	Retrieval	0.224	0.020	11.4	0.00026	0.00008	3.5
	Surprisal	0.141	0.004	37.7	0.16890	0.01767	9.6

Notes: For FPREG z-values are shown, otherwise t-values. FPREG was modelled with a generalized linear model with a binomial link function for EMMA and a generalized linear mixed model by Boston et al. (2011). For all other dependent measures a linear model was used for EMMA's predictions and a linear mixed model by Boston et al. (2011).

effects models on the PSC data and reported significantly positive coefficients for both surprisal and retrieval when predicting SFD, FFD, RPD, TFT, and FPREG. Table 5.3 shows surprisal and retrieval coefficients of regression models on the output of EMMA+rs$_2$ and, where available, the corresponding human data as reported in Boston et al. (2011). Note that the coefficients estimated here and those estimated in Boston et al. (2011) are not directly comparable because the linear models used are different. Boston et al. (2011) used more complex linear mixed models including (apart from surprisal and retrieval word length) word predictability, unigram frequency, and bigram frequency. Item and participant variation were included as random intercepts. Accounting for individual differences is necessary in the case of human data. In our simulations, however, the variance caused by different simulation runs is negligible, which makes the use of mixed models unnecessary. Without accounting for item and participant variation in the human data, however, retrieval effects in particular could not be detected (note the small coefficients for retrieval in the Boston et al. (2011) models).

6 Reanalysis and Underspecification in Sentence Comprehension

Modelling Eye Movements

6.1 Introduction

The previous chapter presented a model of an explicit link between the theory of parsing and memory access by Lewis and Vasishth (2005) and the EMMA model of eye movement control by Salvucci (2001). The model parameters were estimated in an evaluation on the Potsdam Sentence Corpus (Kliegl et al., 2004) using pre-computed values for memory retrieval latency and surprisal from Boston et al. (2011). However, the corpus mainly contained relatively simple, short sentences, which may be of limited value for testing concrete examples of parsing difficulty. In the current chapter, the resulting parameter estimates will therefore be used to generate new predictions for example sentences from the literature. In doing so, the fit between the data and the model can be evaluated by comparing model predictions to empirical data in response to specific types of parsing difficulty. The advantage of the model presented here is that it is integrated with the fully specified parser by Lewis and Vasishth (2005), so that it generates predictions in runtime without the need to pre-compute a retrieval metric. For reasons of simplicity, the focus of this chapter is on effects of memory retrieval and not surprisal.

In addition to Interface I, *Time Out*, that was presented in the previous chapter, three further elementary interfaces are proposed. Interface II, *Reanalysis*, is an early detection of parsing error resulting in a regression similar to "rapid integration failure" in Reichle et al. (2009). A simulation with Interfaces I and II replicates the results of Staub (2010), who found effects of memory and expectation in distinct locations of object- vs. subject-relative clauses. Interface III, *Underspecification*, aborts a costly attachment alternatively to signalling a time out depending on the task-relevance of the attachment relation. A second simulation illustrates how the model predicts that underspecification results from an interaction of eye movement control with parsing and individual differences in working memory capacity. While Interfaces I and II are interventions by the parser that interrupt the otherwise autonomous saccade programming, Interface III is rather an intervention in the other direction: in the case of underspecification, the parser is cut off by time pressure imposed

140

6.2 Modelling Reanalysis

Table 6.1. *ACT-R/EMMA parameter values.*

Simulation	LF	ANS	MAS	MP	VEF	VEE	SPT
5.4 PSC EMMA+r	0.2	0.15	1.5	1.4	0.002	0.4	0.110
6.2 Relative clauses	0.2	0.15	1.5	1.4	0.002	0.4	0.110
6.3 Underspecification	0.2	0.15	3.5	NIL	0.002	0.4	0.110

Note: LF: latency factor, ANS: activation noise, MAS: maximum associative strength, MP: mismatch penalty, VEF: visual encoding factor, VEE: visual encoding exponent, SPT: saccade preparation time.

by eye-movement control. Finally, a possible Interface IV: *Subvocalization* is proposed; this is not discussed in the book but is available in the model code and is discussed in Engelmann (2016). Interface IV serves as another alternative to Time Out; a word ready for integration could be stored in phonological memory (Baddeley, 2003; Baddeley and Hitch, 1974) for a very short time until there is free capacity of the sentence processor. This could be used in future work to model spill-over effects of parsing difficulty.

Table 6.1 summarizes relevant parameter values used in the simulations in this chapter. If not stated otherwise, ACT-R and EMMA parameters were kept constant at the values estimated for Model 4 "EMMA+r" in the corpus study discussed in Chapter 5 or at default values.

6.2 Modelling Reanalysis: Memory and Expectation Processes in Parsing

6.2.1 Memory and Expectation in Relative Clauses

Staub (2010) conducted an experiment that showed effects of both memory retrieval and expectation at different positions within the same sentence. Staub (2010) studied the well-known difference between subject-extracted (SRC) and object-extracted (ORC) relative clauses as in Example (32).

(32) a. The employees that [$_V$ noticed] [$_{NP}$ the fireman] hurried across the open field.
b. The employees that [$_{NP}$ the fireman] [$_V$ noticed] hurried across the open field.

A remarkably consistent fact across many languages is that SRCs are easier to comprehend than ORCs (e.g., Frazier, 1987b; Gibson et al., 2005; King and Just, 1991; Kwon et al., 2010; Schriefers et al., 1995; Traxler et al., 2002).[1]

---

[1] There seem to be some exceptions to this generalization: Basque (Carreiras et al., 2010), Hindi (Vasishth and Lewis, 2006), and Mandarin Chinese (Hsiao and Gibson, 2003) have been argued to either show an ORC advantage or show no indication of a processing difference.

Two major theoretical explanations of this difference in comprehension difficulty are based on memory processes, and on expectation-based processing. Memory-based accounts (Gibson, 1998, 2000; Grodner and Gibson, 2005; Lewis and Vasishth, 2005; Lewis et al., 2006; McElree et al., 2003) predict difficulty in ORCs due to the increased distance between the embedded verb *noticed* and its subject *employees* or memory interference with the intervening noun *fireman*.

According to expectation-based explanations (Gennari and MacDonald, 2009; Hale, 2001; Levy, 2008; Mitchell et al., 1995), SRCs are easier to process because their structure is more frequent and more regular than that of ORCs. For most languages, both accounts predict a preference for the SRC. However, for Mandarin relative clauses the two accounts make opposing predictions, which might be the cause for the long-lasting debate about which relative clause type is easier to process in Mandarin: expectation predicts a subject-relative preference here, too, because SRCs are also more frequent in Mandarin. But as Mandarin is an SVO language and its RCs are pre-nominal, the dependency is more distant in the SRC than in the ORC. Hence, a preference for ORCs is predicted by memory-based accounts in Mandarin.[2]

In his eyetracking experiment, Staub (2010) found increased difficulty at two positions in the ORC (32b): at the embedded noun phrase *the fireman*, an increased probability was found of outgoing first-pass regressions (FPRP), and at the embedded verb *noticed* increased reading times were observed in gaze duration, first-fixation duration (FFD), and go-past time (regression-path duration, RPD). Staub (2010) interpreted the results as evidence for both memory-based and expectation-based explanations for difficulty in ORCs. The difficulty on *the fireman* can be explained by expectation: on seeing the embedded subject noun phrase of the ORC, the expectation for an SRC is violated, which would cause surprise. An effect at *noticed* is predicted according to memory-based accounts due to difficulty integrating the distant dependency with the subject. This analysis was supported by the fact that the two observed effects were qualitatively different: elevated reading times at the ORC verb are compatible with memory-based explanations that predict an increased memory access latency for distant dependencies. More frequent regressions from the subject noun in the ORC could indicate surprise, causing the reader to interrupt reading and potentially revisit previously read material that led to the now-falsified expectation.

---

[2] The case of Mandarin has been investigated closely (Gibson and Wu, 2013; Hsiao and MacDonald, 2013; Jäger et al., 2015; Lin and Bever, 2006; Vasishth et al., 2013; Wu et al., 2017); in our opinion, much of the evidence for the surprising ORC advantage in Mandarin is probably due either to Type M errors, confounded designs, incorrect statistical analyses, or other sources of bias that skewed the conclusions (Vasishth, 2015).

6.2 Modelling Reanalysis 143

The Staub (2010) experiment is a good test case for the model developed in the previous chapter for two reasons. First, relative clauses are possibly the best-studied constructions in psycholinguistics and the subject-relative preference is widely believed to be a cross-linguistically reliable (replicable) result. Second, the cue-based retrieval model not only contains a memory component but also an incremental serial parsing mechanism that commits to one structure at a time. This implicates an expectation component by pre-building the necessary structure, which has to be revised when the parser is garden-pathed. At least in English relative clauses, garden-pathing happens if we encounter an ORC structure when an SRC is expected.[3] Therefore, a natural next step is to implement a mechanism that interfaces moments of garden-path with eye movement behaviour. This is pursued in the next subsection.

6.2.2   Simulation: Modelling the Staub (2010) Data

When integrating a word that is ambiguous in its function in the current parse, an incremental serial parser commits to one possible continuation. By doing so, the parser creates a kind of *expectation* for subsequent words to conform with this commitment. If the upcoming material cannot coherently be integrated, the earlier decision has to be reanalyzed. When encountering a relative pronoun, the Lewis and Vasishth (2005) parser acts according to a subject preference, always creating an SRC structure. When finding an NP to follow the relative pronoun (the subject NP of an ORC), the parsing rules execute a *reanalysis* of the pre-built SRC structure as a *gapped* ORC structure. In particular, this means that the relative pronoun is made available as a filler that can be retrieved as the object at the ORC verb. For that, an additional retrieval of the relativizer DP has to be executed.

This revision process, which occurs at the ORC subject NP, is compatible with the assumptions of expectation-based theories, namely that at this point surprise occurs and expectations have to be revised. The expectation in this case is the syntactic structure built so far, which has to be altered in order to consistently incorporate the present input.

With the Time Out extension presented in the previous chapter, elevated reading times and occasional regressions would be predicted at the ORC subject, because the additional rule firing and retrieval of the revision process

---

[3] Ranked parallel parsers do not assume a revise-on-garden-path mechanism in the sense of Frazier and Rayner (1982), but react by re-ranking possible parses, a process which could be time-consuming. If re-ranking takes times, increased difficulty is predicted just as in the case of a serial parser. However, re-ranking might make different predictions for regressive eye movements than serial parsers: because parallel parsers maintain multiple parses in parallel, it is not necessary to revise previous commitments and, thus, a parallel parsing mechanism may predict only inflated fixations times and no difference in regression probability.

delays the completion of the integration at this point. This would be the case if we assume a "slow integration failure", as Reichle et al. (2009) call it. However, the case of the SRC/ORC revision is better described as what Reichle et al. (2009) call "fast integration failure". In contrast to slow failure, where the integration time simply takes longer than usual, at a revision an error is encountered immediately, with the result that previous material has to be revisited. According to the definition of Reichle et al. (2009)'s fast failure, an immediate attention shift is triggered towards the potential cause of the error. In the SRC/ORC revision, the cause of the error (the violation of expectation) is the structural decision made at the relative pronoun. It is reasonable to assume an attention shift towards previous material in the case of a revision but not in the case of a regular retrieval, because, in a revision, previously attached material changes its role, i.e., its position in the sentence structure.

The Reanalysis interface is defined as follows:

Reanalysis Any rule that changes the attachment of a previously created syntactic object in memory triggers an immediate attention shift towards a point in the sentence that is related to the object in question.

The specific target of the attention shift and the potentially accompanying regression needs further research. As von der Malsburg and Vasishth (2011), von der Malsburg et al. (2015), and others before them (Green and Mitchell, 2006; Meseguer et al., 2002) have pointed out, it is still unclear how regression paths behave in reanalysis. Consequently, for the current simulations, the model is restricted to specifying the source of the regression and not the target. A least-commitment implementation was chosen that selects any target to the left of the current fixation.

6.2.3   Results

Simulations were performed using the parameter values that have been estimated with the Time Out model on the Potsdam Sentence Corpus. Each sentence of Example (32) was run 200 times.

Figure 6.1 shows mean reading times for first-fixation duration, gaze duration, and go-past time in comparison with the data (in gray). In first fixations and gaze durations, the Staub (2010) data shows reading time differences only on the embedded verb, the ORC being slower than the SRC. In go-past times, more regressions occur at this point in the ORC than the SRC.

Qualitatively, the model predicts these patterns exactly in all three eye movement measures. Numerically, there is a remarkably close fit in first-fixation durations. Also in gaze and go-past times, the predictions are numerically in a similar range as the data, but the SRC reading times are underestimated in the predictions by 50–100 milliseconds.

6.2 Modelling Reanalysis

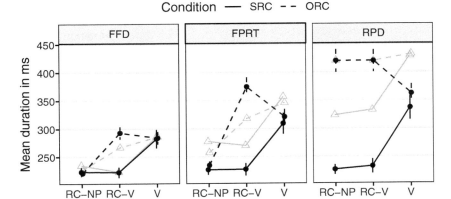

Figure 6.1 Model predictions for reading times in subject- and object-relative clauses at the relative clause NP (RC-NP), the relative clause verb (RC-V), and the main verb (V). The dependent measures are first-fixation durations (FFD), first-pass reading time (FPRT), and regression path duration (RPD). The data are from Table 1 of Staub (2010), and are shown in gray. Error bars represent 95% confidence intervals from the model simulations. This is a zero-parameter fit: no parameter estimation was done to fit the model to the data.

First-pass regression proportions are shown in Figure 6.2. The empirical means are from Table 1 of Staub (2010) and are indicated by the black triangles. They show an increased regression rate in ORCs at the relative clause NP. As for reading times, the model predictions for regressions pattern with the data. The model predicts no first-pass regressions for the SRC at the NP or the verb inside the relative clause; by contrast, the data show regressions in the SRC condition. The model predicts the major empirical finding in Staub (2010) of an increased regression rate at the relative clause NP for the ORC. It does, however, additionally predict a slight increase in regressions at the verb in ORC vs SRC conditions, which has not been found in the data.

6.2.4 Discussion

The simulation tested the model on specific predictions for English relative clauses. No parameter fitting to the data was performed. The model with parameters as estimated on the Potsdam Sentence Corpus generated predictions that qualitatively reproduce the theoretically important patterns in the data. The Time Out interface developed in the previous chapter predicts memory-based differences and magnitudes in three different reading time measures in

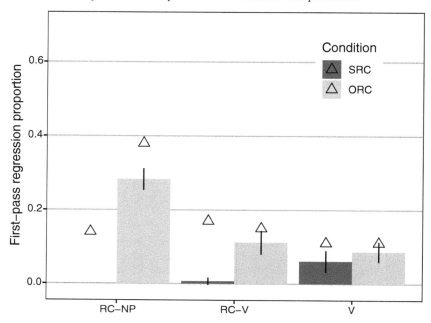

Figure 6.2 Model predictions for first-pass regressions in subject- and object-relative clauses at embedded NP, embedded verb, and main verb. The data are from Staub (2010) and are shown as triangles. Error bars represent 95% confidence intervals from the model simulations. This is a zero-parameter fit: no parameter estimation was done to fit the model to the data.

three regions remarkably well. This shows that the parameter estimates that were computed for the Potsdam Sentence Corpus of German can be used for experimentally controlled comparisons of memory-related complexities in English. The newly introduced Reanalysis interface II, which is similar to Reichle et al. (2009)'s rapid integration failure, correctly predicts increased first-pass regressions due to an invalidated prediction.

In sum, Staub (2010) proposes that the qualitatively distinct effects on the RC noun phrase and the RC verb indicate distinct sources of difficulty, namely expectation and memory, respectively. These two sources of difficulty can be explained within the cue-based retrieval model, without recourse to additional modelling assumptions involving probabilistic predictions. Note that the mechanism of interaction in the model is in both cases the same: the parser intervenes in the forward movement of the eyes, triggering a regression. However, the timing differs in that the intervention happens earlier for violated expectations: memory-induced time outs are triggered after recognition of the next word,

6.2 Modelling Reanalysis

but reanalysis regressions are triggered as soon as the parser detects that the input is unexpected. Due to this timing difference, the time out regressions on the verb are cancelled most of the time before they are executed, because the memory processes are not delayed long enough before normal reading is resumed. The planning and cancelling of regressions thus leads to inflated reading times. By contrast, reanalysis is triggered earlier and the parser has to perform additional actions for revising structure, which leaves enough time for the regression to be completed. This is an example of a simple mechanism producing complex behaviour: the same mechanism – triggering a regression – produces qualitatively different effects under certain circumstances, based on the relative timing between parsing and eye-movement control. One aspect that is not captured in the model is the effect of eye-movement control constraints on regressive eye movements (Engbert et al., 2005). In order to incorporate the effect of eye-movement control, a comprehensive integration of a parsing model and an eye-movement control model like SWIFT is needed. At the time of writing, this research is ongoing (Rabe et al., 2020).

The model predictions thus capture the major findings of Staub's study. However, the model is very simplified and consequently deviates in its predictions in some ways from the data. First, a subject-relative preference is hard-coded into the model, whereas human readers might also expect ORCs in some cases. The underestimation of SRC gaze and go-past durations in the model would be less significant with a probabilistic decision between pursuing an SRC or ORC structure.[4]

Second, first-pass regression proportions are predicted to be slightly increased on the RC verb in the ORC, although the only empirical effect reported was on the RC noun phrase. This indicates that not all of the time out regressions that are triggered at this region were cancelled but some had enough time to be executed, meaning that the model predicts memory-based regressions on the verb which are not supported by Staub's data. However, the biggest effect in the predictions of first-pass regressions is on the ORC subject, consistent with the data.

Third, expectation-based first-pass regressions are only predicted on the determiner of the ORC subject, not on the noun. In the data, however, the effect is found at the determiner *and* the noun. This is most likely a spill-over effect due to delayed parsing in some trials, which is not predicted in this case by the model. It is possible in the model that parsing processes on word n influence the fixation time on word n+1: this happens when a time out is initiated while the eyes have already moved on to word n+1. However, this does

---

[4] In ACT-R, it is possible to learn the utilities of parsing rules over a number of trials, based on the number of successful applications. It would be necessary to simulate reading of a corpus that represents the natural distributions of relative clauses and similar structures.

148   Reanalysis and Underspecification in Sentence Comprehension

not happen in the simulation, because the detection of the validated expectation is instantaneous, meaning it is part of the first parsing production firing at the determiner. Hence, reanalysis is always initiated before the time-out production can fire. This might be a limitation of the model which will have to be addressed in the future. However, an alternative cause for spill-over effects – especially, if they span multiple words – may be that readers delay parsing in order to collect more information before making structural decisions. A likely mechanism for delaying parsing processes in this way is to hold words temporarily in the articulatory loop (Baddeley, 2003; Baddeley and Hitch, 1974). This possibility is explored through a proof-of-concept simulation in Engelmann (2016).

6.3   Modelling Underspecification: The Adaptive Interaction between Parsing, Eye-Movement Control, and Working Memory Capacity

Several researchers, such as Traxler (2007), have proposed that individuals with low working-memory capacity might build less structure than individuals with high working-memory capacity. For example, in sentences like *The sister of the writer that had blond hair arrived this morning*, it isn't clear whether the sister had blond hair or the writer. One proposal is that low-capacity individuals might simply not commit to one or another attachment, leaving the structure underspecified. This proposal implies two distinct strategies for low- vs. high-capacity individuals. In this section, we show how our model, which integrates eye-movement control and parsing processes, can explain such underspecification processes as a function of capacity differences. The model assumes that underspecification occurs as a consequence of low-capacity readers taking longer on average to complete an attachment. Whether an attachment completes or not in a particular trial depends on whether the attachment can be completed fast. If a reader (such as a low-capacity reader) takes longer to read, this will non-deterministically lead to the cancellation of the attachment process, leading to underspecification being observed in some trials. The interesting aspect of the model is that underspecification emerges as a side-effect of the interplay between "normal" reading and working-memory capacity.

6.3.1   Good-Enough Parsing

The good-enough approach to sentence processing (Ferreira et al., 2002; Sanford and Sturt, 2002) suggests that readers strategically adapt their efforts to task demands with the consequence of sometimes not arriving at a complete parse. This implies that readers leave some structural relations underspecified in order to save processing time if the effort does not seem necessary for the task at hand.

6.3 Modelling Underspecification

An example of underspecification is the finding that some ambiguous attachment relations are read faster than their unambiguous counterparts. For example, Traxler et al. (1998) and Traxler (2007) studied sentences like (33c) that were globally ambiguous with regard to the attachment of the relative clause to one of the noun phrases *sister* or *writer* and compared them to sentences where the relative clause was unambiguously attached *high* (33a) or *low* (33b).

(33) a. The writer of the letter/ that had/ blonde hair/ arrived this/ morning.

     b. The letter of the writer/ that had/ blonde hair/ arrived this/ morning.

     c. The sister of the writer/ that had/ blonde hair/ arrived this/ morning.

Both studies found an ambiguity advantage at the disambiguation region *blonde hair*. An analysis of individual working memory capacity in Traxler (2007) revealed that high-capacity readers showed an expected preference for high attachment (NP1). Low-capacity readers, in contrast, showed no such preference. According to Traxler (2007), it might be that low-capacity readers leave the attachment underspecified or the selection of the attachment site is the product of a balance between a high-attachment preference and recency.

Building on work by Just and Carpenter (1992) and MacDonald et al. (1992), among others, Kemper et al. (2004) studied a main clause/relative clause ambiguity such as (34).

(34) a. The experienced soldiers/ warned about the dangers/ before the midnight raid.

     b. The experienced soldiers/ warned about the dangers/ conducted the midnight raid.

     c. The experienced soldiers/ spoke about the dangers/ before the midnight raid.

     d. The experienced soldiers/ who were told about the/ dangers conducted the midnight raid.

In (34a) and (34b), the role of *warned* is temporarily ambiguous between the main verb and the embedded verb of a reduced relative clause. In (34b), the ambiguity is resolved towards the non-preferred reduced-relative reading. In (34c), the verb *spoke* unambiguously induces a main verb reading. Kemper and colleagues found the expected difficulty at *conducted* in the non-preferred condition (34b). However, in contrast to the studies by Traxler and colleagues, they found no ambiguity advantage. An analysis of working memory differences showed that low-capacity readers had more difficulty resolving the ambiguity, which was indicated by slower reading and higher regression rates at the disambiguating region.

A possible account of when attachments are underpecified and thus an explanation for the difference between Traxler's experiments and Kemper et al. (2004) is offered by *construal* (Carreiras and Clifton, 1993; Frazier and Clifton, 1997). This theory differentiates between "primary" and "nonprimary" relations, where primary roughly stands for relations that are obligatory for deriving a coherent message (e.g., verbs and their arguments). The attachment of primary relations is always carried out according to garden-path theory (Frazier, 1987a) while the definite attachment of nonprimary relations can be suspended by loosely associating it with the last theta domain (Frazier and Clifton, 1997).

More evidence for construal and the good-enough account (Ferreira et al., 2002; Sanford and Sturt, 2002) comes from a self-paced reading study by Swets et al. (2008). Similar to Traxler et al. (1998) and Traxler (2007), Swets and colleagues studied ambiguous relative clause attachments as in Example (35).

(35)   a. The maid of the princess who scratched herself in public was terribly humiliated.

   b. The son of the princess who scratched himself in public was terribly humiliated.

   c. The son of the princess who scratched herself in public was terribly humiliated.

Swets et al. (2008) manipulated task demands by using either superficial comprehension questions or questions that specifically queried the interpretation of the relative clause. The results showed an ambiguity advantage in (35a) vs. (b) and (c) at the disambiguating reflexive only when questions were superficial, indicating that question type affected the readers preference to leave the RC attachment underspecified. In addition, in the condition with questions targeting the relative clause (RC question condition), question response times were elevated for ambiguous sentences. This indicates that even in the RC-question condition the attachment was sometimes left unspecified and had to be resolved during the question answering phase. In the RC-question condition, a disambiguation towards NP1 (35b) resulted in longest reading times, pointing to a preference towards NP2 in the initial attachment, which had to be revised at the reflexive. For a detailed analysis of the Swets et al. (2008) data and the compatibility with assumptions about underspecification, see Logačev and Vasishth (2015); Logačev and Vasishth (2016).

In related work, von der Malsburg and Vasishth (2013) investigated the influence of working memory capacity on the preferences for underspecification. They conducted an eyetracking experiment using the stimuli of a Spanish study by Meseguer et al. (2002) and analyzed the participants' individual scanpaths (von der Malsburg and Vasishth, 2011) conditional on working memory capacity. In the sentences studied (Example 37), an adjunct (*cuando los directores...*) was temporarily ambiguous between modifying the main verb

6.3 Modelling Underspecification

dijo as a temporal adverbial clause (high attachment) or the embedded verb *se levantaran* as a conditional (low attachment).

(36)   El   profesor dijo que los alumnos se levantaran del   asiento
       The professor said that the students stand up   from seat

          'The teacher said that the students had to stand up from their seats…'

(37)   a. HIGH

          …cuando los directores **entraron** en la   clase de múusica.
          …when   the directors   entered   in the class of music

          …when the directors entered in the class of music.

       b. LOW

          cuando los directores **entraran** en la   clase de música.
          …when the directors   entered   in the class of music

          …when the directors entered in the class of music.

       c. UNAMB(IGUOUS)

          …**si** los directores entraban en la   clase de música.
          …if the directors   entered in the class of music

          …if the directors entered in the class of music.

The attachment site was disambiguated at the verb *entraron* (indicative) / *entraran* (subjunctive) towards HIGH (37a) or LOW (37b) attachment, respectively. In the unambiguous (UNAMB) condition (37c), using the word *si* ("if") instead of *cuando* ("when"/"if") unambiguously signalled LOW attachment of the adjunct as a conditional.

Von der Malsburg and Vasishth investigated the ambiguity advantage in the pre-verbal region *cuando los directores*. For this design, Traxler (2007) would predict that low-capacity readers underspecify more often. Support for the Traxler (2007) prediction comes from the proportions of rereading of the whole sentence after seeing the disambiguating region (see Figure 6.3). For high-capacity readers, the rereading proportion was highest for condition (a), where the disambiguation was towards the more distant high attachment. In contrast, low-capacity readers showed no statistically significant difference in rereading proportions between conditions. According to von der Malsburg and Vasishth (2013), this suggests that high-capacity readers complete the attachment of the adjunct more often and thus have to reanalyze later, whereas low-capacity readers have no need for reanalysis because they tend to leave the attachment unspecified in the ambiguous conditions. The reason for reanalysis occurring predominantly in the high-attachment condition is that the conditional interpretation with a low attachment is initially preferred with the word *cuando*.

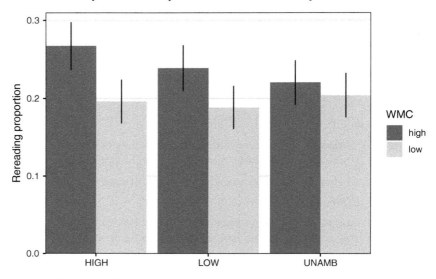

Figure 6.3 Proportions of sentence rereading in the data of von der Malsburg and Vasishth (2013) for ambiguous high (a), low (b), and unambiguous (c) conditions, grouped by high and low working memory capacity. Error bars represent 95% confidence intervals.

The evidence summarized above suggests that ambiguous attachment relations are strategically underspecified, and that readers with low working memory capacity leave an attachment underspecified more often than high-capacity readers do. It is not clear, however, how this adaptation works. Is it necessary to assume that low-capacity readers use a different parsing strategy, or can the difference be explained by a common mechanism? So far, there exists no detailed, computationally implemented model of the good-enough account that could clarify this issue.

Here, we propose that underspecification is a consequence of a single strategy that aims for uninterrupted reading whenever possible. In particular, for nonprimary relations in the sense of Frazier and Clifton (1997), an attachment is treated as non-obligatory and completed only if enough time is left before the next word is ready to be integrated. Thus, underspecification is not a deterministic process but dynamically adapts to the relative timing of the attachment process and autonomous low-level eye movement processes. If an attachment is easy and proceeds fast in relation to the "default" reading speed (in the sense of *uninterrupted* reading), the attachment is completed. If, however, the attachment could not be made without interrupting the progress of the eyes, it is abandoned in a trade-off with reading speed. An influence of working memory

6.3 Modelling Underspecification

differences is predicted by the assumption that, compared to high-capacity readers, low-capacity readers take longer on average to complete the attachment, resulting in more cancellations that leave the attachment underspecified.

6.3.2 Simulation: Modelling the von der Malsburg and Vasishth (2013) Experiment

Here, we report an implementation of the model that defines *good-enough* parsing as the result of an interaction between the parser and eye-movement control, as explained above. For non-obligatory relations, the time to attach is constrained by the time needed by saccade programming and low-level processes to identify the next word:

Underspecification Interface For relations with low utility, an attachment attempt is aborted as soon as the next word is ready for integration, so that reading proceeds uninterrupted.

This implementation naturally predicts an influence of working memory capacity. Here, memory capacity is implemented in terms of the goal buffer source activation parameter W in ACT-R. Working memory capacity has been modelled in this way before: Daily et al. (2001) modelled individual differences in the digit-span task (Lovett et al., 1999) in ACT-R by manipulating the source activation W for the goal buffer. In the context of language comprehension, van Rij et al. (2013) used this method by manipulating W for modelling individual differences in pronoun interpretation. The amount of activation W is equally distributed between sources j in the goal buffer, i.e., the chunks that spread activation to related memory items. Thus, the value of W defines how strongly relevant information from the goal buffer is used for memory retrieval. Therefore, higher values of W improve speed and accuracy of retrieval processes. In this way, the term working memory capacity is defined as a measure of how well an individual is able to separate information in memory that is relevant to the current task from currently irrelevant information – a kind of focussing of cognitive attention.

As an example simulation, the Lewis and Vasishth (2005) model was extended with parsing rules for sentence constructions as used by von der Malsburg and Vasishth (2013) and defined the adjunct attachment as non-obligatory. In particular, when attaching the adjunct, the parser creates the structure for the adjunct clause and then signals that integration is complete, so that no time-out rule will fire. It then attempts to retrieve both potential attachment sites. This process is faster and more accurate for high-capacity readers because, with a high source activation W, the retrieval cues activate the correct retrieval targets more strongly. Thus, high-capacity readers are predicted by the model to underspecify less often than low-capacity readers.

An important observation here is that the mechanism is the same for all readers: as soon as the next word is ready for integration, an ongoing attachment process is abandoned. Following Swets et al. (2008), an abandoned attachment is not corrected later in the sentence. However, if an attachment was made, disambiguating information that contradicts the attachment decision leads to a repair operation, triggering a regression towards the beginning of the sentence (this assumption is based on the finding by von der Malsburg and Vasishth (2013) that repair processes tend to trigger re-reading of a sentence).

Sixty participants were simulated reading the three attachment conditions of von der Malsburg and Vasishth (2013), HIGH, LOW, and UNAMB, 20 times each. EMMA parameters and the latency factor were left at values estimated in the simulations involving the Potsdam Sentence Corpus evaluation. Other parameters were set to the values used in Lewis and Vasishth (2005). However, two parameters were changed for this simulation. First, *mismatch penalty* MP was set to NIL to switch off partial matching. This was done in order to reduce interference and misretrievals as this was not relevant here. Second, the *maximum associative strength* parameter MAS had to be increased from 1.5 to 3.5 in order to have enough spreading activation from the goal buffer for differences in W to have an effect. For simulating individual differences in working memory capacity, the method of Daily et al. (2001) was used to randomly assign to W a value drawn from a normal distribution with mean $= 1.0$ and standard deviation $= 0.25$.

6.3.3   Results

Simulated participants were grouped into high and low capacity with respect to the randomly assigned goal source activation W by using a median split (the median of W was 0.96). This resulted in 30 simulated high-capacity subjects with mean 1.19 and 30 simulated low-capacity subjects with mean 0.75. As in the preceding simulation, no parameter estimation was done to fit the model to the empirical data.

Model predictions for gaze durations for the potentially ambiguous region *cuando/si*[5] are plotted in Figure 6.4. The model predicts an ambiguity advantage which is more pronounced for low-W simulations than for high-W simulations. This is in line with the findings of an ambiguity advantage in previous work.

The timing difference between low- and high-capacity readers in the unambiguous condition predicted by the model is due to different time

---

[5] Predictions are shown for one word only and not for the whole pre-verbal region, because the model currently does not predict any spill-over due to delayed parsing processes. Therefore, the effect of underspecification appears immediately at the critical word. Also see the General Discussion on this point.

6.3 Modelling Underspecification

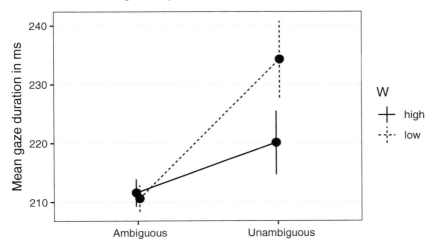

Figure 6.4 Model predictions for gaze durations at *cuando/si* for ambiguous (a and b) and unambiguous (c) conditions, grouped by high and low goal buffer source activation W. Error bars represent 95% confidence intervals.

out proportions in the attachment region, as shown in Figure 6.5. Because attachment is generally slower for low-capacity readers, more time outs (interface I), which make the eyes wait for the completion of integration, are necessary. No time outs are predicted in the ambiguous conditions, since attachment happens as a process of minor importance in this case.

Figure 6.6 shows the proportions of rereading the sentence after seeing the disambiguating verb *entraron/entraran* in the ambiguous conditions or *entraban* in the unambiguous condition. The model predicts rereading almost exclusively in the ambiguous high-attachment condition, because the parser mostly attaches low and reanalysis is therefore mainly needed when the sentence is disambiguated towards high attachment. A second prediction is that high-capacity readers reread in that condition more often than low-capacity readers. The reason for this is that simulated high-capacity subjects attach more often than low-capacity subjects, as is shown in Figure 6.7. This is the case in both ambiguous conditions, and is responsible for the ambiguity advantage seen for both groups. Rereading is, however, only affected in the ambiguous HIGH-disambiguation condition, since only in this case is reanalysis necessary.

There are important differences between the observed patterns in the data and the model predictions. This becomes apparent when we compare the predictions in Figure 6.6 with the data in Figure 6.3. More reading occurs in high-capacity readers in the ambiguous HIGH condition, and this is consistent with the data. However, the predictions show that rereading proportions of

156 Reanalysis and Underspecification in Sentence Comprehension

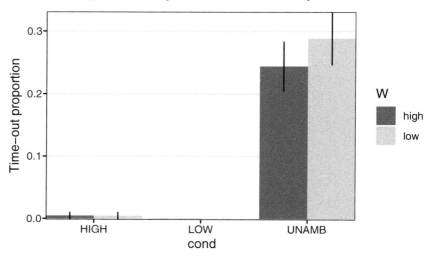

Figure 6.5 Predicted time out proportions for ambiguous high (a), low (b), and unambiguous (c) conditions, grouped by high and low goal buffer source activation W. Error bars represent 95% confidence intervals.

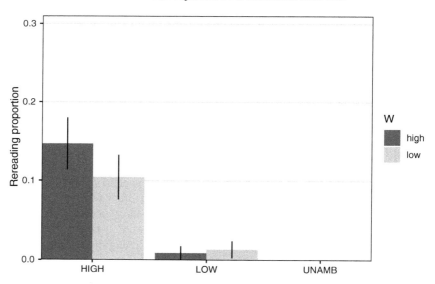

Figure 6.6 Predicted proportions of sentence rereading for ambiguous high (a), low (b), and unambiguous (c) conditions, grouped by high and low goal buffer source activation W. Error bars represent 95% confidence intervals.

6.3 Modelling Underspecification

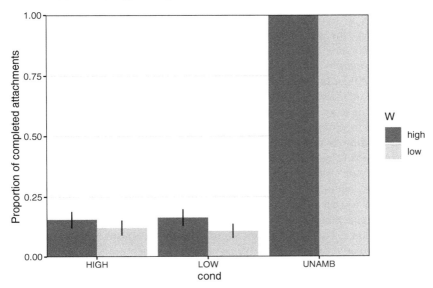

Figure 6.7 Predicted attachment proportions for ambiguous high (a), low (b), and unambiguous (c) conditions, grouped by high and low goal buffer source activation W. Error bars represent 95% confidence intervals.

low-capacity readers are also affected by the conditions, which is not the case in the data. Another difference is that, in the data, there is some rereading in every condition; by contrast, the model predictions show rereading only in the reanalysis condition (a). Both differences are due to the simplified nature of the model, which will be elaborated on in the Discussion.

6.3.4 Discussion

Our simple model of good-enough parsing predicts some of the essential observations: (i) an ambiguity advantage appears at the point of attachment, (ii) low-capacity readers leave an attachment underspecified more often than high-capacity readers, and (iii) high-capacity readers consequently have to reanalyze more often at the point of disambiguation. Interestingly, these predictions are not the result of different strategies for different groups of working memory capacity; rather, these different behaviours emerge from one common strategy that is an adaptive trade-off between attachment accuracy and reading speed, caused simply by the timing of low-level word identification and oculomotor processes. This simple mechanism leads to an adaptive interaction between parsing, eye movement control, and working memory capacity that predicts the observations mentioned above.

158   Reanalysis and Underspecification in Sentence Comprehension

The model used for the above simulation was deliberately kept simple, because the aim was to transparently map predictions to underlying mechanisms. This simplification is responsible for some differences between the model predictions and the empirical observations of von der Malsburg and Vasishth (2013). In the following, four simplifying assumptions in the current model and their implications will be discussed.

Firstly, the model deterministically preferred low attachment (except a small proportion of erroneous retrievals of the high attachment site). This explains why rereading is only predicted in the ambiguous HIGH condition (a). In a more realistic model, a utility value for the attachment productions would simulate a non-deterministic preference that would lead to rereading in both ambiguous conditions. However, there is certainly some amount of rereading that is due to other factors than disambiguation; examples are misreadings, erroneous attachments, and other difficulties due to the length and complexity of the sentence. This is clear from the fact that the data also shows rereading in the unambiguous conditions where no reanalysis is necessary per se.

Secondly, the model deterministically completed the attachment in 100 per cent of the simulation runs in the unambiguous condition. In this condition, the model predicted low-capacity readers to be slower than high-capacity readers, because attachment takes longer for the former. For simplicity, underspecification was only allowed in the model for the specific relation of adjunct attachment. In a more sophisticated model, the trade-off between time out (the eyes wait for the parser) and attachment underspecification (the eyes cut off the parser) would be defined by a utility value which is learned for different attachment relations by reading experience. Thus, unambiguous and obligatory relations would also have some possibility for being underspecified. A possible model would be the following: For every relation, there is a utility value that decides between the two possibilities, time-out (completing the attachment) and cut-off (underspecification). These values are adjusted after every sentence by a positive or negative *reward* according to a task such as answering comprehension questions. An incorrect response to the task will shift the utility towards more accuracy making the completion of attachments more important. A high number of time outs during the sentence reading will, however, shift the utility towards speed, reducing the importance of attachments, leading to more underspecified relations. The utility learning module of ACT-R would be suitable for this kind of model. In ACT-R, when a reward is triggered, the utility values U of all productions that fired since the last reward are updated with emphasis on more recent productions as defined in Eq. (6.1):

$$U_i(n) = U_i(n-1) + \alpha[R_i(n) - U_i(n-1)], \qquad (6.1)$$

where α is the learning rate set by a parameter and $R_i(n)$ is the reward value given to production i at time n.

6.3 Modelling Underspecification

This mechanism would ensure a balance between speed and accuracy according to individual differences and task demands. For low capacity readers, the utility for attachment would automatically turn out generally lower and thus compensate for slower memory processes. As a result, reading speed of low-capacity readers would be more or less the same as of high-capacity readers. This adaptive yet simple mechanism of global good-enough processing makes the prediction that low-capacity readers do not generally read slower than high-capacity readers; this prediction should be tested in future work. In addition, a model like this would predict the results of Swets et al. (2008) who found indications for underspecification only in sessions when superficial comprehension questions were asked. The adaptation of utility values according to response accuracy would lead to more attachments for comprehension questions targeting the ambiguous relation and more underspecification for easy questions. This adaptation would occur over time and would predict trial effects.

A third simplifying model assumption regards the generation of differences in working memory capacity. Although the data shows qualitative differences in the ambiguity advantage (there is no indication of an ambiguity advantage for high-capacity readers) and rereading proportions (there is no indication of a difference by condition for low-capacity readers), the model rather predicts differences in the magnitude of the ambiguity advantage by capacity level: the ambiguity advantage is predicted to have a larger magnitude for low-capacity readers, and differences in rereading proportions are more pronounced for high-capacity readers. This is a result of the choice made during modelling regarding the variability in capacity between subjects (for the simulations, W is sampled from a normal distribution around 1 with standard deviation 0.25). Choosing a greater variance would increase the differences between capacity groups. The variance for W could be based on the empirical variance in scores of the working memory test that assesses individual working memory capacity. We leave this for future work.

The fourth (and final) point relates to the immediacy of the predicted effects. In other words, effects are generally predicted at the word that causes them. What is needed is a mechanism that allows for somewhat delayed parsing processes and predicts spill-over as observed, e.g., in the expectation-based first-pass regressions in Staub (2010) or the ambiguity advantage in gaze durations across the pre-verbal region in von der Malsburg and Vasishth (2013).

In summary, the model assumes that a simple common mechanism leads to an interaction between parsing, eye movements, and individual differences predicting observations that are attributed to good-enough processing. Further, a more sophisticated model is sketched out that uses adaptive utilities that predict an interaction of underspecifications with task demands.

6.4 General Discussion

In this chapter, three additional interfaces between parsing and eye movement control have been defined and tested. Including the Time Out interface introduced earlier, the framework now comprises three interfaces, which are summarized below:

(i) Time Out: Short regressions compensate for slow syntactic integration, simulation using the Potsdam Sentence Corpus
(ii) Reanalysis: Immediate attention shift to previous material when structure has to be revised (the simulation of the Staub (2010) data)
(iii) Underspecification: For structural relations with low utility, time-consuming attachments are aborted as soon as the next word is ready for integration, such that reading proceeds uninterrupted (the simulation of the von der Malsburg and Vasishth (2013) data)

The first two interfaces, Time Out and Reanalysis, cause parser-triggered *interruptions* of the reading process, whereas Underspecification provides mechanisms that abort or delay parsing to ensure *uninterrupted* reading. Time Out is a relatively straight-forward implementation of a well-defined mechanism. However, the other two interfaces are simplifying descriptions of more complex mechanisms. The Reanalysis interface leaves open the question of where regressions are targeted and how the target position is determined. Interface III predicts *when* attachment is aborted due to an interaction of parsing difficulty, word identification timing, and individual differences, but it lacks a definition of *which* relations are eligible candidates for potential underspecification. As discussed above, construal theory provides an orientation for this question, but a continuous experience- and context-based utility value for syntactic relations would be a more realistic model.

The idea of capacity-constrained sentence comprehension is not new; e.g., the CC READER model (Just and Varma, 2002; Varma, 2016) also has a notion of constrained capacity inducing individual differences in sentence comprehensive behaviour. This model is currently not in active development or use, but understanding the predictions of the CC READER model for underspecification data would be a very informative research direction. A completely different way in which capacity could be seen as constrained is by assuming that readers have different amounts of parallelism in the number of states that the parser can maintain at any choice point (Boston et al., 2011; Jurafsky, 1996). For example, if we assume that individuals have different amounts of bandwidth for maintaining states in parallel, this could potentially explain individual-level differences. These are all interesting future directions that could be pursued in order to evaluate alternative ways to realize individual-level differences in behaviour in underspecification configurations.

7 Competing Accounts of Interference in Sentence Processing

The different cue-based retrieval models presented in the preceding chapters of this book are not the only way to implement retrieval processes in sentence processing. An interesting competing proposal comes from McElree (2000) and Van Dyke and McElree (2006). For a long time, the Lewis and Vasishth activation model and the McElree direct-access model were considered to be notational variants (e.g., see Lewis et al., 2006; Parker et al., 2017). Unfortunately, the direct-access model was never implemented as a computational process model; this made it difficult to unpack the underlying latent processes assumed there.

One way to compare the predictions of the model discussed in this book and the direct-access model is to implement a simplified statistical process model that abstracts away from some of the more complex aspects of the models (especially the Lewis and Vasishth model). The principal reason to simplify the model is convenience; a fully implemented process model for direct-access, programmed in the same cognitive architecture as the Lewis and Vasishth model, should be a longer-term goal.

Nicenboim and Vasishth (2018) were the first to implement the Lewis and Vasishth model and the direct-access model as statistical models and to quantitatively compare the predictions of these two models of retrieval. In this chapter, we present some of the work relating to these model comparisons. The models are implemented using the Stan programming language (www.mc-stan.org).

7.1 The Direct-Access Model

The direct-access model was motivated by research from the cognitive psychology literature (McElree, 2000, 2006; Van Dyke and McElree, 2006), which shows that accessing items from memory is driven by a content-addressable memory system. That is, as in the activation model, retrieval cues (bundles of feature-value pairs) are used to carry out a search. Sentence processing is

162   Competing Accounts of Interference in Sentence Processing

assumed to be constrained by the same general memory system that constrains other types of information processing (McElree, 1993).[1]

The term "direct-access" refers to the assumption that search in memory is driven by directly accessing items in memory that match the features used as retrieval cues. The time taken to complete a retrieval is assumed to be constant regardless of when the item was previously encountered. Lewis et al. (2006) point out that "[t]he estimate of memory retrieval times from the SAT [Speed-accuracy tradeoff] studies is about 80–90 ms." This type of search process is often referred to as a content-addressable cue-based search. The term content-addressable refers to the use of retrieval cues (bundles of feature-value specifications such as [subject: yes, animate: yes]) to search for items in memory using their feature specifications.

The memory-access process assumed in the computationally implemented version of the direct-access model (Nicenboim and Vasishth, 2018) is perhaps most easily understood if we consider how inhibitory interference effects arise in the model. We use example (38) to explain model assumptions.

(38)   a. The worker was surprised that the resident$_{+subject}^{+animate}$ who was living near the dangerous neighbour$_{-subject}^{+animate}$ was complaining $\{_{subject}^{animate}\}$ about the investigation.

        b. The worker was surprised that the resident$_{+subject}^{+animate}$ who was living near the dangerous warehouse$_{-subject}^{-animate}$ was complaining $\{_{subject}^{animate}\}$ about the investigation.

As shown schematically in Figure 7.1, for sentence (38a) the model assumes that when the retrieval cues [subject: yes, animate: yes] are used to access the subject noun in memory, these cues match the noun "resident", but they also partially match the noun "neighbour" on one feature (animate). This leads to a cue overload as in the activation model. The consequence of this cue overload is that in most trials the subject "resident" will be retrieved, but in some proportion of trials the incorrect noun "neighbour" will be misretrieved. In both cases the time taken to complete the retrieval is the same, say β milliseconds. In trials where the incorrect noun is retrieved, in some proportion of the cases a second retrieval attempt (referred to as reanalysis) is carried out which costs a certain amount of time, say δ ms. In contrast to (38a), in (38b) when the retrieval cues [subject: yes, animate: yes] are used to access the subject noun in memory, only one noun ("resident") matches these cues and most of the retrievals succeed immediately. Thus, in (38a) the probability of a misretrieval followed by a reanalysis step is higher than in (38b), and since reanalysis costs δ ms, sentence (38a) takes longer to read than (38b).

[1] This chapter contains text used with permission from Vasishth et al. (2019), Copyright (2019) Elsevier; license numbers 4740780688305 and 4740790181694.

7.1 The Direct-Access Model

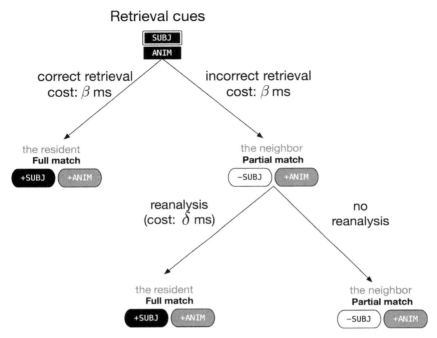

Figure 7.1 A schematic illustration of the direct-access model. For sentences like (38a), the model assumes that once a search is initiated in memory using a set of retrieval cues (here, subject and animate), one of two events can happen. Either the correct item is retrieved from memory, or the incorrect item, which matches some of the retrieval cues, is misretrieved. In the case of a misretrieval, either processing ends with a misretrieval, or a reanalysis step is initiated that leads to a correct retrieval. This reanalysis step costs time, and therefore leads to slowdowns in processing on average.

An important difference from the activation model is that in the direct-access model, cue overload affects only the probability of retrieving an item from memory; the retrieval time per se is constant. In the direct-access model, the increased reading time observed due to cue overload is a consequence of the reanalysis time. By contrast, in the activation model, cue overload redistributes the activation of items, dampening activation for all items that (partly) match the retrieval cues. Since activation affects retrieval accuracy as well as retrieval time, the direct consequence of cue overload is increased retrieval time.

Formally, the direct-access model can therefore be seen as a two-component finite mixture process (Frühwirth-Schnatter, 2006; McLachlan and Peel, 2004), with some proportion of trials representing a successful retrieval in the first

164 Competing Accounts of Interference in Sentence Processing

attempt, and some proportion representing a slower retrieval that is the consequence of an initially unsuccessful retrieval in the first attempt followed by a subsequent reanalysis step (Nicenboim and Vasishth, 2018). A formalization in terms of a mixture process is as follows.

Let y be the reading time in milliseconds and β the mean time in log milliseconds taken for a successful retrieval, with standard deviation σ. Such a successful retrieval happens with probability p. Retrieval is assumed to fail with probability $(1 - p)$, and the extra cost of re-attempting and successfully carrying out retrieval is δ log ms. For the full, hierarchically specified model, see Nicenboim and Vasishth (2018).

$$y \sim \begin{cases} LogNormal(\beta, \sigma^2), & \text{retrieval succeeds, probability } p \\ LogNormal(\beta + \delta, \sigma^2), & \text{retrieval fails initially, probability } 1 - p. \end{cases}$$
(7.1)

We can now determine whether the observed data are underlyingly coming from a two-component mixture (the direct-access model) or from the activation model, and whether a mixture distribution yields better predictions with respect to the data.

The Nicenboim and Vasishth (2018) computational implementation of the direct-access model in Stan (Carpenter et al., 2016) is available from the book's home page: https://vasishth.github.io/RetrievalModels/.

7.2 Comparing the Predictive Performance of the Models

7.2.1 Inhibitory Interference

Nicenboim et al. (2018) carried out a self-paced reading study in German. The critical items are shown below. Examples (39) show sentences where the verb phrase 'had greeted' requires a subject noun with singular, animate marking. In (39a), two other nouns match the singular number cue, increasing the fan to three; by contrast, in (39b), only the subject matches the number cue of the verb. For this design, the activation model predicts an inhibitory interference effect (a slowdown) at the verb in (39a) vs. (39b) because of the fan effect.

(39)   a.   HIGH INTERFERENCE

   Der   **Wohltäter**,   der   den   Assistenten
   The.sg.nom philanthropist, who.sg.nom the.sg.acc assistant

       des   Direktors **begrüßt hatte**,   saß   später im
   (of) the.sg.gen director   **greeted had.sg**, sat.sg later in the
   Spendenausschuss.
   donations committee.

7.2 Comparing the Predictive Performance of the Models 165

'The philanthropist, who had greeted the assistant of the director, sat later in the donations committee.'

b. LOW INTERFERENCE

Der   Wohltäter,   der   die   Assistenten
The.sg.nom philanthropist, who.sg.nom the.pl.acc assistant(s)

  der   Direktoren **begrüßt hatte,** saß   später im
(of) the.pl.gen director(s) **greeted had.sg,** sat.sg later in the

Spendenausschuss.
donations committee.

'The philanthropist, who had greeted the assistants of the directors, sat later in the donations committee.'

After each trial, Nicenboim et al. (2018) also asked participants who carried out the action implied in the main clause. Four options were given as possible answers; see (40) and (41).

(40) QUESTION

a. (MV) Wer saß später im Spendenausschuss?

Who sat in the donations committee?

b. (EVS) Wer hatte jemanden begrüßt?

Who had greeted someone?

c. (EVO) Wen hatte jemand begrüßt?

Whom had someone greeted?

· (41) MULTIPLE-CHOICE OPTIONS

a. (1) der/die Wohltäter (MV-EVS); (2) der/die Assistent/en (EVO); (3) der/die Direktor/en; (4) Ich weiß es nicht

(1) the philanthropist(s) (MV-EVS); (2) the assistant(s) (EVO); (3) the director(s); (4) I don't know

As a consequence, for each trial, participants provided a reading time at the verb phrase, and either a correct response or one of three possible incorrect responses.

The experiment showed the expected inhibitory interference effect; the estimated slowdown in (39a) vs. (39b) was 9 ms, with a 95% credible interval spanning 0–18 ms.

In order to evaluate the relative predictive accuracy of the activation model and the direct-access model, Nicenboim and Vasishth (2018) carried out a model comparison using the above data. The predictive performance of the two models was evaluated using k-fold cross-validation (Vehtari et al., 2017, 2012).

Figure 7.2 shows a comparison of the relative predictive fits from the hierarchical Bayesian models implementing the activation model, and McElree's

166   Competing Accounts of Interference in Sentence Processing

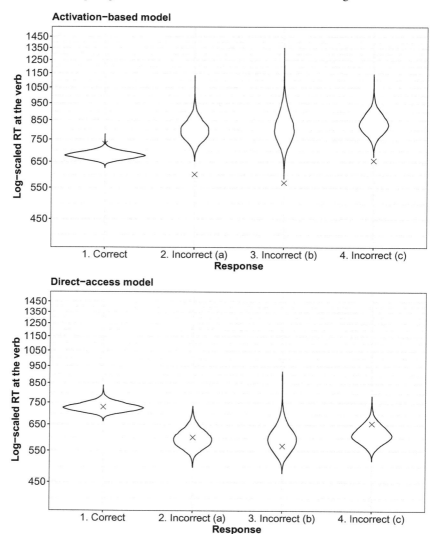

Figure 7.2 A comparison of observed sample means with the posterior predictive distributions of the activation-based model, and the direct-access model. The figure is adapted from the online materials available from a StanCon 2017 conference talk by Bruno Nicenboim and Shravan Vasishth, which are under a CC-BY 4.0 licence.

7.2 Comparing the Predictive Performance of the Models 167

direct-access model as a finite mixture process. The violin plots show posterior predictive distributions from the model; their width represents the density of the predicted mean reading times. The black circles show the empirically observed mean reading times. The four types of reading times refer to four different kinds of question responses that the participants could give in the experiment (Nicenboim et al., 2018).

The figure shows that the activation model overestimates the reading times in the incorrect responses, compared to the direct-access model. Although not shown here, this overestimation is due to the activation model assuming a single variance component for both correct and incorrect responses. When that assumption is relaxed, both models show similar predictive accuracy (Nicenboim and Vasishth, 2018).

In summary, the direct-access model exhibited a better predictive performance compared to the activation model. The reason that the direct-access model outperformed the activation model is that the latter predicts that in inhibitory interference experimental designs, retrievals of the incorrect chunk should be slower than the retrievals of the correct chunk. In the data-set used for model comparison (Nicenboim et al., 2018), incorrect retrievals had faster reading time than correct retrievals. This pattern is predicted by the direct-access model because correct retrievals are a mixture of an initially correct retrieval and an initial retrieval failure followed by a second retrieval attempt; the presence of trials with a costly second retrieval attempt take more time on average than incorrect trials.

The direct-access mode and the activation model should be compared on other data as well; ideally, we need a broad range of benchmark data to carry out a thorough evaluation. The first step in this direction is reported in Chapter 8 (Section 8.3).

7.2.2 Relative Clauses in Chinese

In Section 6.2, we presented a model of subject vs. object relative clause processing in English. There, we were mainly interested in demonstrating how eye-movement control and parsing interact; the broader goal was to show how expectation and memory effects play a role in parsing.

In this section, we use the statistical modelling approach discussed above to answer a different question. Of the two competing theories of retrieval, the Lewis and Vasishth model and the direct-access model, which theory can better explain the empirical facts about Chinese relative clause processing?

It is widely accepted in psycholinguistics that English subject relative clauses are easier to process than object relatives (e.g., Grodner and Gibson, 2005). For example, in (42), reading times at the relative clause verb *invited* would be shorter in subject vs. object relatives.

168   Competing Accounts of Interference in Sentence Processing

(42)   a. Subject relative
           The official who invited the tycoon has bad intentions.

       b. Object relative
           The official who the tycoon invited has bad intentions.

One of the explanations for this observed difference is decay in working memory: the distance between the subject and the relative clause verb is larger in object relatives than subject relatives; this leads to the decay in activation of the subject, causing greater retrieval difficulty at the relative clause verb (Gibson, 2000). Another alternative explanation is in terms of the fan effect discussed earlier: in object relatives, two nouns match the retrieval cues set at the relative clause verb, whereas in subject relatives only one noun matches the retrieval cues. We will refer to the decay or interference explanations as the distance account, because both depend on whether or not an intervener appears between the subject and the verb.

Interestingly, the distance account predicts that in Chinese, object relatives should be *easier* than subject relatives – this would be the opposite pattern to that found for English. As shown in (43), Chinese relative clauses are prenominal: they appear before the head noun, not after (as is the case in English). This has the consequence that the distance between the gap and the relative clause head noun is larger in the subject relative than in the object relative.

(43)   a. Subject relative

           [GAP$_i$ yaoqing fuhao   de] guanyuan$_i$ xinhuaibugui
           GAP   invite   tycoon DE official   have bad intentions

           'The official who invited the tycoon has bad intentions.'

       b. Object relative

           [fuhao yaoqing GAP$_i$ de] guanyuan$_i$ xinhuaibugui
           tycoon invite   GAP DE official   have bad intentions

           'The official who the tycoon invited has bad intentions.'

The distance account therefore predicts that in Chinese, the head noun should be read slower in subject relatives compared to object relatives. We will refer to this as the object relative advantage. The first study to claim that this expected pattern is indeed observed in Chinese is Hsiao and Gibson (2003). A subsequent study (Gibson and Wu, 2013) also showed the same object-relative advantage, and this pattern was replicated in a direct replication attempt (Vasishth et al., 2013). There are several empirical difficulties with the claimed object relative advantage; these are discussed in Vasishth et al. (2013), Wu et al. (2017), and Jäger et al. (2015).

7.2 Comparing the Predictive Performance of the Models

For the present purposes, we focus on the observed object relative advantage reported in Gibson and Wu (2013) and the replication reported in Vasishth et al. (2013); the data from Hsiao and Gibson (2003) were not available. Vasishth et al. (2017b) asked the question: is the observed object relative advantage explained better by the distance account, or by the direct-access model as defined above? One can use k-fold cross-validation to answer this question.

Vasishth et al. (2017b) implemented the distance account and the direct-access model as hierarchical models in Stan and compared the predictive performance of the two models against held-out data from the two data-sets. Four models were defined:

- M0: A standard hierarchical linear model (no mixture). This corresponds to a test of Gibson's DLT and Lewis and Vasishth's cue-based retrieval account.
- M1: This model assumes a mixture distribution in both subject and object relatives. The model also assumes that there is no difference in retrieval time in ORs vs. SRs, but only in the probability of successful retrieval. The variances of the success and reanalysis distributions are assumed to be identical (homogeneous variances).
- M2: This model assumes a mixture in both relative clause types just like M1. It differs from M1 in that the variances of the success and reanalysis distributions are assumed to be different (heterogeneous variances).
- M3: This model assumes that retrieval time in SRs and ORs is different, and that the variances of the two distributions are different (heterogeneous variance). Thus, M3 is like M2, but with the additional assumption that distance may affect dependency completion time, as proposed by Gibson and others. This model is therefore a hybrid of the two proposals.

The results of the k-fold cross-validation for the Gibson and Wu (2013) data are shown in Table 7.1. The quantity shown is the difference (Δ) in expected log pointwise density (ELPD) between the two models. ELPD is a measure of deviance; a positive difference represents a better fit.

Table 7.1. *Model comparison using K-fold cross-validation for the Gibson and Wu 2013 data. Shown are the differences in $\widehat{elpd}$, along with standard errors of the differences. In a comparison between a model A vs B, a positive $\Delta \widehat{elpd}$ favours model A.*

	models	$\Delta \widehat{elpd}$	se
1	M1 vs M0	118.00	13.82
2	M2 vs M1	29.61	9.28
3	M3 vs M2	−2.05	2.52

170   Competing Accounts of Interference in Sentence Processing

Table 7.2. *Model comparison using k-fold cross-validation for the Vasishth et al. (2013) replication of the Gibson and Wu (2013) study.*

	models	elpd_diff	se
1	M1 vs M0	107.78	18.56
2	M2 vs M1	51.46	16.25
3	M3 vs M2	0.13	3.48

As shown in the table, model M1 has a better fit than M0, and M2 is better than M1; there is no improvement in fit between M3 and M2. This implies that for the Gibson and Wu (2013) data, the heterogeneous variance version of the direct-access model exhibits a better predictive performance than the distance account. There isn't any evidence for a hybrid model that includes both the direct-access assumption or reanalysis-driven cost and the distance account's assumption of distance-driven cost.

The replication data from Vasishth et al. (2013) also show a similar pattern: superior predictive performance of the direct-access model over the distance accounts; see Table 7.2.

7.2.3   Discussion

It is interesting that the direct-access model can outperform the Lewis and Vasishth model on three data-sets. This suggests that a wider investigation of these two models is needed; we are currently carrying out further model comparisons with new data-sets (Lissón et al., 2021).

One important limitation of the direct-access model is that all the published work relating to this model has focussed on inhibitory interference effects (Vasishth et al., 2019). What are the model's predictions regarding facilitatory interference effects? The model assumes that slower reading times occur due to a reanalysis step that results in the correct item being retrieved. However, in ungrammatical sentences, there is no correct item to retrieve. The direct-access model is underspecified regarding the processing steps taken in this situation (Nicenboim and Vasishth, 2018). It is therefore likely that additional assumptions will be needed to account for the speedups discussed earlier in connection with the activation model. Extending the direct-access model is a potentially interesting topic for future research.

Continuing with our exploration of competing accounts of retrieval, we explore an idea, proposed by Villata and Franck (2016), that encoding interference rather than retrieval interference might be a better explanation for the agreement attraction effects discussed earlier in the book.

7.3 Encoding Interference in Agreement Attraction

As discussed earlier in the book, sentences such as (44a) can lead to an illusion of grammaticality.[2] The sentence is ungrammatical because of the lack of number agreement between the subject *key* and the auxiliary *are*. Note that the second noun, *cabinets*, and the auxiliary *are* agree in number, but no syntactic agreement is possible between these two elements.

(44) a. The key to the cabinets are on the table.

   b. The key to the cabinet are on the table.

The illusion has the effect that the auxiliary *are* is read faster in (44a) compared to the equally ungrammatical sentence (44b) (see Jäger et al., 2017 for a review). In contrast to (44a), in (44b) the second noun (*cabinet*) is singular and does not agree with the auxilary in number.

Several explanations have been proposed for the illusion of grammaticality in (44a) vs. (44b). We discuss two of these here.

The feature percolation account proposes that in (44a) the plural feature on *cabinets* can, in some proportion of trials, move or percolate up to the head noun *key* (see Patson and Husband, 2016, for recent evidence for this model). The head noun now has the plural feature, leading to an illusion of grammaticality compared to (44b), where no such feature percolation occurs. Another prominent explanation, due to Wagers et al. (2009), is the retrieval interference account. Here, in ungrammatical sentences like (44a), a singular verb would be predicted; but when the plural verb *are* is encountered, a cue-based retrieval process is triggered: the verb triggers a search for a noun that is plural marked and is a subject. A parallel cue-based associative memory access leads to the retrieval of a partially matching noun in memory (*cabinets*) that agrees in number but is not the subject. This partial match leads to a successful retrieval and an illusion of grammaticality.[3]

There is evidence for both these accounts: a facilitatory effect is generally present in the published data. A question then arises: if we take the position that a dependency between *cabinets* and *are* is not plausible, could there be an explanation for the facilitation that does not need reference to a cue-based retrieval process?

As discussed earlier in Chapter 2, the facilitatory effect is more or less clearly seen in at least 10 published studies (self-paced reading or eyetracking). The

---

[2] An extended version of this section appeared as Vasishth et al. (2017a) in the Proceedings of the International Conference on Cognitive Modelling, held at the University of Warwick, Coventry, UK.

[3] Notice that the cue-based retrieval account may a priori be implausible because it predicts that an incorrect dependency is built between *cabinets* and *are*; building such a dependency would imply that the sentence has the implausible meaning that the cabinets are on the table. The reader should detect such an implausible meaning and this should lead to a slowdown rather than facilitation.

172 Competing Accounts of Interference in Sentence Processing

explanation we presented in Chapter 3 was in terms of a race process within the ACT-R based model. Next, we consider an alternative explanation in terms of encoding interference.

Consider the ungrammatical example sentences again. In example (44b), both the nouns are marked singular, whereas in example (44a) the nouns have different number marking. As discussed in Villata and Franck (2016), the similarity in number of the two nouns in (44b) could be the underlying cause for increased processing difficulty, compared to (44a). The identical number marking in (44b) could lead to increased confusability between the two nouns, leading to longer reading times at the moment when a subject noun is to be accessed at the auxiliary verb. The feature overwriting model of Nairne (1990) formalizes this idea. To quote (p. 252): "An individual feature of a primary memory trace is assumed to be overwritten, with probability F, if that feature is matched in a subsequently occurring event. Interference occurs on a feature-by-feature basis, so that, if feature b matches feature a, the latter will be lost with probability F."

The Nairne proposal has a natural interpretation as a finite mixture process. Specifically, feature overwriting could occur with a higher probability in example (44b) compared to (44a). This assumption implies that the reading times in both (44b) and (44a) are generated from a mixture of two distributions. In a particular trial, if no feature overwriting occurs, the reading time would come from a LogNormal distribution with some location and scale parameters; this situation would result in minimal processing difficulty in carrying out a retrieval and detecting the ungrammaticality. In other trials, when feature overwriting does occur, the reading time would have a larger location parameter, and possibly also a larger scale parameter; this would represent the cases where additional difficulty occurred due to feature overwriting.

An explicit assumption here is that feature overwriting could occur in both (44b) and (44a), but the proportion would be higher in (44b). It is also possible to assume that feature overwriting only occurs in (44b), but we leave the investigation of this and other alternative models to future work.

Thus, in the mixture model implementation of the Nairne proposal, one distribution will have a larger location parameter (and perhaps also a larger scale parameter). In the modelling presented below, one goal is to estimate the mixing proportions of these distributions. When reporting the results below, we will refer to the proportion of the slow reading time distributions in (44b) as `prob_hi`, and in (44a) `prob_lo`. The suffixes `hi` and `lo` here refer to whether we expect confusability to be high or low.

To summarize, the feature percolation, cue-based retrieval, and feature over-writing models all predict facilitation in the ungrammatical sentences (44a) compared to (44b), but the underlying generative process assumed in each model is different. Feature percolation and feature overwriting can be seen as

7.3 Encoding Interference in Agreement Attraction 173

finite mixture models of different types, and cue-based retrieval can be seen as implemented by the standard hierarchical model. Our goal here is to implement all the three proposals as statistical models and then compare their relative fit to the data in order to adjudicate between them.

7.3.1 An Evaluation of the Nairne Proposal

We fit homogeneous and heterogeneous variance hierarchical mixture models to the 10 reading time data-sets that compared reading times at the auxiliary or the following region for sentences like (44a) and (44b).

The data were assumed to be generated from a two-mixture LogNormal distribution with either a homogeneous variance in both mixture distributions, or heterogeneous variances. Thus, for the high confusability condition (44b), we considered two models:

Homogeneous variance feature overwriting model

$$
\begin{aligned}
y_{ij} \sim &\text{prob\_hi} \cdot LogNormal(\beta + \delta + u_i + w_j, \sigma_e^2) + \\
&(1 - \text{prob\_hi}) \cdot LogNormal(\beta + u_i + w_j, \sigma_e^2) \\
&\text{where:} \\
&u_i \sim Normal(0, \sigma_u^2), w_k \sim Normal(0, \sigma_w^2)
\end{aligned} \tag{7.2}
$$

Heterogeneous variance feature overwriting model

$$
\begin{aligned}
y_{ij} \sim &\text{prob\_hi} \cdot LogNormal(\beta + \delta + u_i + w_j, \sigma_{e'}^2) + \\
&(1 - \text{prob\_hi}) \cdot LogNormal(\beta + u_i + w_j, \sigma_e^2) \\
&\text{where:} \\
&u_i \sim Normal(0, \sigma_u^2), w_k \sim Normal(0, \sigma_w^2)
\end{aligned} \tag{7.3}
$$

In both models, y_{ij} is the reading time in milliseconds from subject i and item j. The probability `prob_hi` represents the mixing probability of the distribution that generates the slow reading times corresponding to trials where feature overwriting occurred (44b). Although not shown, another mixture distribution is defined for example (44a); here, `prob_lo` represents the mixing probability of the distribution that generates the slower reading times corresponding to the trials where feature overwriting occurred.

The homogeneous variance model assumes that both mixture distributions have the same standard deviation σ_e. The heterogeneous mixture model assumes that the mixture distribution that leads to the slower reading times is assumed to have both a different mean ($\beta + \delta$) and a different standard deviation ($\sigma_{e'}$) than the other distribution. Alternative models can be fit that relax these assumptions, but we leave these extensions for future work.

174   Competing Accounts of Interference in Sentence Processing

As a baseline, we fit a model corresponding to the retrieval interference account, and the feature percolation proposal. The latter also assumes a mixture distribution, but only for the condition corresponding to example (44a). Recall that the claim is that in ungrammatical sentences, in some proportion of trials the plural feature on the distractor *cabinets* moves up to the head noun. In (44b), no such mixture process should occur because percolation never occurs; hence a standard hierarchical LogNormal distribution can be assumed here. We therefore defined the following generative process for (44a):

$$\text{Feature percolation model}$$

$$y_{ij} \sim \text{prob\_perc} \cdot LogNormal(\beta + \gamma + u_i + w_j, \sigma_e^2) +$$

$$(1 - \text{prob\_perc}) \cdot LogNormal(\beta + u_i + w_j, \sigma_e^2) \qquad (7.4)$$

$$\text{where:}$$

$$u_i \sim Normal(0, \sigma_u^2), w_k \sim Normal(0, \sigma_w^2), \gamma < 0$$

Note that in the specification above the parameter γ, which represents the change in the location parameter, is constrained in the model to be negative; this is because the assumption in the feature percolation proposal is that percolation leads to faster reading time.

For sentences like (44b), in which no percolation is assumed to occur, we simply assumed a LogNormal generative process:

$$y_{ij} \sim LogNormal(\beta + u_i + w_j, \sigma_e^2), \qquad (7.5)$$

7.3.2   Model Comparison

Having fit the homogeneous and heterogeneous variance models, as well as the baseline models (the cue-based retrieval and feature percolation models), we evaluate the predictive fit of the competing models using $\widehat{elpd}$ as in the preceding section.

Table 7.3 shows that apart from study 1, the homogeneous variance feature overwriting model is clearly superior to the retrieval interference model because it has higher $\widehat{elpd}$ values. Table 7.3 also shows that the homogeneous variance feature overwriting model furnishes a better fit than the feature percolation model. Finally, the table shows that, except for study 1, the heterogeneous variance model is superior to the homogeneous variance model.

Since the model comparisons are transitive (if model A is better than B, and B is better than C, then A is better than C), we can conclude that, among the models compared, the heterogeneous variance feature overwriting model characterizes these data the best. In summary, overall there is good motivation to assume that in the condition with two singular nouns (Example 44b), a proportion of trials comes from a distribution with a larger mean and larger

7.3 Encoding Interference in Agreement Attraction

Table 7.3. *Comparison of the 10 sets of hierarchical models. Shown are the differences in $\widehat{elpd}$ between (a) the standard hierarchical model and the homogeneous variance mixture model; (b) the feature percolation model and the homogeneous variance mixture model; and (c) the homogeneous vs. heterogeneous variance mixture model. Also shown are standard errors for each comparison. If the difference in $\widehat{elpd}$ is positive, this is evidence in favour of the second model. The pairwise model comparisons are transitive. These comparisons show that the heterogeneous variance mixture model has the best predictive performance.*

Study	(a) Standard HLM vs. Homogeneous variance mixture model		(b) Percolation vs. Homogeneous variance mixture model		(c) Homogeneous variance vs. Heterogeneous variance mixture model	
	elpd_diff	SE	elpd_diff	SE	elpd_diff	SE
1	−0.29	1.67	29.55	6.97	0.57	1.09
2	56.98	13.57	76.34	14.26	15.20	6.07
3	97.62	16.10	112.40	17.43	57.12	11.11
4	71.29	14.08	84.78	14.12	19.66	8.77
5	112.74	18.17	120.45	18.56	63.28	18.12
6	66.84	12.59	85.97	13.88	43.58	12.18
7	72.45	13.76	80.93	14.72	80.92	14.41
8	88.50	14.60	90.22	14.77	40.17	11.87
9	78.35	14.21	108.10	16.04	26.21	7.76
10	90.08	14.14	105.23	15.02	33.59	11.95

standard deviation, and this proportion is higher than in the condition with one singular and one plural noun (Example 44b).

7.3.3 Discussion

We implemented as a statistical model the proposal that nouns with similar feature marking (here, number) may be more confusable due to feature over-writing in some proportion of trials, which in turn leads to occasional increase in difficulty in accessing the correct noun when a dependency is to be completed between the subject and the verb. By fitting Bayesian hierarchical two-mixture models, we showed that 9 out of the 10 data-sets showed evidence for this increased confusability in one condition over the other.

The feature overwriting account for the ungrammatical sentences (44a, 44b) appears to be superior to both the retrieval interference and feature percolation accounts.

Some Limitations An interesting future direction would be to evaluate the predictions of these models for grammatical sentences such as those

176   Competing Accounts of Interference in Sentence Processing

considered in Villata and Franck (2016). The overall pattern observed in the literature is that, with one exception (Nicenboim et al., 2018), no differences are seen in the grammatical conditions (see, e.g., the meta-analysis results reported in Jäger et al., 2017). However, as discussed in Chapter 1, it is likely that the studies that investigated the grammatical constructions were underpowered; if so, there may not be enough data from each study to draw any conclusions from the absence of an effect. Nevertheless, in principle it is possible that the feature overwriting process can explain the data better than the alternative accounts.

As mentioned earlier, the retrieval interference proposal has an a priori difficulty that may rule it out: it implies that whenever *cabinets* is erroneously retrieved in (44a), the reader should conclude that the cabinets are on the table. This interpretation should make no sense to the reader because cabinets are usually not placed on tables. Thus, even if the reader misretrieves *cabinets* in (44a), they should register that something is wrong with the resulting meaning. As a consequence, if subjects do register this anomaly and assuming that this step costs time, facilitation (faster reading time) may not necessarily be observed at the verb (auxiliary or main verb, depending on the experiment) or a subsequent region in (44a) vs. (44b). One could, however, defend the cue-based retrieval account on the grounds that the comprehender is not interpreting the meaning of the sentence but is relying only on some type of syntactic local coherence (Tabor et al., 2004) to parse the sentence. Given the evidence in the literature for underspecification in comprehension (Swets et al., 2008; von der Malsburg and Vasishth, 2013), this could be an argument for the cue-based retrieval account. Future research should focus on disentangling these two competing accounts.

One argument against the feature overwriting account is that one cannot explain the facilitatory interference effects found in Cunnings and Sturt (2018); see the discussion relating to Example 28 on page 106. In the Cunnings and Sturt design, there cannot be a feature overwrite between the nouns in question that can explain the differences in reading time observed at the verb.

Finally, new data-sets on agreement attraction have recently become available (Avetisyan et al., 2020; Jäger et al., 2020). A more extensive investigation is being carried out to evaluate whether the feature overwriting model can explain such data better as well (Paape et al., 2020).

7.4   Summary

In this chapter, we reported some attempts at understanding the cue-based retrieval model's predictions from a model comparison perspective. In order to carry out these model comparisons, hierarchical statistical models were implemented of competing theories of cognitive processes. Then, their predictive performance was compared quantitatively. This comparison-based approach to

7.4 Summary

model evaluation is superior to the standard approach that we took in the earlier chapters of this book, that of only evaluating one's own favoured model against data. The model comparison approach is superior because it establishes model performance relative to a baseline model. If all models are wrong, we want to identify the models that are less wrong. We hope that future researchers will focus on model comparison based evaluations, so that we can engage in "strong inference" (Platt, 1964) and focus on the models that show the best performance.

8   Modelling Sentence Comprehension Deficits in Aphasia

Aphasia is an acquired disorder of language processing that arises from lesions in the speech and language areas in the brain. These lesions occur due to cerebrovascular and other diseases or other injuries. Studies on aphasia have shown that two distinct types of aphasia arise depending on the area of the brain that develops lesions. Broca's aphasia involves lesions to the left lateral frontal region (the so-called Broca's area) and Wernicke's aphasia involves lesions to the left posterior temporal lobe (Wernicke's area). Classical definitions of sub-types of aphasia are defined around syndromes. Broca's aphasia involves difficulties in language production and moderate problems in syntactic comprehension. Spontaneous speech can be nonfluent, and repeating sentences back can be difficult. Wernicke's aphasia involves severe comprehension and repetition difficulties, and difficulty in finding words. Some other sub-types are global aphasia (complete loss of language); conduction aphasia (relative intact comprehension and production but difficulties in repetition); and anomic aphasia (comprehension intact, but difficulty in finding words).

Because aphasia is an acquired disorder, from the computational modelling perspective it is natural to ask whether models of sentence processing can help us understand what the nature of the impairment(s) is. Focussing only on sentence comprehension, several attempts have been made to "damage" a computational model of unimpaired processing in various ways to simulate disorders of comprehension. We summarize some of the important models and theories next.[1]

8.1   Theories and Models of Sentence Comprehension Deficits

Theories of sentence processing deficits in aphasia have been traditionally categorized as either representational deficit accounts or processing deficit accounts (for an overview, see Caplan, 2009). Representational or specific deficit accounts ascribe the impairment to disturbances in underlying syntactic

---

[1] The next section is reproduced with permission from Patil et al. (2016a), Copyright (2016) Wiley; license number 4736540285736.

8.1 Theories and Models of Sentence Comprehension Deficits

representations, i.e., they assume that patients suffer from a breakdown in their knowledge of the grammar; in traditional linguistic terms, the deficit is in their competence as opposed to performance. For example, the Trace Deletion Hypothesis (TDH, Grodzinsky, 1995, 2000, 2006) proposes that aphasic patients have lost the ability to represent traces of syntactic movement. Hence, for noncanonical structures such as passives, they have no information about the theta-role of a moved NP and they need to rely on a default cognitive strategy which assigns the AGENT theta-role to the first NP in a sentence. However, the patients' syntactic representation also contains another AGENT, the one assigned to the unmoved subject NP in base position, which forces them to simply guess which of the two NPs is assigned the role of AGENT in a reversible noncanonical sentence. Besides the TDH, other accounts exist that relate syntactic comprehension disorders to disruptions in constructing fully intact syntactic representations (for example, Beretta and Munn, 1998; Hickok and Avrutin, 1995; Mauner et al., 1993). These accounts ascribe patients' sentence comprehension deficits to a breakdown in syntactic chain formation. In summary, representational deficit accounts generally equate "breakdown in knowledge of grammar" with the loss in the ability to track head-dependent relations (such as the relation between a noun phrase and its trace) or the ability to keep track of the derivational history of a syntactic structure, where derivational history is construed in classical Chomskyan terms. It is by no means clear that such a breakdown is not due to processing difficulty; that is, the failure to keep track of dependencies (which may be equivalent to deleting traces) may be a processing problem arising due to stochastic variability or less efficient retrieval processes in parsing.

We turn next to theories that have traditionally been termed processing deficit accounts. These assume that the underlying grammatical knowledge of patients is preserved, but the syntactic processing system is affected by processing (or capacity) limitations. Thus, these theories ascribe patients' difficulties with noncanonical sentences to a processing breakdown in parsing.

There exist various processing accounts that differ in how exactly they conceptualize processing limitations in syntactic parsing: (i) timing deficits; (ii) reduction in memory; (iii) intermittent deficiency; (iv) weakened syntax; (v) slow syntax; (vi) lexical integration deficit; and (vii) lexical access deficits.

Timing deficit accounts have been articulated in some detail in computationally implemented models; the others remain verbally stated theories. We discuss each of these theories below.

8.1.1 Timing Deficit

A representative of the timing deficit accounts is the work by Haarmann and Kolk (1991). They proposed a computational model of aphasic language

180 Modelling Sentence Comprehension Deficits in Aphasia

breakdown, called SYNCHRON. This model implements the hypothesis by Kolk and Van Grunsven (1985) that parsing fails in agrammatic aphasics because syntactic representational elements that need to be simultaneously active in working memory are often not coactive because of disturbances in timing due to brain damage. The model is provided with a predefined phrase-structure representation of a sentence and it determines whether the complete construction of this phrase-structure representation is possible given a set of temporal constraints. The model constructs the phrase-structure representation as a bottom-up chain of retrievals – input words cause the retrieval of word forms, word forms cause the retrieval of associated lexical categories and lexical categories cause the retrieval of phrasal categories. The retrieval of a phrasal category is possible only if all its constituent categories are available in memory, which is the *computational simultaneity* constraint in the model.

SYNCHRON assumes that aphasics have a temporal disorder – either the retrieval time, the time required to retrieve an element, is longer than normal, or the memory time, the amount of time a retrieved element remains available for further processing, is shorter than normal. A different way to characterize these constraints is in terms of slowed retrieval and faster than normal decay of items in memory. This temporal disorder disrupts computational simultaneity among elements of the phrasal category, causing parsing failures. Haarmann and Kolk (1991) showed that assuming a temporal disorder is sufficient to model the combined effects of the degree of severity and sentence complexity in agrammatic aphasics described in Schwartz et al. (1980) and in a replication study by Kolk and Van Grunsven (1985). Although SYNCHRON was successful in modelling aphasic behaviour on simpler sentence types, its capabilities are limited due to the absence of a parsing process. It also lacked a mechanism for thematic role assignment, which is a crucial issue in sentence processing.

8.1.2 Reduction in Memory

In later work, Haarmann et al. (1997) proposed an enhanced model of aphasic sentence processing, the Capacity Constrained Resource Deficit (CCRD) model. It is implemented in the 3CAPS architecture (Just and Carpenter, 1980) and is derived from the Resource Reduction Hypothesis (Miyake et al., 1994). This hypothesis proposes that the impairment in aphasia is an extension of sentence processing limitations in low working memory capacity of unimpaired individuals. CCRD focusses on deriving thematic roles assigned by the verb in the sentence. CCRD is composed of three main subsystems that accomplish thematic role assignment by carrying out three different sub-tasks in sentence processing: performing lexical access, constructing the parse tree and mapping thematic roles. The functionality of each component subsystem is achieved through a set of production rules. Production rules temporarily activate the

8.1 Theories and Models of Sentence Comprehension Deficits

working memory elements that lead to various sentence representations. The rules in the thematic role component use the parse tree representation of a sentence to generate thematic roles between words in the sentence. Once the processing of a sentence is completed, the levels of activation of the working memory elements representing the thematic role bindings are recorded. Sentence comprehension accuracy is indicated by the average activation of these memory elements.

Both storage and computation of information need to draw from available activation. If enough activation is not available, this leads to a breakdown in sentence comprehension. The hypothesis for aphasic patients is that they share a deficit of pathologically reduced working memory capacity. A more complex sentence has higher storage and computational demands, and the reduction in the available activation in aphasics induces a breakdown in processing. The model was shown to reproduce the sentence complexity effect obtained by Caplan et al. (1985) across nine sentence types, as well as the interaction between the sentence complexity effect and the degree of severity of aphasia in the data from Kolk and Van Grunsven (1985). All simulations involved modelling the offline measure of sentence comprehension accuracy by fitting the memory capacity parameter along with several other parameters.

Apart from SYNCHRON and CCRD, other attempts at modelling aphasic sentence comprehension are the HOPE model proposed by Gigley (1986), the UNIFICATION SPACE model proposed by Kempen and Vosse (1989) and Vosse and Kempen (2000), and the ACT-R based model proposed by Crescentini and Stocco (2005). While these models differ considerably in their details, they are consistent with the assumption that aphasic sentence comprehension is not a result of any breakdown in the knowledge of the grammar, but rather a deficit in the processing of this knowledge. As observed by (Haarmann et al., 1997, p. 82), all these previous models share the common assumptions that "(i) knowledge representation and processing are activation driven, (ii) successful sentence comprehension requires the co-activation of certain critical representational elements, and (iii) in aphasia, co-activation is disturbed by an immediate or emergent timing deficit."

8.1.3 Intermittent Deficiency

Support for intermittent deficiency comes from recent online studies with aphasics. In a self-paced listening study combined with a sentence-picture matching and grammaticality judgement task, Caplan et al. (2007) found normal online performance for patients when they provided correct offline responses. In contrast, incorrect offline responses were associated with abnormal online performance. This result is (arguably) unexpected under the TDH, which does not predict systematic differences in online processes underlying correct and erroneous responses. Caplan and colleagues concluded that patients cannot be suffering from constant impairments in an underlying grammatical structure (e.g., deleted traces), or from a total breakdown in specific parsing operations (e.g., associating a trace with its filler). Instead, they argued that sentence comprehension deficits should better be conceptualized as reflecting intermittent deficiencies in resources necessary for syntactic parsing. These intermittent reductions are then seen in divergent self-paced listening data and lead the patient to end up with an erroneous sentence interpretation. These claims are consistent with the results of former sentence processing studies by Caplan and Waters (2003, 1995). In recent work, Hanne et al. (2011) also provided evidence for the systematic differences between correct vs. incorrect parses, pointing to intermittent deficiencies.

8.1.4 Weakened Syntax

Weakened syntax has received support from sentence comprehension studies using eyetracking (e.g., Choy and Thompson, 2010; Dickey et al., 2007; Dickey and Thompson, 2009; Hanne et al., 2011; Meyer et al., 2012; Thompson and Choy, 2009); for eyetracking studies on sentence production in aphasia, see also Cho and Thompson (2010) and Lee and Thompson (2011a,b). Through a series of studies in the visual world paradigm, Thompson and colleagues explored patients' online parsing abilities for structures like yes-no questions, wh-questions, and object clefts (Dickey et al. (2007); Thompson et al. (2004)). For correctly answered wh-questions, aphasics showed the same eye movement patterns as controls – anticipatory eye movements to a potential filler (the moved object) for the gap when they heard the verb. When the offline response was incorrect, they showed increased looks to the subject competitor towards the end of the sentence. According to the authors, the anticipatory eye movements reflect the participants' incremental, automatic gap-filling during sentence comprehension. This suggests that "resolving wh-dependencies was relatively unimpaired in the patients" (Dickey et al., 2007, p. 14). Moreover, because patients' eye movements during correct responses were similar to controls' in speed and the overall pattern, the results are inconsistent with a slowdown in aphasics' online processing. Referring to Avrutin (2006), the authors suggested a weakened-syntax view of sentence comprehension disorders, which holds that syntactic representations in aphasia are (largely) undamaged and processing operations such as gap filling function with the same speed as in controls, but the resulting syntactic structures are not strong enough to inhibit competition from other sources (such as competing extra-linguistic heuristics) (Dickey et al., 2007). To replicate and extend these initial results, Dickey and Thompson (2006, 2009) evaluated patients' online processing in sentences with two different types of syntactic movement – wh-movement

8.1 Theories and Models of Sentence Comprehension Deficits 183

in object relative clauses and NP-movement in passives. Although the results showed that patients can successfully resolve wh-movement dependencies, gap-filling in object relative clauses was slightly delayed. These results are different from earlier findings involving wh-questions. Hence, the process of gap filling may be delayed in patients at least for some syntactic structures involving movement. Moreover, this process was disrupted by the late-emerging influence of syntactically unlicensed competitor interpretations. This position is closely related to the idea of slow syntax (Burkhardt et al., 2003), discussed next.

8.1.5 Slow Syntax

As mentioned above, there is some evidence that gap-filling is delayed in patients. Further evidence consistent with slow syntax comes from Hanne et al. (2011), who investigated online processing of Broca's aphasics on German reversible canonical (SVO) sentences and their noncanonical counterparts (OVS) using a classical sentence-picture matching task in the visual world paradigm. Online (eye movements) and offline (accuracy and response time) data were collected simultaneously during the task. Patients' accuracy reflected the expected pattern. On average, they performed worse than controls, and comprehension for noncanonical sentences was significantly lower than for canonical sentences. Reaction times were significantly longer in patients than in controls, and noncanonical sentences elicited longer latencies than canonical ones. Fixation patterns showed systematic differences in correct vs. incorrect offline responses. For correctly answered trials, patients' eye movement patterns were very similar to those of controls (in terms of relative fixation probabilities). For incorrectly answered trials, patients' eye movements were clearly deviant from those of controls. Interestingly, patients' eye movement patterns were delayed compared to controls, which is suggestive of a slowdown in online sentence processing. Following Caplan and colleagues, they also came to the conclusion that these preserved processing routines are not always available because of intermittent deficiencies of parsing operations. Thus, the data of Hanne et al. are consistent with the independently motivated idea of a slowdown in syntactic processing in aphasia and with intermittent deficiency, although there may well be other underlying factors that lead to a slowdown, such as increased uncertainty under noisy memory representations. Using eyetracking with sentence-picture matching, Meyer et al. (2012) investigated the processing of English active and passive sentences in aphasics and age-matched controls. They found that, in active sentences as well as correctly comprehended passive sentences, on average aphasics' eye movements converged to the correct picture a little bit later than controls. Such delays could be interpreted as slow syntactic processing or, as Meyer et al. interpreted them, as delayed lexical integration, which is discussed next.

8.1.6 Lexical Integration Deficit

Thompson and colleagues are the main proponents of lexical integration difficulties. In a comprehensive summary of their eyetracking experiments, Thompson and Choy (2009) concluded that sentence comprehension impairments in aphasia are unlikely to be "related to an inability to form, or compute, syntactic representations" (p. 278). They further emphasized that although slight delays in gap-filling were seen for some syntactic structures, no delayed syntactic processing was found for patients' dependency resolution in pronominal constructions as well as in wh-questions, making a general delay in syntactic computation unlikely. Instead, given the consistent finding of the late-emerging influence of competitor interpretations in patients' incorrect responses, the authors argued for a lexical integration deficit in aphasia, i.e., an impairment in the ability to integrate already accessed lexical information into a syntactic or a higher-level semantic representation. Work by Hagoort et al. (1996) and Swaab et al. (1997) makes similar claims.

8.1.7 Lexical Access Deficits

Some authors attribute patients' syntactic difficulties to an earlier stage in language processing – lexical access. Prather et al. (1997), using a list priming paradigm, found slower than normal activation of word meanings in Broca's patients. They suggested that this effect directly connects to reduced and/or absent activation effects found at gap sites during real-time sentence processing (Zurif et al., 1994). In subsequent studies using a cross-modal lexical priming paradigm with Broca's aphasics, Love and colleagues (Love et al., 2001; Swinney et al., 1996) found that priming of a filler at its gap site in syntactic movement structures is not absent, but delayed. The late reactivation of the antecedent was taken as evidence that patients can associate a moved element with a trace; however, this process is pathologically slow. In another study (Love et al., 2008), when the speech rate of the auditory input was slowed, patients showed immediate priming effects at the gap site. They also showed delays in lexical activation when a moved NP was first overtly encountered in a sentence. Love and colleagues interpreted their findings as evidence that "the formation of a syntactic dependency involving a moved constituent is selectively vulnerable, not because it's a syntactic operation, but because if lexical reactivation is not accomplished within a normal time frame, a non-grammatical heuristic kicks in to provide a conflicting interpretation" (Love et al., 2008, p. 216). Further, Ferrill et al. (2012) showed that in patients, lexical activation is slower not only in syntactic structures containing movement dependencies but also in canonical sentences without dislocated NPs. However, it remains unclear why comprehension of canonical structures is less (or even not at all) affected in aphasia.

8.1 Theories and Models of Sentence Comprehension Deficits   185

It is also worth noting that the lexical access account and the lexical integration deficit account may be difficult to disentangle. The lexical access account is in principle distinct from Thompson and colleagues' proposal of a deficit in lexical integration. Thompson and colleagues observed no or only slight delays in the reactivation of antecedents at their gap sites (at least for correct trials) across experiments involving different movement structures (Choy and Thompson, 2010; Meyer et al., 2012; Thompson and Choy, 2009). This absence of an effect, together with the observation of aberrant sentence-end effects of lexical competitors, led Thompson and colleagues to propose an impairment in integrating already accessed lexical information into the syntax or a higher-level semantic representation. According to them, this account could explain deficits in comprehending both pronominal and movement structures. However, Thompson and colleagues' findings could also be interpreted as evidence towards a delay in lexical access. For example, in experiment one in Thompson and Choy (2009) (see also Choy and Thompson, 2010), patients showed delayed looks to overtly mentioned (unmoved) nouns in a sentence compared to controls. Dickey et al. (2007) observed similar effects at the subject in yes-no-questions (see also experiment two reported in Thompson and Choy, 2009). In addition, Love et al. (2008) pointed out that the auditory sentences used, for example, in Dickey et al. (2007) were spoken at a slower than normal speech rate, which might have confounded the results because the slow input could have compensated for the delay in aphasics' lexical activation. Furthermore, Yee et al. (2008) showed evidence for reduced lexical activation in Broca's aphasia rather than delays in reaching a certain activation threshold value; this points to impairments in lexical activation levels rather than the time course of this activation. Finally, Blumstein et al. (1998), found no delays but successful priming of a filler at its gap site using a within-modality priming paradigm (auditory-auditory lexical decision). In this study, Broca's patients even patterned with unimpaired participants. Given the diverging results, it is currently still unclear whether and how impairments in sentence comprehension are caused by failures at the stage of lexical access or lexical integration.

We have summarized above the various theories about sentence comprehension deficits in aphasia; but it may be helpful to see the connections, similarities and differences between these theories by trying to identify some of the key proposals in these theories. We present such a comparison next.

8.1.8   A Comparison of Theories of Impaired Processing, and Their Relation to Theories of Unimpaired Processing

The theories of sentence processing deficits mentioned above address essentially the same issues that theories of unimpaired populations address (one difference is that the effect of the various determinants of processing difficulty

186 Modelling Sentence Comprehension Deficits in Aphasia

Table 8.1. *A matrix showing how the models relate to each other along dimensions of the three working-memory related events – delays, forgetting (or failure to retrieve), and misretrieval – that have been investigated in sentence comprehension research.*

Model	Delays	Forgetting	Misretrieval
TDH	x	x	
SYNCHRON	x	x	
CCRD		x	
intermittent deficiency		x	x
weakened syntax		x	
slow syntax	x	x	
lexical integration deficit		x	x
delayed lexical access	x	x	

may be amplified in impaired populations). This becomes clear when we consider how theories of unimpaired sentence processing that focus on the effect of working memory are characterized; here, comprehension difficulty (i.e., delays) can arise in the integration of lexical items due to decay or interference (Van Dyke and Lewis, 2003), or working-memory capacity differences (Just and Carpenter, 1992); dependencies may be forgotten (Frank et al., 2015; Tabor et al., 2004; Vasishth et al., 2010), which may or may not lead to parse failure; and there may be occasional misparses (Badecker and Straub, 2002; Cunnings and Felser, 2013; Patil et al., 2016b; Vasishth et al., 2008; Wagers et al., 2009), due to interference effects or stochastic noise. As Table 8.1 shows, classifying the theories mentioned above along these three dimensions – delay, forgetting, and misretrieval – demonstrates that while all the theories of sentence comprehension deficits in aphasia try to characterize forgetting in different ways, some try to also develop a theory of why processes are delayed, and why misretrievals happen:

(i) In TDH, trace deletion has the effect that the relationship between a filler and a gap, which originally was present, is forgotten. Possibly, delays could also occur if the parser carries out extra steps to complete a heuristic strategy to decide on thematic roles for arguments.

(ii) SYNCHRON implements delays and forgetting by inducing timing deficits that make retrieval slower and that make items in memory decay faster.

(iii) CCRD induces capacity limitations, which lead to forgetting.

(iv) Intermittent deficiency, as discussed by Caplan and others, is mainly concerned with occasional forgetting and misretrieval, although the precise nature of the deficiency is not defined.

8.2 Modelling Individual-Level Differences

(v) Weakened syntax assumes that syntactic structures do not have strong enough representations, which may be a way to implement forgetting.

(vi) Slow syntax assumes slowed down parsing processes, which would cause delays, and occasional parsing failures.

(vii) The lexical integration deficit proposal, as developed by Thompson and colleagues, assumes a failure to retrieve a lexical item into a higher-level representation; this could be seen as implementing forgetting and possibly also misretrieval.

(viii) The delayed lexical access model assumes that accessing an item in memory in the service of completing a dependency will lead to delays and failures.

Framing existing theories of sentence comprehension deficits in the context of delay, forgetting, and misretrieval also highlights the fact that (a) no one theory seems to cover all three events, and (b) one could re-classify theories as either being about delays (more generally, slowed processing), occasional failures to retrieve, or misretrievals. As an aside, note that none of the theories has any formalization of prediction cost (e.g., Hale, 2001; Levy, 2008); researchers in aphasia have largely neglected this topic in the past, but it is likely to become a focus of research in the coming years (see Clark, 2012, for an interesting recent attempt using the storage cost metric from the Dependency Locality Theory).

In summary, a useful way to understand the various theories of sentence comprehension deficits is in terms of their attempt to characterize delays, forgetting, and misretrievals. The fact that theories of unimpaired sentence comprehension that depend on working memory concepts are also focussed on these same events suggests a natural classification of theories of impairment that makes contact with a more general theory of unimpaired processing.

8.2 Modelling Individual-Level Differences

In healthy adults, sentence comprehension has long been argued to be influenced by individual differences; a commonly assumed source is differences in working memory capacity (Daneman and Carpenter, 1980; Just and Carpenter, 1992). Other factors such as age (Caplan and Waters, 2005) and cognitive control (Novick et al., 2005) have also been implicated.[2]

An important question that has not received much attention in the computational psycholinguistics literature is: what are sources of individual differences in healthy adults versus impaired populations, such as individuals with aphasia (IWA)?

---

[2] This section reuses material from Mätzig et al. (2018), reproduced with permission, license number 4740821189889, Copyright 2018 Cognitive Science Society, Inc.

188 Modelling Sentence Comprehension Deficits in Aphasia

It is well-known that individuals with aphasia often experience difficulties in comprehending sentences. These difficulties are mainly observable as lower accuracy scores in comprehension tasks such as sentence-picture matching, in which a picture must be selected in accordance with the meaning of a sentence, or in object-manipulation task, in which the meaning of a sentence must be reenacted with figurines (see literature review in Patil et al., 2016a). Furthermore, eyetracking during comprehension studies have revealed that IWA exhibit slower overall processing times (Hanne et al., 2011).

Two factors that are known to affect performance in sentence comprehension tasks (such as sentence-picture-matching, see Hanne et al., 2011) are canonicity (i.e., word order) and reversibility of thematic roles of animate nouns. Comprehension difficulties in IWA are selective in nature and particularly pronounced in sentences that are semantically reversible and have noncanonical word order, for example passives or object relative clauses. For these sentence structures, response accuracy is often indistinguishable from guessing (50% accuracy). Such a pattern is referred to as chance performance.[3] On the other hand, performance for canonical structures (e.g., actives or subject relative clauses) and irreversible sentences is often within normal range (Hanne et al., 2011). While chance performance is a typical trait of Broca's aphasia, it can be observed in other aphasia syndromes as well.

In this section, we evaluate three of the proposals discussed earlier, which seek to explain why sentence processing deficits arise in individuals with aphasia:

(i) *Slowed processing*: Burkhardt et al. (2003) argue that a slowdown in parsing mechanisms can best explain the processing deficit.
(ii) *Intermittent deficiencies*: Caplan et al. (2015) suggest that occasional temporal breakdowns of parsing mechanisms capture the observed behaviour.
(iii) *Resource reduction*: A further hypothesis, due to Caplan (2012), is that the deficit is caused by a reduction in resources related to sentence comprehension.

Computational modelling can help evaluate these different proposals quantitatively. The Lewis and Vasishth (2005) model is a useful framework for investigating processing deficits in aphasia because several of its numerical parameters (which are part of the general ACT-R framework) can be interpreted as implementing the three proposals mentioned above.

The objective of the work presented here is to demonstrate that it is possible to map the three types of deficits mentioned above to three distinct parameters (described below) of the ACT-R architecture, and to use, for each individual

---

[3] As an aside, we note that this way of thinking is misleading; if one tosses a fair coin 10 times and gets 9 heads out of 10, this has happened by chance (the coin is fair).

8.2 Modelling Individual-Level Differences

IWA, the best-fitting values of these parameters as a means to distinguish between impaired and unimpaired individuals.

In Patil et al. (2016a), the Lewis and Vasishth (2005) architecture was used to model aphasic sentence processing on a small scale, using data from seven IWA. They modelled proportions of fixations in a visual world task, response accuracies and response times for empirical data of a sentence-picture matching experiment by Hanne et al. (2011). Their goal was to test two of the three hypotheses of sentence comprehension deficits mentioned above, slowed processing and intermittent deficiency. Their results revealed the best fit for the model that implemented both of the accounts, compared to models that only implemented one. Further, the results lead to the conclusion that IWA exhibit deficits to differing amounts.

One major limitation of the Patil et al. study was the limited data it was based on: seven IWA. In this section, we provide a proof-of-concept study that goes beyond Patil et al. (2016a) in two respects: first, we use a much larger data-set from Caplan et al. (2015), with 56 IWA and 46 matched controls; and second, we evaluate the evidence for all the three hypotheses mentioned above.

When fitting individual participants, we vary three parameters that map to the three theoretical proposals mentioned above. The goal is to determine whether the distributions of optimal parameter values computed for individual participants furnish any support for any of the three sources of deficits in processing. If there is a tendency in one parameter to show nondefault values in individual model fits for IWA, for example slowed processing, then there is support for the claim that slowed processing is an underlying source of processing difficulty in IWA. Similar predictions hold for the other two constructs (intermittent deficiency and resource reduction), and for combinations of the three proposals.

8.2.1 Mapping ACT-R Parameters to Sources of Deficits

As discussed earlier in detail, in ACT-R, the retrieval of a chunk from memory depends on its activation level, which is determined by several constraints. We revisit a subset of these next. Let C be the set of all chunks in declarative memory. The total activation of a chunk $i \in C$ equals

$$A_i = B_i + S_i + \epsilon, \tag{8.1}$$

where B_i is the base-level or resting-state activation of the chunk i; the second summand S_i represents the spreading activation that a chunk i receives during a particular retrieval event; and ϵ is noise that is logistically distributed, approximating a normal distribution, with mean 0 and standard deviation ANS; the noise term is generated at each new retrieval request. The time it takes for a chunk i to be retrieved T_i depends on its activation A_i via $T_i = Fexp(-A_i)$, where F is a scaling constant which we kept constant at 0.2 here.

190   Modelling Sentence Comprehension Deficits in Aphasia

The parameter ANS of the logistic distribution from which ϵ is generated can be interpreted as implementing the intermittent deficiency hypothesis, because higher values of ANS will tend to lead to more fluctuations in activation of a chunk and therefore higher rates of unsuccessful retrievals.[4] Increasing ANS leads to a larger influence of random fluctuation in activation on a chunk's activation, which represents the core idea of intermittent deficiency: that there is not a constantly present damage to the processing system, but rather that the deficit occasionally interferes with parsing, leading to more errors.

The second summand in (8.1) represents the process of spreading activation within the ACT-R framework. For a given chunk i to be retrieved, and given retrieval cues $j \in \{1, \ldots, J\}$, the amount of activation spread to the chunk i as a function of the retrieval cues is quantified by computing:

$$S_i = \sum_{j=1}^{J} W_j S_{ji}. \tag{8.2}$$

The weighting term W_j is assumed by default to be $\frac{GA}{J}$, where GA is an ACT-R parameter[5] and S_{ji} is a value that reflects the strength of association between the retrieval cue j and the chunk i. To give a simplified example of what spreading activation does, assume that two chunks i_1 and i_2 are in memory, and there are two retrieval cues c_1 and c_2 that are being used to search for a chunk. Chunk i_1 matches fully with the two retrieval cues, and chunk i_2 matches with only one of the retrieval cues, say c_2. Suppose also that the strength of association S_{ji} between a retrieval cue j and a chunk i is 1 if the retrieval cue matches a feature on the chunk, and 0 otherwise. Assume that GA is 1. Then, the activation spread to item i_1 as a function of the two retrieval cues is

$$S_{i_1} = W_1 S_{11} + W_2 S_{21} = 1/2 \times 1 + 1/2 \times 1 = 1, \tag{8.3}$$

and the activation spread to item i_2 is

$$S_{i_2} = W_1 S_{12} + W_2 S_{22} = 1/2 \times 1 + 1/2 \times 0 = 1/2. \tag{8.4}$$

More activation is spread to chunk i_1 than to chunk i_2 due to a full match with the retrieval cues. Now consider the case where $GA = 2$. Now, $S_{i_1} = 2/2 \times 1 + 2/2 \times 1 = 2$ and $S_{i_2} = 2/2 \times 1 + 2/2 \times 0 = 1$. Thus, with a higher GA value, more activation is spread to a chunk in memory when it matches the retrieval cues.

The parameter GA therefore determines the total amount of activation increase in a chunk as a function of the number of retrieval cues it matches.

---

[4] Note that Patil et al. (2016a) implemented intermittent deficiency using another source of noise in the model, which affects not activation levels but rather the odds of a processing operation being chosen.
[5] GA stands for goal activation in ACT-R, for reasons that are not relevant here.

8.2 Modelling Individual-Level Differences

It is a free parameter in ACT-R. As discussed in Chapter 6, this parameter has been used to model individual differences in working memory capacity (see, for example, Daily et al., 2001). The lower the GA value, the lower the increase in activation of the chunk i due to a match with the retrieval cues. Low GA values thus model low working memory capacity: when an item needs to be retrieved from memory using certain retrieval cues, the probability of successful retrieval will go down if GA is lower. Similarly, higher GA values model higher working memory capacity. Thus, it can be seen as one way (although by no means the only way) to implement the resource reduction hypothesis.

Finally, the hypothesis of slowed processing can be mapped to the default action time (DAT) parameter in ACT-R. This defines the constant amount of time it takes a selected parsing rule to "fire", i.e., to start the actions specified in the action part of the rule. Higher values would lead to a greater delay in firing of parsing rules. Due to decay, retrieval may be slower and more failed retrieval attempts may occur.

In the following section, we evaluate the model's performance on the empirical data for IWA and unimpaired individuals, implementing the three theoretical claims by varying the three parameters described above.

8.2.2 Simulations

In this section, we describe our modelling method and the procedure we use for fitting the model results to the empirical data from Caplan et al. (2015).

Materials We used the data from 56 IWA and 46 matched controls published in Caplan et al. (2015). In this data-set, participants listened to recordings of sentences presented word by word; they paced themselves through the sentence, providing self-paced listening data. Participants processed 20 examples of 11 spoken sentence types and indicated which of two pictures corresponded to the meaning of each sentence. This yielded accuracy data for each sentence type.

Out of the 11 sentence types, we chose the subject/object relative clause contrast for the current simulation: subject relatives (*The woman who hugged the girl washed the boy*) represent the arguments of the sentence (woman, girl) in canonical order, whereas in object relatives (*The woman who the girl hugged washed the boy*), they occur in noncanonical order. We chose relative clauses for two reasons. First, relative clauses have been very well studied in psycholinguistics and serve as a typical example where processing difficulty is (arguably) experienced due to deviations in canonical word ordering (Just and Carpenter, 1992). Second, the Lewis and Vasishth (2005) model already has productions defined for these constructions, so the relative clause data serve as a good test of the model as it currently stands.

192   Modelling Sentence Comprehension Deficits in Aphasia

Parameter Estimation We used grid search to find the best fitting parameters. We refer to the parameter space Π_i as the set of all vectors (GA, DAT, ANS) with GA, DAT, ANS $\in \mathbb{R}$. For computational convenience, we chose a discretization of Π by defining a step-width and lower and upper boundaries for each parameter. In this discretized space Π', we chose GA $\in \{0.2, 0.3, \ldots, 1.1\}$, DAT $\in \{0.05, 0.06, \ldots, 0.1\}$, and ANS $\in \{0.15, 0.2, \ldots, 0.45\}$.[6] Π' could be visualized as a three-dimensional grid of 420 dots, which are the elements $p' \in \Pi'$.

The default parameter values were included in Π'. This means that models that vary only one or two of the three parameters were included in the simulations.

For all participants in the Caplan et al. (2015) data-set, we calculated comprehension question response accuracies, averaged over all items of the subject/object relative clause condition. For each $p' \in \Pi'$, we ran the model for 1,000 iterations for the subject and object relative tasks. From the model output, we determined whether the model made the correct attachment in each iteration, i.e., whether the correct noun was selected as subject of the embedded verb, and calculated the accuracy in a simulation for a given parameter $p' \in \Pi'$ as the proportion of iterations where the model made the correct attachment. We counted a parsing failure, where the model did not create the target dependency, as an incorrect response.

The problem of finding the best fit for each subject can be phrased as follows: for all subjects, find the parameter vector that minimizes the absolute distance between the model accuracy for that parameter vector and each subject's accuracy. Because there might not always be a unique p' that solves this problem, the solution can be a set of parameter vectors. If for any one participant multiple optimal parameters were calculated, we averaged each parameter value to obtain a unique parameter vector. This transforms the parameter estimates from the discretized space Π' to the original parameter space Π.

8.2.3   Results

In this section, we present the results of the simulations and the fit to the data. First, we describe the general pattern of results reflected by the distribution of nondefault parameter estimates per subject. Following that, we test whether tighter clustering occurs in controls.

Distribution of parameter value estimates Table 8.2 shows the number of participants for which a nondefault parameter value was predicted. We refer

---

[6] The standard settings in the Lewis and Vasishth (2005) model are GA $= 1$, DAT $= 0.05$ (or 50 ms), and ANS $= 0.15$.

8.2 Modelling Individual-Level Differences

to the values GA = 1, DAT = 0.05 (or 50 ms), and ANS = 0.15 as the default values, as set in the ACT-R architecture. It is clear that, as expected, the number of subjects with nondefault parameter values is always larger for IWA vs. controls, but controls show nondefault values unexpectedly often. In controls, the main difference between subject and object relatives is a clear increase in elevated noise values in object relatives.

For IWA in subject relatives, the single-parameter models are very similar, whereas in simple object relatives, most IWA (95%) exhibit elevated noise values, while a far smaller proportion (71%) showed reduced goal activation values.

Figures 8.1 and 8.2 illustrate the smoothed marginal distributions of parameter value estimates for subject and object relative clauses, respectively. Most importantly, it is visible in both subject and object relatives that the distributions of controls' estimates have their point of highest density around the default

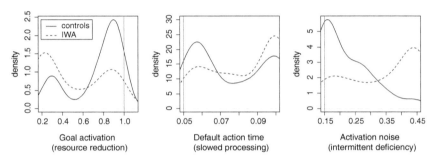

Figure 8.1 Marginal distributions of each of the three parameters for subject relatives in controls (solid lines) vs. IWA (dotted lines). The vertical line shows the default setting for the respective parameter.

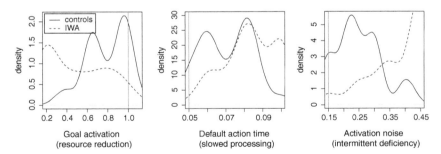

Figure 8.2 Marginal distributions of each of the three parameters for object relatives in controls (solid lines) vs. IWA (dotted lines). The vertical line shows the default setting for the respective parameter.

194   Modelling Sentence Comprehension Deficits in Aphasia

Table 8.2. *The number of participants in subject/object relatives (SR/OR) for which nondefault parameter values were predicted, in the subject vs. object relative tasks, respectively; for goal activation (GA), default action time (DAT), and noise (ANS) parameters.*

		GA	DAT	ANS	GA & DAT	GA & ANS	DAT & ANS	GA & DAT & ANS
SR	control	19	24	18	18	11	16	10
	IWA	38	41	42	32	33	36	27
OR	control	21	26	36	21	20	25	20
	IWA	40	48	53	38	40	48	38

value of the respective parameter. Deviations from this observation are mainly visible in the distributions for object relatives, where a second peak further away from the default is visible for each parameter. Distributions for IWA, on the other hand, are much flatter, and most density is concentrated relatively far away from the default parameter setting. This situation is exacerbated in object relatives compared to subject relatives.

Overall, most IWA exhibit nondefault parameter settings ANS and DAT, and to a lesser extent in GA. Table 8.2 shows further that the only combined model (i.e., the model that varied two or more parameters instead of keeping the other two at their default value) that matches the single variation model for DAT or ANS is the one combining DAT and ANS. We suspect that the lower number of IWA for which nondefault GA values were estimated are due to GA and ANS eliciting similar model behaviour. We address this point in the Discussion.

Cluster analysis In order to investigate the predicted clustering of parameter estimates, we performed a cluster analysis on the data to investigate the degree to which controls and IWA could be discriminated. If our prediction is correct that, compared to IWA, clustering is tighter in controls, we expect that a higher proportion of the data should be correctly assigned to one of two clusters, one corresponding to controls, the other one corresponding to IWA. We chose hierarchical clustering to test this prediction (Friedman et al., 2001).

We combined the data for subject and object relatives into one respective data-set. We calculated the dendrogram and cut the tree at 2, because we are only looking for the discrimination between controls and IWA. The results of this are shown in Table 8.3. The clustering is able to identify controls better than IWA, but in object relatives the identification of IWA is only a little bit better than chance (50%). Discriminative ability might improve if all 11 constructions in Caplan et al. (2015) were to be used; this will be investigated in future work.

8.2 Modelling Individual-Level Differences

Table 8.3. *Discrimination ability of hierarchical clustering on the combined data for subject/object relatives. Numbers in bold show the number of correctly clustered data points. The bottom row shows the percentage accuracy.*

	Subject relatives		Object relatives	
predicted group	controls	IWA	controls	IWA
control	**34**	21	**42**	24
IWA	12	**35**	4	**32**
accuracy	74%	63%	91%	57%

8.2.4 Discussion

The simulations and cluster analysis from Mätzig et al. (2018) demonstrate overall tighter clustering in parameter estimates for controls, and more variance in IWA. This is evident from the clustering results in Table 8.3. These findings are consistent with the predictions of the small-scale study in Patil et al. (2016a). However, there is considerable variability even in the parameter estimates for controls, more than expected based on the results of Patil et al. (2016a).

The distribution of nondefault parameter estimates (see Figures 8.1 and 8.2 and Table 8.2) suggest that all three hypotheses are possible explanations for the patterns in our simulation results: compared to controls, estimates for IWA tend to include higher default action times and activation noise scales, and lower goal activation. These effects generally appear to be more pronounced in object relatives vs. subject relatives. This means that all the three hypotheses can be considered viable candidate explanations. Overall, more IWA than controls display nondefault parameter settings. Although there is evidence that many IWA are affected by all three impairments in our implementation, there are also many patients that show only one or two nondefault parameter values. Again, this is more the case in object relatives than in subject relatives.

In general, there is evidence that all three deficits are plausible to some degree. However, IWA differ in the degree of the deficits, and they have a broader range of parameter values than controls. Nevertheless, even the controls show a broad range of differences in parameter values, and even though these are not as variable as IWA, this suggests that some of the unimpaired controls can be seen as showing slowed processing, intermittent deficiencies, and resource reduction to some degree.

There are several problems with the current modelling method. First, using the ACT-R framework with its multiple free parameters has the risk of over-fitting. We plan to address this problem in three ways in future research: (1)

Testing more constructions from the Caplan et al. (2015) data-set might show whether the current estimates are unique to this kind of construction, or if they are generalisable. (2) We plan to create a new data-set analogous to Caplan's, using German as the test language (Pregla et al., 2020a,b). Once the English data-set has been analyzed and the conclusions about the different candidate hypotheses have been tested on English, a crucial test of the conclusions would be cross-linguistic generalisability. A systematic model comparison method such as k-fold cross-validation might serve as a means to formally compare the implementations of the theoretical claims of aphasic sentence processing.

Second, the use of accuracies as modelling measure has some drawbacks. Informally, in an accuracy value there is less information encoded than in, for example, reading or listening times. In future work, we aim to implement an approach modelling both accuracies and listening times (Nicenboim and Vasishth, 2018). Also, counting each parsing failure as "wrong" might yield overly conservative accuracy values for the model; this can be addressed by assigning a random component into the calculation. This reflects more closely a participant who guesses if he/she did not fully comprehend the sentence.

Third, related to the overfitting problem addressed above, at least two of the varied parameters – goal activation and activation noise – lead to similar effects when manipulated in the way described here. More specifically, the decision to use the ANS parameter makes the assumption that the high noise levels for IWA influence all declarative memory retrieval processes, and thus the whole memory, not only the production system. Similarly, assuming lower GA values for IWA amounts to assuming generally lower working memory capacity in those participants, not specifically lower verbal working memory. Both parameters lead to a higher rate of retrieval failures. Because of this, it will be worth investigating in future work whether other sources of noise in the ACT-R framework may be a better way to model intermittent deficiencies (see Patil et al., 2016a for an example).

Lastly, simulating the subject vs. object relative tasks separately yields the undesirable interpretation of participants' parameters varying across sentence types. While this is not totally implausible, estimating only one set of parameters for all sentence types would reduce the necessity of making additional theoretical assumptions on the underlying mechanisms, and allow for easier comparisons between different syntactic constructions. We plan to do this in future work.

Although our method, as a proof of concept, showed that all three hypotheses are supported to some degree, it is worth investigating more thoroughly how different ACT-R mechanisms are influenced by changes in the three varied parameters in the present work. Implementing more of the constructions from Caplan et al. (2015) will, for example, enable us to explore how the different hypotheses interact with each other in our implementation.

8.3 Competing Models of Retrieval in Aphasia

One possible way to delve deeper into identifying the sources of individual variability in IWA could be to investigate whether sub-clusters show up within the IWA parameter estimates. For example, different IWA being grouped together by high noise values could be interpreted as these patients sharing a common source of their sentence processing deficit (in this hypothetical case, our implementation of intermittent deficiencies). We will address this question once we have simulated data for more constructions of the Caplan et al. (2015) data-set.

To sum up, we evaluated three well-known verbally stated hypotheses about causes of deficits in sentence comprehension in aphasia: slowed processing, intermittent deficiency, and resource reduction. We implemented these hypotheses within the Lewis and Vasishth (2005) model of cue-based retrieval. The three hypotheses can be implemented by changing the default values of three different parameter values within the Lewis and Vasishth model. Using a relatively large data-set from IWA and unimpaired controls, we estimated the optimal values for each of these parameters for each individual separately. We found that, compared to controls, IWA have more variable optimal parameter values than controls, and that IWA show differential degrees of deficit, where a deficit is considered to exist if an optimal parameter value for an individual deviates from the default value of the parameter. Thus, all three hypotheses about deficits in sentence comprehension may be viable explanations of processing difficulty; however, for each individual, the degree of impairment along each of these dimensions of slowed processing, intermittent deficiency, and resource reduction is likely to differ. An important implication is that it is not meaningful to state hypotheses about deficits in IWA in terms of average behaviour: multiple causes of deficit may exist in any one individual, and the degree of deficit along each dimension in each individual may differ. Understanding deficits in IWA requires shifting the focus towards understanding the nature of the variability between individuals.

Next, we report a first attempt to leverage Caplan et al. (2015) to compare the predictive fit of the direct-access model and the activation-based model.

8.3 Competing Models of Retrieval in Aphasia

8.3.1 Materials

Lissón et al. (2021) investigated the two competing models of retrieval discussed in Chapter 7, the direct-access model and the activation-based model. The data used was the self-paced listening data-set Caplan et al. (2015) described in Section 8.2.2. Here, the dependent variable was summed-up listening times at the verb and the noun inside the relative clause; this region was chosen because we are interested in the retrieval events that happen at the

198 Modelling Sentence Comprehension Deficits in Aphasia

moment that the verb region is processed. The listening times were summed up in these two regions in order to make the comparison between the English subject and relative clause processing times comparable; in English, the position of the verb is different in subject vs. object relatives (see Examples 45a and 45b below).

(45) a. **Subject Relative (SR):** The girl who **chased the mother** hugged the boy.

  b. **Object Relative (OR):** The girl who **the mother chased** hugged the boy.

One assumption made in the implementations of the direct-access and activation-based models was that the picture-selection accuracy would be taken to indicate whether the participant interpreted the relative clause correctly. Since only 10 out of the 20 items in the Caplan et al. (2015) had pictures corresponding to the correct vs. incorrect interpretations of the relative clause verb (the other items targeted the main clause verb), the modelling was restricted to these 10 items.

8.3.2 *Results and Discussion*

Model comparison using the k-fold cross-validation method discussed in Chapter 7 showed that the activation-based model has a somewhat better predictive performance than the direct-access model; the $\widehat{elpd}$ difference between the two models was 115 ($SE = 69$), in favour of the activation-based model. The relative differences in $\widehat{elpd}$ for each data-point are shown in Figure 8.3.

Figure 8.3 shows that the activation-based model does somewhat better than the direct-access model for the denser regions of the plots, but the difference is not really decisive even when the difference in $\widehat{elpd}$ is viewed graphically in this form.

One problem in interpreting this slight advantage for the activation-based model is the fact that the data used are relatively sparse compared to standard psycholinguistics data-sets; the data of only 33 IWAs and 46 controls were used. Eight IWAs were excluded because they were in the early post-acute phase, and fifteen others had been classified as IWAs but showed no apparent symptoms of aphasia. For a decisive model comparison, a larger-sample data-set is needed from IWAs and controls.

8.4 Concluding Remarks

In this chapter, we reported some of our recent attempts at using the largest data-set currently in existence on individuals with aphasia (IWAs) and controls

8.4 Concluding Remarks

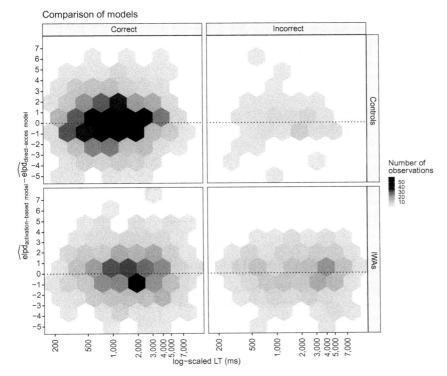

Figure 8.3 Shown are the differences between the two models in expected pointwise log density for each data-point. Points above the zero line show an advantage for the activation-based model, and points below the zero line an advantage for the direct-access model. The darkness in the hexagons represents density, with darker hexagons representing more dense data-points. The figure is under a CC-BY 4.0 license, https://doi.org/10.6084/m9.figshare.12114075.v1.

(the Caplan et al. (2015) data-set). One study investigated individual differences in the behaviour of IWAs vs. controls, quantified through the filter of the model's parameters (Mätzig et al., 2018). The second study (Lissón et al., 2021) compared the predictions of two competing models of retrieval processes. These approaches open up some very promising directions for future research, when larger data-sets become available.

9 Future Directions

In this closing chapter, we briefly discuss what we see as some of the important open problems that we made some progress in solving, and the problems that still need to be addressed. In Section 1.5, we discussed four gaps in the literature. In this book, to what extent did we succeed in addressing these gaps?

9.1 Developing Implemented Computational Models

We have presented several models covering a broad range of empirical phenomena: subject-verb dependencies (agreement and non-agreement), negative polarity items, antecedent-reflexive and -reciprocal dependencies, attachment ambiguities, the effect of prominence and cue-associativity, expectation, reanalysis, and underspecification effects, and relative clause processing. The models were unfortunately not all developed in exactly the same framework; sometimes we implemented full models, at other times simplified models. This mixture of modelling types is a consequence of the fact that the models were developed over many years in different research contexts. Future work should attempt to model the phenomena under a unified framework. It is possible that the python-based implementation of Brasoveanu and Dotlačil (2020) is the most appropriate one for future work (rather than Common Lisp, the language that ACT-R was originally written in). It would also be very useful if competing models of the phenomena we discuss are also implemented, so that formal model comparison can be carried out.

9.2 An Excessive Focus on Average Behaviour

As discussed earlier, many researchers have pointed out the importance of modelling not just mean differences but also individual-level differences. Our first attempts in this direction have focussed on individuals with aphasia; this was because group analyses may make less sense in this population. We also showed how capacity differences between participants can be modelled within the framework presented. However, much more can be done with the ACT-R

9.3 Model Evaluation and Comparison using Benchmark Data 201

framework when it comes to understanding the underlying causes of individual-level variation. This line of work has only just begun in our lab (Yadav et al., 2020).

9.3 Creating Higher-Precision Benchmark Data-Sets for Model Evaluation and Comparison

Several classes of problems have been studied in sentence processing. A probably incomplete list is:

   (i) Local attachment ambiguities (garden-path constructions)
  (ii) Constraints on dependency completion
 (iii) Shallow vs. deep processing (good-enough processing and underspecification)
  (iv) Serial vs. parallel parsing
   (v) The use of syntactic vs. semantic (pragmatic/phonological/prosodic) cues in sentence comprehension
  (vi) Illusions of grammaticality/ungrammaticality
 (vii) Similarity-based interference effects
(viii) Expectation-based effects
  (ix) Large-scale comprehension data on processing differences between unimpaired and impaired populations.

Unfortuntely, psycholinguistics has generally neglected power considerations in most of the published literature; as a consequence of the generally low power of published studies, many papers end up reporting overestimates that never replicate. There is an urgent need to revisit the empirical base of psycholinguistics and to establish larger-sample benchmark data so that model evaluation and model comparison is meaningful.

In recent empirical work we have carried out, we have made some modest attempts to systematically create benchmark reading data available specifically on similarity-based interference effects. Examples are Jäger et al. (2020), Mertzen et al. (2020b,c,a); Vasishth et al. (2018). We have also tried to systematically synthesize existing evidence in particular areas of sentence processing using meta-analysis (Bürki et al., 2020; Jäger et al., 2017).

An important task that remains for the field is to systematically create a repository of such data-sets for the different phenomenaa listed above, with the goal that the predictions of competing models of sentence processing be tested against as broad a class of phenomena as possible.

9.4 Developing Better Criteria for Evaluating Model Fit

The Roberts and Pashler (2000) criteria for what constitutes a good fit have generally been ignored in psycholinguistics. An important goal, which we only partly accomplished in this book, is to constrain model predictions so that the model evaluation against data is meaningful. An important part of such evaluations is to take a model comparison approach.

In our work (e.g., Lissón et al., 2021; Nicenboim and Vasishth, 2018), we have made some initial attempts to quantitatively compare the predictions of the Lewis and Vasishth activation-based model and McElree's direct-access model against benchmark data. However, a broader investigation that takes a model comparison perspective is yet to be carried out.

There is also a need to compare the predictive performance of the activation model with other competing modelling approaches, such as SOPARSE (Smith et al., 2018). In order to conduct a fair model comparison across completely different approaches such as these, a principled approach needs to be developed for defining which lexical features are relevant for retrieval; currently, this decision is made on an ad hoc basis. Smith and Vasishth (2020) have taken the first steps towards such a principled approach using large-scale corpora. Such a principled specification of lexical features will be very useful for future attempts at comparing competing models against benchmark data.

9.5 In Closing

This book attempts to address some of the important open problems in sentence comprehension, admittedly with varying degrees of success and varying degrees of uniformity. Nevertheless, the last 20 years of work on retrieval models, starting with the pioneering work of Rick Lewis, have taught us a lot about the role that general information processing principles play in explaining aspects of sentence comprehension. We hope that other researchers will find useful at least some of the ideas presented in this book. We hope that our first steps, reported in this book, will help others develop the next generation of computational models of sentence processing.

Bibliography

Anderson, J. R. 1974. Retrieval of propositional information from long-term memory. *Cognitive Psychology*, **6**(4), 451–474.

Anderson, J. R., Bothell, D., Byrne, M. D., Douglass, S., Lebiere, C., and Qin, Y. 2004. An integrated theory of the mind. *Psychological Review*, **111**(4), 1036–1060.

Anderson, John R., and Lebiere, Christian. 1998. *Atomic Components of Thought*. Hillsdale, NJ: Lawrence Erlbaum Associates, Inc.

Ariel, M. 1990. *Accessing Noun-Phrase Antecedents*. London: Routledge.

Arnold, D. 2007. Non-restrictive relatives are not orphans. *Journal of Linguistics*, **43**(2), 271–309.

Arnold, J. E. 2001. The effect of thematic roles on pronoun use and frequency of reference continuation. *Discourse Processes*, **31**, 137–162.

Avetisyan, S., Lago, S., and Vasishth, S. 2020. Does case marking affect agreement attraction in comprehension? *Journal of Memory and Language*, **112**. https://doi .org/10.1016/j.jml.2020.104087.

Avrutin, S. 2006. Weak syntax. In Y. Grodzinsky and K. Amunts, eds., *Broca's Region*. New York: Oxford University Press, pp. 49–62.

Baayen, R. H., Milin, P., Djurdjević, D. F., Hendrix, P., and Marelli, M. 2011. An amorphous model for morphological processing in visual comprehension based on naive discriminative learning. *Psychological Review*, **118**(3), 438.

Baayen, R. H., Piepenbrock, R., and van Rijn, H. 1993. *The CELEX lexical data base on CD-ROM*. Philadelphia: Linguistic Data Consortium, University of Pennsylvania.

Baddeley, A. D. 2003. Working memory: Looking back and looking forward. *Nature Reviews Neuroscience*, **4**(10), 829–839.

Baddeley, A. D., and Hitch, G. J. 1974. Working memory. In G. A. Bower, ed., *The Psychology of Learning and Motivation*. Vol. 8. New York: Academic Press, pp. 47–89.

Badecker, W., and Straub, K. 2002. The processing role of structural constraints on the interpretation of pronouns and anaphors. *Journal of Experimental Psychology: Learning, Memory, and Cognition*, **28**(4), 748–769.

Bader, M. 2016. Complex center embedding in German – The effect of sentence position. In S. Featherston and Y. Versley, eds., *Quantitative Approaches to Grammar and Grammatical Change: Perspectives from Germanic*. Berlin/Potsdam: DeGruyter Mouton, pp. 9–31.

Bartek, B., Lewis, R. L., Vasishth, S., and Smith, M. R. 2011. In search of on-line locality effects in sentence comprehension. *Journal of Experimental Psychology: Learning, Memory, and Cognition*, **37**(5), 1178–1198.

204   Bibliography

Beretta, A., and Munn, A. 1998. Double-agents and trace-deletion in agrammatism. *Brain and Language*, **65**(3), 404–421.

Berman, M. G., Jonides, J., and Lewis, R. L. 2009. In search of decay in verbal short-term memory. *Journal of Experimental Psychology: Learning, Memory, and Cognition*, **35**(2), 317.

Berwick, R., and Weinberg, A. 1984. *The Grammatical Basis of Linguistic Performance*. Cambridge, MA: MIT Press.

Bicknell, K., and Levy, R. 2010. A rational model of eye movement control in reading. In *Proceedings of the 48th Annual Meeting of the Association for Computational Linguistics*. Uppsala, Sweden: Association for Computational Linguistics, pp. 1168–1178.

Binder, K. S., Duffy, S. A., and Rayner, K. 2001. The effects of thematic fit and discourse context on syntactic ambiguity resolution. *Journal of Memory and Language*, **44**(2), 297–324.

Blastland, M., and Spiegelhalter, D. 2014. *The Norm Chronicles: Stories and Numbers about Danger and Death*. London: Profile Books.

Blitzstein, Joseph K, and Hwang, Jessica. 2014. *Introduction to Probability*. Boca Raton, FL: Chapman and Hall/CRC.

Blumstein, S. E., Byma, G., Kurowski, K., Hourihan, J., Brown, T., and Hutchinson, A. 1998. On-line processing of filler-gap construction in aphasia. *Brain and Language*, **61**(2), 149–168.

Booth, R. W., and Weger, U. W. 2013. The function of regressions in reading: Backward eye movements allow rereading. *Memory and Cognition*, **41**(1), 82–97.

Boston, M. F., Hale, J. T., Patil, U., Kliegl, R., and Vasishth, S. 2008. Parsing costs as predictors of reading difficulty: An evaluation using the Potsdam Sentence Corpus. *Journal of Eye Movement Research*, **2**(1), 1–12.

Boston, M. F., Hale, J. T., Vasishth, S., and Kliegl, R. 2011. Parallel processing and sentence comprehension difficulty. *Language and Cognitive Processes*, **26**(3), 301–349.

Brasoveanu, Adrian, and Dotlačil, Jakub. 2020. *Computational Cognitive Modeling and Linguistic Theory*. New York: Springer-Verlag.

Brennan, S. E. 1995. Centering attention in discourse. *Language and Cognitive Processes*, **10**(2), 137–167.

Brown, J. 1958. Some tests of the decay theory of immediate memory. *Quarterly Journal of Experimental Psychology*, **10**, 173–189.

Budiu, R., and Anderson, J. 2004. Interpretation-based processing: A unified theory of semantic sentence comprehension. *Cognitive Science*, **28**(1), 1–44.

Burkhardt, P., Piñango, M. M., and Wong, K. 2003. The role of the anterior left hemisphere in real-time sentence comprehension: Evidence from split intransitivity. *Brain and Language*, **86**(1), 9–22.

Bürki, Audrey, Elbuy, Shereen, Madec, Sylvain, and Vasishth, Shravan. 2020. What did we learn from forty years of research on semantic interference? A Bayesian meta-analysis. *Journal of Memory and Language*. https://doi.org/10.1016/j.jml.2020.104125.

Busemeyer, J. R., and Diederich, A. 2010. *Cognitive Modeling*. Thousand Oaks, CA: Sage.

Bybee, J. L. 2006. From usage to grammar: The mind's response to repetition. *Language*, **82**(4), 711–733.

Caplan, D. 2009. The neural basis of syntactic processing. In M. S. Gazzaniga, ed., *The Cognitive Neurosciences*, 4th ed. Cambridge, MA: MIT Press, pp. 805–816.

Caplan, D. 2012. Resource reduction accounts of syntactically based comprehension disorders. In R. Bastiaanse and C. K. Thompson, eds., *Perspectives on Agrammatism*. Hove, East Sussex: Psychology Press, pp. 48–62.

Caplan, D., Baker, C., and Dehaut, F. 1985. Syntactic determinants of sentence comprehension in aphasia. *Cognition*, **21**(2), 117–175.

Caplan, D., Michaud, J., and Hufford, R. 2015. Mechanisms underlying syntactic comprehension deficits in vascular aphasia: New evidence from self-paced listening. *Cognitive Neuropsychology*, **32**(5), 283–313.

Caplan, D., and Waters, G. 2003. On-line syntactic processing in aphasia: Studies with auditory moving window presentation. *Brain and Language*, **84**(2), 222–249.

Caplan, D., and Waters, G. 2005. The relationship between age, processing speed, working memory capacity, and language comprehension. *Memory*, **13**(3–4), 403–413.

Caplan, D., Waters, G., Dede, G., Michaud, J., and Reddy, A. 2007. A study of syntactic processing in aphasia I: Behavioral (psycholinguistic) aspects. *Brain and Language*, **101**(2), 103–150.

Caplan, D., and Waters, G. S. 1995. Aphasic disorders of syntactic comprehension and working memory capacity. *Cognitive Neuropsychology*, **12**(6), 637–649.

Carminati, M. N. 2005. Processing reflexes of the Feature Hierarchy (Person > Number > Gender) and implications for linguistic theory. *Lingua*, **115**(3), 259–285.

Carpenter, B., Gelman, A., Hoffman, M., Lee, D., Goodrich, B., Betancourt, M., Brubaker, M. A., Guo, J., Li, P., and Riddell, A. 2016. Stan: A probabilistic programming language. *Journal of Statistical Software*, **20**, 1–37.

Carreiras, M., and Clifton, C., Jr. 1993. Relative clause interpretation preferences in Spanish and English. *Language and Speech*, **36**(4), 353–372.

Carreiras, M., Duñabeitia, J. A., Vergara, M., de la Cruz-Pavía, I., and Laka, I. 2010. Subject relative clauses are not universally easier to process: Evidence from Basque. *Cognition*, **115**(1), 79–92.

Chafe, W. L. 1976. Givenness, contrastiveness, definiteness, subjects, topics, and point of view. In C. N. Li, ed., *Subject and Topic*. New York: Academic Press, pp. 25–56.

Cho, P. W., Goldrick, M., and Smolensky, P. 2017. Incremental parsing in a continuous dynamical system: Sentence processing in Gradient Symbolic Computation. *Linguistics Vanguard*, **3**(1). https://doi.org/10.1515/lingvan-2016-0105.

Cho, S., and Thompson, C. K. 2010. What goes wrong during passive sentence production in agrammatic aphasia: An eyetracking study. *Aphasiology*, **24**(12), 1576–1592.

Chomsky, N. 1981. *Lectures on Government and Binding*. Dordrecht: Foris.

Chomsky, N. 1986. *Knowledge of Language: Its Nature, Origin, and Use*. New York: Praeger.

Choy, J. Janet, and Thompson, C. K. 2010. Binding in agrammatic aphasia: Processing to comprehension. *Aphasiology*, **24**(5), 551–579.

Clark, D. G. 2012. Storage costs and heuristics interact to produce patterns of aphasic sentence comprehension performance. *Frontiers in Psychology*, **3**, 1–19.

206   Bibliography

Cohen, J. 1962. The statistical power of abnormal-social psychological research: A review. *Journal of Abnormal and Social Psychology*, **65**(3), 145.

Cowan, N. 2001. The magical number 4 in short-term memory: a reconsideration of mental storage capacity. *Behavioral and Brain Sciences*, **24**(1), 87–114.

Cowles, H. W., Walenski, M., and Kluender, R. 2007. Linguistic and cognitive prominence in anaphor resolution: Topic, contrastive focus and pronouns. *Topoi*, **26**(1), 3–18.

Crescentini, C., and Stocco, A. 2005. Agrammatism as a failure in the lexical activation process. In B. Bara, L. Barsalou, and M. Bucciarelli, M., eds., *Proceedings of the 27th Annual Conference of the Cognitive Science Society*. Mahwah, NJ: Lawrence Erlbaum Associates.

Cunnings, I., and Felser, C. 2013. The role of working memory in the processing of reflexives. *Language and Cognitive Processes*, **28**(1–2), 188–219.

Cunnings, I., and Sturt, P. 2018. Retrieval interference and sentence interpretation. *Journal of Memory and Language*, **102**, 16–27.

Daily, L. Z., Lovett, M. C., and Reder, L. M. 2001. Modeling individual differences in working memory performance: A source activation account. *Cognitive Science*, **25**(3), 315–353.

Daneman, M., and Carpenter, P. A. 1980. Individual differences in working memory and reading. *Journal of Verbal Learning and Verbal Behavior*, **19**(4), 450–466.

Demberg, V., and Keller, F. 2008. Data from eye-tracking corpora as evidence for theories of syntactic processing complexity. *Cognition*, **109**(2), 193–210.

Dickey, M. W., Choy, J. J., and Thompson, C. K. 2007. Real-time comprehension of wh- movement in aphasia: Evidence from eyetracking while listening. *Brain and Language*, **100**(1), 1–22.

Dickey, M. W., and Thompson, C. K. 2006. Automatic processing of wh- and NP-movement in agrammatic aphasia: Evidence from eyetracking. *Brain and Language*, **99**(1–2), 63–64.

Dickey, M. W., and Thompson, C. K. 2009. Automatic processing of wh- and NP-movement in agrammatic aphasia: Evidence from eyetracking. *Journal of Neurolinguistics*, **22**(6), 563–583.

Dillon, B. 2011. *Structured Access in Sentence Comprehension*. PhD thesis, University of Maryland, College Park.

Dillon, B., Mishler, A., Sloggett, S., and Phillips, C. 2013. Contrasting intrusion profiles for agreement and anaphora: Experimental and modeling evidence. *Journal of Memory and Language*, **69**(2), 85–103.

Du Bois, J. W. 2003. Argument structure: Grammar in use. In J. W. Du Bois, L. E. Kumpf, and W. J. Ashby, eds., *Studies in Discourse and Grammar. Vol. 14: Preferred Argument Structure: Grammar as Architecture for Function*. Amsterdam: John Benjamins, pp. 11–60.

Eberhard, K. M., Cutting, J. C., and Bock, K. 2005. Making syntax of sense: Number agreement in sentence production. *Psychological Review*, **112**(3), 531.

Elman, J. L., Hare, M., and McRae, K. 2004. Cues, constraints, and competition in sentence processing. In M. Tomasello and D. I. Slobin, eds., *Beyond Nature–Nurture: Essays in Honor of Elizabeth Bates*. Mahwah, NJ: Lawrence Erlbaum Associates, pp. 111–138.

Engbert, R., Longtin, A., and Kliegl, R. 2002. A dynamical model of saccade generation in reading based on spatially distributed lexical processing. *Vision Research*, **42**(5), 621–636.

Engbert, R., Nuthmann, A., Richter, E. M., and Kliegl, R. 2005. SWIFT: A dynamical model of saccade generation during reading. *Psychological Review*, **112**(4), 777–813.

Engelmann, F. 2016. *Toward an Integrated Model of Sentence Processing in Reading*. Doctoral thesis, Universität Potsdam, Germany.

Engelmann, F., Jäger, L. A., and Vasishth, S. 2020. The effect of prominence and cue association in retrieval processes: A computational account. *Cognitive Science*. https://doi.org/10.1111/cogs.12800.

Engelmann, F., and Vasishth, S. 2009. Processing grammatical and ungrammatical center embeddings in English and German: A computational model. In A. Howes, D. Peebles, and R. P. Cooper, eds., *Proceedings of 9th International Conference on Cognitive Modeling, ICCM*. University of Manchester.

Engelmann, F., Vasishth, S., Engbert, R., and Kliegl, R. 2013. A framework for modeling the interaction of syntactic processing and eye movement control. *Topics in Cognitive Science*, **5**(3), 452–474.

Epstein, J. M. 2008. Why model? *Journal of Artificial Societies and Social Simulation*, **11**(4), 12.

Farrell, S., and Lewandowsky, S. 2018. *Computational Modeling of Cognition and Behavior*. Cambridge: Cambridge University Press.

Ferreira, F., Ferraro, V., and Bailey, K. G. D. 2002. Good-enough representations in language comprehension. *Current Directions in Psychological Science*, **11**, 11–15.

Ferrill, M., Love, T., Walenski, M., and Shapiro, L. P. 2012. The time-course of lexical activation during sentence comprehension in people with aphasia. *American Journal of Speech-Language Pathology*, **21**(2), 179–189.

Francis, W., and Kucera, H. 1982. *Frequency Analysis of English Usage: Lexicon and Grammar*. Boston, MA: Houghton Mifflin.

Frank, S. 2009. Surprisal-based comparison between a symbolic and a connectionist model of sentence processing. In N. Taatgen and H. van Rijn, eds., *Proceedings of the 31st Annual Conference of the Cognitive Science Society*, Amsterdam, pp. 1139–1144.

Frank, S. L., Trompenaars, T., and Vasishth, S. 2015. Cross-linguistic differences in processing double-embedded relative clauses: Working-memory constraints or language statistics? *Cognitive Science*, **40**(3), 554–578.

Frazier, L. 1979. *On Comprehending Sentences: Syntactic Parsing Strategies*. PhD thesis, University of Massachusetts, Amherst.

Frazier, L. 1985. Syntactic complexity. In David R. Dowty, Lauri Kartunnen, and Arnold M. Zwicky, eds., *Natural Language Parsing: Psychological, Computational, and Theoretical Perspectives*. Cambridge: Cambridge University Press, pp. 129–189.

Frazier, L. 1987a. Sentence processing: A tutorial review. In M. Coltheart, ed., *Attention and Performance 12: The Psychology of Reading*. Hillsdale, NJ: Lawrence Erlbaum, pp. 559–586.

Frazier, L. 1987b. Syntactic processing: Evidence from Dutch. *Natural Language and Linguistic Theory*, **5**(4), 519–559.

208 Bibliography

Frazier, L., and Clifton, C., Jr. 1997. Construal: Overview, motivation, and some new evidence. *Journal of Psycholinguistic Research*, **26**(3), 277–295.

Frazier, L., and Rayner, K. 1982. Making and correcting errors during sentence comprehension: Eye movements in the analysis of structurally ambiguous sentences. *Cognitive Psychology*, **14**(2), 178–210.

Freedman, L. S., Lowe, D., and Macaskill, P. 1984. Stopping rules for clinical trials incorporating clinical opinion. *Biometrics*, **40**(3), 575–586.

Friedman, J., Hastie, T., and Tibshirani, R. 2001. *Springer Series in Statistics. Vol 1: The Elements of Statistical Learning*. New York: Springer.

Frühwirth-Schnatter, S. 2006. *Finite Mixture and Markov Switching Models*. New York: Springer Science and Business Media.

Fukumura, K., and van Gompel, R. P. G. 2011. The effect of animacy on the choice of referring expression. *Language and Cognitive Processes*, **26**(10), 1472–1504.

Gelman, A., and Carlin, J. 2014. Beyond power calculations assessing Type S (sign) and Type M (magnitude) errors. *Perspectives on Psychological Science*, **9**(6), 641–651.

Gelman, A., Carlin, J. B., Stern, H. S., Dunson, D. B., Vehtari, A., and Rubin, D. B. 2014. *Bayesian Data Analysis*, 3rd ed. Boca Raton, FL: Chapman and Hall/CRC.

Gennari, S. P., and MacDonald, M. C. 2009. Linking production and comprehension processes: The case of relative clauses. *Cognition*, **111**(1), 1–23.

Gernsbacher, M. A., and Hargreaves, D. J. 1988. Accessing sentence participants: The advantage of first mention. *Journal of Memory and Language*, **27**, 699–717.

Gibson, E. 1998. Linguistic complexity: Locality of syntactic dependencies. *Cognition*, **68**(1), 1–76.

Gibson, E. 2000. The dependency locality theory: A distance-based theory of linguistic complexity. In A. Marantz, Y. Miyashita, and W. O'Neil, eds., *Image, Language, Brain*. Cambridge, MA: MIT Press, pp. 95–126.

Gibson, E., Desmet, T., Grodner, D., Watson, D., and Ko, K. 2005. Reading relative clauses in English. *Cognitive Linguistics*, **16**(2), 313–353.

Gibson, E., Pearlmutter, N., Canseco-Gonzales, E., and Hickock, G. 1996. Recency preference in the human sentence processing mechanism. *Cognition*, **59**, 23–59.

Gibson, E., and Thomas, J. 1997. *The complexity of nested structures in English: Evidence for the syntactic prediction locality theory of linguistic complexity*. Unpublished manuscript, MIT.

Gibson, E., and Wu, H.-H. I. 2013. Processing Chinese relative clauses in context. *Language and Cognitive Processes*, **28**(1–2), 125–155.

Gigley, H. M. 1986. Studies in artificial aphasia: Experiments in processing change. *Computer Methods and Programs in Biomedicine*, **22**(1), 43–50.

Green, M. J., and Mitchell, D. C. 2006. Absence of real evidence against competition during syntactic ambiguity resolution. *Journal of Memory and Language*, **55**(1), 1–17.

Grodner, D., and Gibson, E. 2005. Consequences of the serial nature of linguistic input. *Cognitive Science*, **29**(2), 261–290.

Grodzinsky, Y. 1995. A restrictive theory of agrammatic comprehension. *Brain and Language*, **50**(1), 27–51.

Grodzinsky, Y. 2000. The neurology of syntax: Language use without Broca's area. *Behavioral and Brain Sciences*, **23**(1), 1–71.

Grodzinsky, Y. 2006. The language faculty, Broca's region, and the mirror system. *Cortex*, **42**(4), 464–468.

Grosz, B. J., Joshi, A. K., and Weinstein, S. 1995. Centering: A framework for modeling the local coherence of discourse. *Computational Linguistics*, **21**(2), 203–225.

Haarmann, H. J., Just, M. A., and Carpenter, P. A. 1997. Aphasic sentence comprehension as a resource deficit: A computational approach. *Brain and Language*, **59**(1), 76–120.

Haarmann, H. J., and Kolk, H. H. J. 1991. A computer model of the temporal course of agrammatic sentence understanding: The effects of variation in severity and sentence complexity. *Cognitive Science*, **15**(1), 49–87.

Hagoort, P., Brown, C. M., and Swaab, T. Y. 1996. Lexical-semantic event-related potential effects in patients with left hemisphere lesions and aphasia, and patients with right hemisphere lesions without aphasia. *Brain*, **119**(2), 627–649.

Hale, J. T. 2001. A probabilistic Earley parser as a psycholinguistic model. In *Proceedings of the 2nd Meeting of the North American Chapter of the Association for Computational Linguistics*. Pittsburgh: Association for Computational Linguistics, pp. 159–166.

Hale, J. T. 2011. What a rational parser would do. *Cognitive Science*, **35**(3), 399–443.

Hammerly, C., Staub, A., and Dillon, B. 2019. The grammaticality asymmetry in agreement attraction reflects response bias: Experimental and modeling evidence. *Cognitive Psychology*, **110**, 70–104.

Hanne, S., Sekerina, I. A., Vasishth, S., Burchert, F., and De Bleser, R. 2011. Chance in agrammatic sentence comprehension: What does it really mean? Evidence from eye movements of German agrammatic aphasics. *Aphasiology*, **25**, 221–244.

Hickok, G., and Avrutin, S. 1995. Representation, referentiality, and processing in agrammatic comprehension: Two case studies. *Brain and Language*, **50**(1), 10–26.

Hoenig, J. M., and Heisey, D. M. 2001. The abuse of power: The pervasive fallacy of power calculations for data analysis. *American Statistician*, **55**(1), 19–24.

Hofmeister, P. 2007. *Representational Complexity and Memory Retrieval in Language Comprehension*. PhD thesis, Stanford University.

Hofmeister, P. 2011. Representational complexity and memory retrieval in language comprehension. *Language and Cognitive Processes*, **26**(3), 376–405.

Hofmeister, P., and Vasishth, S. 2014. Distinctiveness and encoding effects in online sentence comprehension. *Frontiers in Psychology*, **5**, 1–13. Article 1237. https://doi .org/10.3389/fpsyg.2014.01237.

Hsiao, F., and Gibson, E. 2003. Processing relative clauses in Chinese. *Cognition*, **90**(1), 3–27.

Hsiao, Y., and MacDonald, M. C. 2013. Experience and generalization in a connectionist model of Mandarin Chinese relative clause processing. *Frontiers in Psychology*, **4**(767). https://doi.org/10.3389/fpsyg.2013.00767.

Husain, S., Vasishth, S., and Srinivasan, N. 2014. Strong expectations cancel locality effects: Evidence from Hindi. *PLoS ONE*, **9**(7), 1–14.

Husain, S., Vasishth, S., and Srinivasan, N. 2015. Integration and prediction difficulty in Hindi sentence comprehension: Evidence from an eye-tracking corpus. *Journal of Eye Movement Research*, **8**(2), 1–12.

210   Bibliography

Inhoff, A. W., and Weger, U. W. 2005. Memory for word location during reading: Eye movements to previously read words are spatially selective but not precise. *Memory and Cognition*, **33**(3), 447–461.

Jäger, L. A., Chen, Z., Li, Q., Lin, C. J. C., and Vasishth, S. 2015. The subject-relative advantage in Chinese: Evidence for expectation-based processing. *Journal of Memory and Language*, **79**, 97–120.

Jäger, L. A., Engelmann, F., and Vasishth, S. 2015. Retrieval interference in reflexive processing: Experimental evidence from Mandarin, and computational modeling. *Frontiers in Psychology*, **6**(617). https://doi.org/10.3389/fpsyg.2015.00617.

Jäger, L. A., Engelmann, F., and Vasishth, S. 2017. Similarity-based interference in sentence comprehension: Literature review and Bayesian meta-analysis. *Journal of Memory and Language*, **94**, 316–339.

Jäger, L. A., Mertzen, D., Van Dyke, J. A., and Vasishth, S. 2020. Interference patterns in subject-verb agreement and reflexives revisited: A large-sample study. *Journal of Memory and Language*, **111**. https://doi.org/10.1016/j.jml.2019.104063.

Jurafsky, D. 1996. A probabilistic model of lexical and syntactic access and disambiguation. *Cognitive Science*, **20**, 137–194.

Just, M. A., and Carpenter, P. A. 1980. A theory of reading: From eye fixations to comprehension. *Psychological Review*, **87**(4), 329–354.

Just, M. A., and Carpenter, P. A. 1992. A capacity theory of comprehension: Individual differences in working memory. *Psychological Review*, **99**(1), 122–149.

Just, M. A., Carpenter, P. A., and Varma, S. 1999. Computational modeling of high-level cognition and brain function. *Human Brain Mapping*, **8**, 128–136.

Just, M. A., and Varma, S. 2002. A hybrid architecture for working memory: Reply to MacDonald and Christiansen (2002). *Psychological Review*, **109**(1), 55–65.

Just, Marcel Adam, and Varma, Sashank. 2007. The organization of thinking: What functional brain imaging reveals about the neuroarchitecture of complex cognition. *Cognitive, Affective, and Behavioral Neuroscience*, **7**(3), 153–191.

Keenan, E. L., and Comrie, B. 1977. Noun phrase accessibility and universal grammar. *Linguistic Inquiry*, **8**(1), 63–99.

Kempen, G., and Vosse, T. 1989. Incremental syntactic tree formation in human sentence processing: A cognitive architecture based on activation decay and simulated annealing. *Connection Science*, **1**(3), 273–290.

Kemper, S., Crow, A., and Kemtes, K. 2004. Eye fixation patterns of high and low span young and older adults: Down the garden path and back again. *Psychology and Aging*, **19**, 157–170.

Keppel, G., and Underwood, B. J. 1962. Proactive inhibition in short-term retention of single items. *Journal of Verbal Learning and Verbal Behavior*, **1**, 153–161.

Kidd, E., Donnelly, S., and Christiansen, M. H. 2018. Individual differences in language acquisition and processing. *Trends in Cognitive Sciences*, **22**(2), 154–169.

King, J., and Just, M. A. 1991. Individual differences in syntactic processing: The role of working memory. *Journal of Memory and Language*, **30**(5), 580–602.

Kliegl, R., Grabner, E., Rolfs, M., and Engbert, R. 2004. Length, frequency, and predictability effects of words on eye movements in reading. *European Journal of Cognitive Psychology*, **16**(1), 262–284.

Kolk, H. H. J., and Van Grunsven, M. M. F. 1985. Agrammatism as a variable phenomenon. *Cognitive Neuropsychology*, **2**(4), 347–384.

Konieczny, L. 2000. Locality and parsing complexity. *Journal of Psycholinguistic Research*, **29**(6), 627–645.

Konieczny, L., and Döring, P. 2003. Anticipation of clause-final heads: Evidence from eye-tracking and SRNs. In P. P. Slezak, ed., *Proceedings of the ICCS/ASCS Joint International Conference on Cognitive Science*. Sydney: University of New South Wales, pp. 330–335.

Kruschke, J. 2014. *Doing Bayesian Data Analysis: A Tutorial with R, JAGS, and Stan*. London: Academic Press.

Kush, D., and Phillips, C. 2014. Local anaphor licensing in an SOV language: Implications for retrieval strategies. *Frontiers in Psychology*, **5**(1252). https://doi.org/10.3389/fpsyg.2014.01252.

Kwon, N., Gordon, P. C., Lee, Y., Kluender, R., and Polinsky, M. 2010. Cognitive and linguistic factors affecting subject/object asymmetry: An eye-tracking study of prenominal relative clauses in Korean. *Language*, **86**(3), 546–582.

Lago, S., Shalom, D. E., Sigman, M., Lau, E. F., and Phillips, C. 2015. Agreement attraction in Spanish comprehension. *Journal of Memory and Language*, **82**, 133–149.

Laird, J. E. 2012. *The Soar Cognitive Architecture*. Cambridge, MA: MIT Press.

Langacker, R. W. 1987. *Foundations of Cognitive Grammar: Theoretical Prerequisites*, Vol. 1. Stanford, CA: Stanford University Press.

Lee, J., and Thompson, C. K. 2011a. Real-time production of arguments and adjuncts in normal and agrammatic speakers. *Language and Cognitive Processes*, **26**(8), 985–1021.

Lee, J., and Thompson, C. K. 2011b. Real-time production of unergative and unaccusative sentences in normal and agrammatic speakers: An eyetracking study. *Aphasiology*, **25**(6–7), 813–825.

Lee, M. D., and Wagenmakers, E.-J. 2014. *Bayesian Cognitive Modeling: A Practical Course*. Cambridge: Cambridge University Press.

Legge, G. E., Hooven, T. A., Klitz, T. S., Mansfield, S. J., and Tjan, B. S. 2002. Mr. Chips 2002: New insights from an ideal-observer model of reading. *Vision Research*, **42**(18), 2219–2234.

Levy, R. 2008. Expectation-based syntactic comprehension. *Cognition*, **106**, 1126–1177.

Levy, R., Fedorenko, E., Breen, M., and Gibson, E. 2012. The processing of extraposed structures in English. *Cognition*, **122**(1), 12–36.

Levy, R., Fedorenko, E., and Gibson, E. 2013. The syntactic complexity of Russian relative clauses. *Journal of Memory and Language*, **69**(4), 461–495.

Levy, R., and Keller, F. 2013. Expectation and locality effects in German verb-final structures. *Journal of Memory and Language*, **68**(2), 199–222.

Lewandowsky, S., Geiger, S. M., and Oberauer, K. 2008. Interference-based forgetting in verbal short-term memory. *Journal of Memory and Language*, **59**, 200–222.

Lewis, R. L. 1993. *An Architecturally-Based Theory of Human Sentence Comprehension*. PhD thesis, Carnegie Mellon University, Pittsburgh.

Lewis, R. L. 1996. Interference in short-term memory: The magical number two (or three) in sentence processing. *Journal of Psycholinguistic Research*, **25**, 93–115.

Lewis, R. L. 2000. Cognitive modeling, symbolic. In R. Wilson and F. Keil, eds., *The MIT Encyclopedia of the Cognitive Sciences*. Cambridge, MA: MIT Press.

212 Bibliography

Lewis, R. L., and Vasishth, S. 2005. An activation-based model of sentence processing as skilled memory retrieval. *Cognitive Science*, **29**(3), 375–419.

Lewis, R. L., Vasishth, S., and Van Dyke, J. A. 2006. Computational principles of working memory in sentence comprehension. *Trends in Cognitive Sciences*, **10**(10), 447–454.

Lin, C.-J. C., and Bever, T. G. 2006. Subject preference in the processing of relative clauses in Chinese. In D. Baumer, D. Montero, and M. Scanlon, eds., *Proceedings of the 25th West Coast Conference on Formal Linguistics*. Somerville, MA: Cascadilla Press, pp. 254–260.

Linzen, T., and Jaeger, T. F. 2016. Uncertainty and expectation in sentence processing: Evidence from subcategorization distributions. *Cognitive Science*, **40**, 1382–1411.

Linzen, T., and Leonard, B. 2018. Distinct patterns of syntactic agreement errors in recurrent networks and humans. *arXiv preprint arXiv:1807.06882*.

Lissón, Paula, van het Nederend, Mick, Nicenboim, Bruno, Paape, Dario, Pregla, Dorothea, Burchert, Frank, Stadie, Nicole, Caplan, David, and Vasishth, Shravan. 2021. A computational evaluation of two models of retrieval processes in sentence processing: The case of aphasia. *Cognitive Science*. Accepted pending minor revisions.

Logačev, P., and Vasishth, S. 2015. A multiple-channel model of task-dependent ambiguity resolution in sentence comprehension. *Cognitive Science*, **40**, 266–298.

Logačev, P., and Vasishth, S. 2016. Understanding underspecification: A comparison of two computational implementations. *Quarterly Journal of Experimental Psychology*, **69**(5), 996–1012.

Love, T., Swinney, D., Walenski, M., and Zurif, E. 2008. How left inferior frontal cortex participates in syntactic processing: Evidence from aphasia. *Brain and Language*, **107**(3), 203–219.

Love, T., Swinney, D., and Zurif, E. B. 2001. Aphasia and the time-course of processing long-distance dependencies. *Brain and Language*, **79**, 169–170.

Lovett, M. C., Reder, L. M., and Lebiere, C. 1999. Modeling working memory in a unified architecture. In A. Miyake and P. Shah, eds., *Models of Working Memory: Mechanisms of Active Maintenance and Executive Control*. Cambridge: Cambridge University Press, pp. 135–182.

Lunn, D., Jackson, C., Spiegelhalter, D. J., Best, N., and Thomas, A. 2012. *The BUGS Book: A Practical Introduction to Bayesian Analysis*. Boca Raton, FL: CRC Press.

MacDonald, M. C., and Christiansen, M. H. 2002. Reassessing working memory: Comment on Just and Carpenter (1992) and Waters and Caplan (1996). *Psychological Review*, **109**(1), 35–54.

MacDonald, Maryellen C., Just, Marcel Adam, and Carpenter, Patricia A. 1992. Working memory constraints on the processing of syntactic ambiguity. *Cognitive Psychology*, **24**(1), 56–98.

Mätzig, P., Vasishth, S., Engelmann, F., Caplan, D., and Burchert, F. 2018. A computational investigation of sources of variability in sentence comprehension difficulty in aphasia. *Topics in Cognitive Science*, **10**(1), 161–174.

Mauner, G., Fromkin, V. A., and Cornell, T. L. 1993. Comprehension and acceptability judgments in agrammatism: Disruptions in the syntax of referential dependency. *Brain and Language*, **45**(3), 340–370.

Bibliography

McElree, B. 1993. The locus of lexical preference effects in sentence comprehension: A time-course analysis. *Journal of Memory and Language*, **32**(4), 536–571.

McElree, B. 2000. Sentence comprehension is mediated by content-addressable memory structures. *Journal of Psycholinguistic Research*, **29**(2), 111–123.

McElree, B. 2006. Accessing recent events. In B. H. Ross, ed., *The Psychology of Learning and Motivation. Vol. 46: Advances in Research and Theory*. San Diego, CA: Elsevier, pp. 155–200.

McElree, B., Foraker, S., and Dyer, L. 2003. Memory structures that subserve sentence comprehension. *Journal of Memory and Language*, **48**, 67–91.

McLachlan, G., and Peel, D. 2004. *Finite mixture models*. New York: John Wiley and Sons.

McRae, K., Spivey-Knowlton, M. J., and Tanenhaus, M. K. 1998. Modeling the influence of thematic fit (and other constraints) in on-line sentence comprehension. *Journal of Memory and Language*, **38**, 283–312.

Mertzen, Daniela, Dillon, Brian W., Engbert, Ralf, and Vasishth, Shravan. 2020a. *A cross-linguistic investigation of retroactive similarity-based interference in sentence comprehension*. Technical report.

Mertzen, Daniela, Dillon, Brian W., Engbert, Ralf, and Vasishth, Shravan. 2020b. *An investigation of proactive and retroactive interference in sentence comprehension*. Technical report.

Mertzen, Daniela, Laurinavichyute, Anna, Dillon, Brian W., Engbert, Ralf, and Vasishth, Shravan. 2020c. *A cross-linguistic investigation of proactive, similarity-based retrieval interference in sentence comprehension: No support from English, German and Russian eye-tracking data*. Unpublished manuscript.

Meseguer, E., Carreiras, M., and Clifton, C., Jr.. 2002. Overt reanalysis strategies and eye movements during the reading of mild garden path sentences. *Memory and Cognition*, **30**(4), 551–561.

Meyer, A. M., Mack, J. E., and Thompson, C. K. 2012. Tracking passive sentence comprehension in agrammatic aphasia. *Journal of Neurolinguistics*, **25**(1), 31–43.

Miller, G. A. 1956. The magical number seven, plus or minus two: Some limits on our capacity for processing information. *Psychological Review*, **63**(2), 81.

Miller, G. A., and Chomsky, N. 1963. Finitary models of language users. In R. D. Luce, R. R. Bush, and E. Galanter, eds., *Handbook of Mathematical Psychology*, Vol. 2. New York: John Wiley, pp. 419–492.

Mitchell, D. C., Cuetos, F., Corley, M. M. B., and Brysbaert, M. 1995. Exposure-based models of human parsing: Evidence for the use of coarse-grained (non-lexical) statistical records. *Journal of Psycholinguistic Research*, **24**, 469–488.

Mitchell, D. C., Shen, X., Green, M. J., and Hodgson, T. L. 2008. Accounting for regressive eye-movements in models of sentence processing: A reappraisal of the selective reanalysis hypothesis. *Journal of Memory and Language*, **59**(3), 266–293.

Miyake, A., Carpenter, P. A., and Just, M. A. 1994. A capacity approach to syntactic comprehension disorders: Making normal adults perform like aphasic patients. *Cognitive Neuropsychology*, **11**(6), 671–717.

Nairne, J. S. 1988. A framework for interpreting recency effects in immediate serial recall. *Memory and Cognition*, **16**(4), 343–352.

Nairne, J. S. 1990. A feature model of immediate memory. *Memory and Cognition*, **18**(3), 251–269.

214   Bibliography

Newell, A. 1973. *Production systems: Models of control structures.* Technical report, DTIC.

Newell, A. 1978. *Harpy, production systems and human cognition.* Technical report, Carnegie Mellon University.

Nicenboim, B., Logačev, P., Gattei, C., and Vasishth, S. 2016. When high-capacity readers slow down and low-capacity readers speed up: Working memory differences in unbounded dependencies. *Frontiers in Psychology*, **7**, 280. Special Issue on Encoding and Navigating Linguistic Representations in Memory.

Nicenboim, B., and Vasishth, S. 2016. Statistical methods for linguistic research: Foundational Ideas – Part II. *Language and Linguistics Compass*, **10**, 591–613.

Nicenboim, B., and Vasishth, S. 2018. Models of retrieval in sentence comprehension: A computational evaluation using Bayesian hierarchical modeling. *Journal of Memory and Language*, **99**, 1–34.

Nicenboim, B., Vasishth, S., Engelmann, F., and Suckow, K. 2018. Exploratory and confirmatory analyses in sentence processing: A case study of number interference in German. *Cognitive Science*, **42**, 1075–1100.

Nicenboim, B., Vasishth, S., and Rösler, F. 2020. Are words pre-activated probabilistically during sentence comprehension? Evidence from new data and a Bayesian random-effects meta-analysis using publicly available data. *Neuropsychologia.* https://doi.org/10.1016/j.neuropsychologia.2020.107427.

Nicenboim, Bruno, Schad, Daniel, and Vasishth, Shravan. 2021. *Introduction to Bayesian Data Analysis for Cognitive Science.* Boca Raton, FL: CRC Press. Under contract with Chapman and Hall/CRC Statistics in the Social and Behavioral Sciences Series.

Nicol, J. 1988. *Coreference Processing during Sentence Comprehension.* PhD thesis, Massachusetts Institute of Technology, Cambridge.

Nilsson, M., and Nivre, J. 2010. Towards a data-driven model of eye movement control in reading. In J. T. Hale, ed., *Proceedings of the 2010 Workshop on Cognitive Modeling and Computational Linguistics, ACL 2010.* Uppsala, Sweden: Association for Computational Linguistics, pp. 63–71.

Novick, J. M., Trueswell, J. C., and Thompson-Schill, S. L. 2005. Cognitive control and parsing: Reexamining the role of Brocaâ£™s area in sentence comprehension. *Cognitive, Affective, and Behavioral Neuroscience*, **5**(3), 263–281.

Oakley, J. E., and O'Hagan, A. 2010. *SHELF: The Sheffield Elicitation Framework (Version 2.0).* School of Mathematics and Statistics, University of Sheffield.

Oberauer, K., and Kliegl, R. 2006. A formal model of capacity limits in working memory. *Journal of Memory and Language*, **55**, 601–626.

Oberauer, K., and Lewandowsky, S. 2013. Evidence against decay in verbal working memory. *Journal of Experimental Psychology: General*, **142**(2), 380.

Oberauer, Klaus, and Lewandowsky, Stephan. 2014. Further evidence against decay in working memory. *Journal of Memory and Language*, **73**(1), 15–30.

O'Hagan, A., Buck, C. E., Daneshkhah, A., Eiser, J. R., Garthwaite, P. H., Jenkinson, D. J., Oakley, J. E., and Rakow, T. 2006. *Uncertain Judgements: Eliciting Experts' Probabilities.* Chichester, West Sussex: John Wiley and Sons.

Paape, Dario, Avetisyan, Serine, Lago, Sol, and Vasishth, Shravan. 2020. *Modeling misretrieval and feature substitution in agreement attraction: A computational evaluation.* Unpublished manuscript. https://psyarxiv.com/957e3/.

Palestro, J. J., Sederberg, P. B., Osth, A. F, Van Zandt, T., and Turner, B. M. 2018. *Likelihood-Free Methods for Cognitive Science*. Cham, Switzerland: Springer.

Parker, D. 2019. Cue combinatorics in memory retrieval for anaphora. *Cognitive Science*, **43**(3), e12715. https://doi.org/10.1111/cogs.12715.

Parker, D., and Phillips, C. 2014. Selective priority for structure in memory retrieval. *Proceedings of the 27th Annual CUNY Conference on Human Sentence Processing*. Columbus: Ohio State University, p. 100.

Parker, D., and Phillips, C. 2017. Reflexive attraction in comprehension is selective. *Journal of Memory and Language*, **94**, 272–290.

Parker, D., Shvartsman, M., and Van Dyke, J. A. 2017. The cue-based retrieval theory of sentence comprehension: New findings and new challenges. In L. Escobar, V. Torrens, and T. Parodi, eds., *Language Processing and Disorders*. Newcastle upon Tyne: Cambridge Scholars, pp. 121–144.

Patil, U., Hanne, S., Burchert, F., De Bleser, R., and Vasishth, S. 2016a. A computational evaluation of sentence comprehension deficits in aphasia. *Cognitive Science*, **40**, 5–50.

Patil, U., Vasishth, S., and Kliegl, R. 2009. Compound effect of probabilistic disambiguation and memory retrievals on sentence processing: Evidence from an eye-tracking corpus. In A. Howes, D. Peebles, and R. P. Cooper, eds., *Proceedings of the 9th International Conference on Cognitive Modeling*. University of Manchester.

Patil, U., Vasishth, S., and Lewis, R. L. 2012. *Retrieval interference in syntactic processing: The case of reflexive binding in English*. Manuscript submitted.

Patil, U., Vasishth, S., and Lewis, R. L. 2016b. Retrieval interference in syntactic processing: The case of reflexive binding in English. *Frontiers in Psychology*, **7**, 329. Special Issue on Encoding and Navigating Linguistic Representations in Memory.

Patson, N. D., and Husband, E. M. 2016. Misinterpretations in agreement and agreement attraction. *Quarterly Journal of Experimental Psychology*, **69**(5), 950–971.

Pearlmutter, N. J., Garnsey, S. M., and Bock, K. 1999. Agreement processes in sentence comprehension. *Journal of Memory and Language*, **41**, 427–456.

Peterson, L. R., and Peterson, M. J. 1959. Short-term retention of individual items. *Journal of Experimental Psychology*, **61**, 12–21.

Pickering, M. J., and Van Gompel, R. P. G. 2006. Syntactic parsing. In M. J. Traxler and M. A. Gernsbacher, eds., *Handbook of Psycholinguistics*, 2nd ed. New York: Academic Press, pp. 455–503.

Platt, John R. 1964. Strong inference. *Science*, **146**(3642), 347–353.

Prather, P. A., Zurif, E., Love, T., and Brownell, H. 1997. Speed of lexical activation in nonfluent Broca's aphasia and fluent Wernicke's aphasia. *Brain and Language*, **59**(3), 391–411.

Pregla, Dorothea, Lissón, Paula, Vasishth, Shravan, Burchert, Frank, and Stadie, Nicole. 2020a. Variability in sentence comprehension in aphasia in German. *Brain and Language*. Under review.

Pregla, Dorothea, Lissón, Paula, Vasishth, Shravan, Stadie, Nicole, and Burchert, Frank. 2020b. *Individual differences in visual world eye-tracking in aphasia in German*. Technical report.

R Core Team. 2012. *R: A Language and Environment for Statistical Computing*. Vienna: R Foundation for Statistical Computing.

Bibliography

R Core Team. 2016. *R: A Language and Environment for Statistical Computing*. Vienna: R Foundation for Statistical Computing.

Raab, D. H. 1962. Statistical facilitation of simple reaction times. *Transactions of the New York Academy of Sciences*, **24**(5 Series II), 574–590.

Rabe, Maximilian M., Chandra, Johan, Krügel, André, Seelig, Stefan A., Vasishth, Shravan, and Engbert, Ralf. 2020. A Bayesian approach to dynamical modeling of eye-movement control in reading of normal, mirrored, and scrambled texts. *Psychological Review*. In press.

Rabovsky, M., and McRae, K. 2014. Simulating the N400 ERP component as semantic network error: Insights from a feature-based connectionist attractor model of word meaning. *Cognition*, **132**(1), 68–89.

Rasmussen, N. E., and Schuler, W. 2017. Left-corner parsing with distributed associative memory produces surprisal and locality effects. *Cognitive Science*, **42**(S4), 1009–1042. Special Issue in Sentence Processing.

Ratcliff, R. 1978. A theory of memory retrieval. *Psychological Review*, **85**(2), 59.

Rayner, K., Kambe, G., and Duffy, S. A. 2000. The effect of clause wrap-up on eye movements during reading. *Quarterly Journal of Experimental Psychology*, **53A**(4), 1061–80.

Reichle, E. D., Pollatsek, A., Fisher, D. L., and Rayner, K. 1998. Toward a model of eye movement control in reading. *Psychological Review*, **105**(1), 125–157.

Reichle, E. D., Pollatsek, A., and Rayner, K. 2006. E-Z Reader: A cognitive-control, serial-attention model of eye-movement behavior during reading. *Cognitive Systems Research*, **7**(1), 4–22.

Reichle, E. D., Rayner, K., and Pollatsek, A. 2003. The E-Z reader model of eye-movement control in reading: Comparisons to other models. *Behavioral and Brain Sciences*, **26**(4), 445–476.

Reichle, E. D., Warren, T., and McConnell, K. 2009. Using E-Z Reader to model the effects of higher-level language processing on eye movements during reading. *Psychonomic Bulletin and Review*, **16**(1), 1–21.

Reilly, R. G., and Radach, R. 2006. Some empirical tests of an interactive activation model of eye movement control in reading. *Cognitive Systems Research*, **7**(1), 34–55.

Rescorla, R. A., and Wagner, A. R. 1972. A theory of Pavlovian conditioning: Variations in the effectiveness of reinforcement and nonreinforcement. In A. H. Black and W. F. Prokasy, eds., *Classical Conditioning II: Current Research and Theory*, Vol. 2. New York: Appleton-Century-Crofts, pp. 64–99.

Resnik, P. 1992. Left–corner parsing and psychological plausibility. In *Proceedings of COLING*, pp. 191–197.

Richter, E. M., Engbert, R., and Kliegl, R. 2006. Current advances in SWIFT. *Cognitive Systems Research*, **7**, 23–33.

Roberts, S., and Pashler, H. 2000. How persuasive is a good fit? A comment on theory testing. *Psychological Review*, **107**(2), 358–367.

Safavi, M. S., Husain, S., and Vasishth, S. 2016. Dependency resolution difficulty increases with distance in Persian separable complex predicates: Implications for expectation and memory-based accounts. *Frontiers in Psychology*, **7**, 403.

Salvucci, D. 2001. An integrated model of eye movements and visual encoding. *Cognitive Systems Research*, **1**(4), 201–220.

Bibliography

Sanford, A. J., and Sturt, P. 2002. Depth of processing in language comprehension: Not noticing the evidence. *Trends in Cognitive Sciences*, **6**(9), 382–386.

Schad, D. J., Betancourt, M., and Vasishth, S. 2020a. Towards a principled Bayesian workflow: A tutorial for cognitive science. *Psychological Methods*, **26**(1), 103–126.

Schad, D. J., Hohenstein, S., Vasishth, S., and Kliegl, R. 2020b. How to capitalize on a priori contrasts in linear (mixed) models: A tutorial. *Journal of Memory and Language*, **110**. https://doi.org/10.1016/j.jml.2019.104038.

Schilling, H. E. H., Rayner, K., and Chumbley, J. I. 1998. Comparing naming, lexical decision, and eye fixation times: Word frequency effects and individual differences. *Memory and Cognition*, **26**(6), 1270–1281.

Schneider, D. W., and Anderson, J. R. 2012. Modeling fan effects on the time course of associative recognition. *Cognitive Psychology*, **64**(3), 127–160.

Schriefers, H., Friederici, A. D., and Kuhn, K. 1995. The processing of locally ambiguous relative clauses in German. *Journal of Memory and Language*, **34**(4), 499–520.

Schwartz, M. F., Saffran, E. M., and Marin, O. S. M. 1980. The word order problem in agrammatism: I. Comprehension. *Brain and Language*, **10**(2), 249–262.

Sisson, S. A., Fan, Y., and Beaumont, M. A. 2019. *Handbook of Approximate Bayesian Computation*. Boca Raton, FL: Chapman and Hall/CRC.

Smaldino, P. E. 2017. Models are stupid, and we need more of them. In Robin R. Vallacher, Stephen J. Read, and Andrzej Nowak, eds., *Computational Social Psychology*. Routledge, pp. 311–331.

Smith, G., Franck, J., and Tabor, W. 2018. A self-organizing approach to subject-verb number agreement. *Cognitive Science*, **42**(4)Suppl, 1043–1074.

Smith, G., and Vasishth, S. 2020. A principled approach to feature selection in models of sentence processing. *Cognitive Science*, **44**(12). https://doi.org/10.1111/cogs.12918.

Spiegelhalter, D. J., Abrams, K. R., and Myles, J. P. 2004. *Statistics in Practice. Vol. 13: Bayesian Approaches to Clinical Trials and Health-Care Evaluation*. Chichester, West Sussex: John Wiley and Sons.

Spiegelhalter, D. J., Freedman, L. S., and Parmar, M. K. B. 1994. Bayesian approaches to randomized trials. *Journal of the Royal Statistical Society. Series A (Statistics in Society)*, **157**(3), 357–387.

Spivey, M. J., and Tanenhaus, M. K. 1998. Syntactic ambiguity resolution in discourse: Modeling the effects of referential context and lexical frequency. *Journal of Experimental Psychology: Learning, Memory, and Cognition*, **24**(6), 1521–1543.

Stack, C. M. H., James, A. N., and Watson, D. G. 2018. A failure to replicate rapid syntactic adaptation in comprehension. *Memory and Cognition*, **46**(6), 864–877.

Staub, A. 2010. Eye movements and processing difficulty in object relative clauses. *Cognition*, **116**(1), 71–86.

Sternberg, S. 1966. High-speed scanning in human memory. *Science*, **153**(3736), 652–654.

Sternberg, S. 1969. Memory-scanning: Mental processes revealed by reaction-time experiments. *American Scientist*, **57**, 421–457.

Sturt, P. 2003. The time-course of the application of binding constraints in reference resolution. *Journal of Memory and Language*, **48**(3), 542–562.

Bibliography

Swaab, T. Y., Brown, C. M., and Hagoort, P. 1997. Spoken sentence comprehension in aphasia: Event-related potential evidence for a lexical integration deficit. *Journal of Cognitive Neuroscience*, **9**, 39–66.

Swets, B., Desmet, T., Clifton, C., Jr., and Ferreira, F. 2008. Underspecification of syntactic ambiguities: Evidence from self-paced reading. *Memory and Cognition*, **36**(1), 201–216.

Swinney, D., Zurif, E. B., Prather, P., and Love, T. 1996. Neurological distribution of processing operations underlying language comprehension. *Journal of Cognitive Neuroscience*, **8**, 174–184.

Tabor, W., Galantucci, B., and Richardson, D. 2004. Effects of merely local syntactic coherence on sentence processing. *Journal of Memory and Language*, **50**, 355–370.

Thompson, C. K., and Choy, J. 2009. Pronominal resolution and gap filling in agrammatic aphasia: Evidence from eye movements. *Journal of Psycholinguistic Research*, **38**(3), 255–283.

Thompson, C. K., Dickey, M. W., and Choy, J. J. 2004. Complexity in the comprehension of wh-movement structures in agrammatic Broca's aphasia: Evidence from eyetracking. *Brain and Language*, **91**(1), 124–125.

Tomasello, M. 2003. *Constructing a Language: A Usage-Based Account of Language Acquisition*. Cambridge, MA: Harvard University Press.

Traxler, M. J. 2007. Working memory contributions to relative clause attachment processing: A hierarchical linear modeling analysis. *Memory and Cognition*, **35**(5), 1107–1121.

Traxler, M. J. 2014. Trends in syntactic parsing: Anticipation, Bayesian estimation, and good-enough parsing. *Trends in Cognitive Sciences*, **18**(11), 605–611.

Traxler, M. J., Morris, R. K., and Seely, R. E. 2002. Processing subject and object relative clauses: Evidence from eye movements. *Journal of Memory and Language*, **47**(1), 69–90.

Traxler, M. J., Pickering, M. J., and Clifton, C., Jr. 1998. Adjunct attachment is not a form of lexical ambiguity resolution. *Journal of Memory and Language*, **39**(4), 558–592.

Tucker, M. A., Idrissi, A., and Almeida, D. 2015. Representing number in the real-time processing of agreement: Self-paced reading evidence from Arabic. *Frontiers in Psychology*, **6**(347). https://doi.org/10.3389/fpsyg.2015.00347.

Van Dyke, J. A. 2007. Interference effects from grammatically unavailable constituents during sentence processing. *Journal of Experimental Psychology. Learning, Memory, and Cognition*, **33**(2), 407–430.

Van Dyke, J. A., and Lewis, R. L. 2003. Distinguishing effects of structure and decay on attachment and repair: A cue-based parsing account of recovery from misanalyzed ambiguities. *Journal of Memory and Language*, **49**(3), 285–316.

Van Dyke, J. A., and McElree, B. 2006. Retrieval interference in sentence comprehension. *Journal of Memory and Language*, **55**(2), 157–166.

Van Dyke, J. A., and McElree, B. 2011. Cue-dependent interference in comprehension. *Journal of Memory and Language*, **65**(3), 247–263.

Van Dyke, J. A., Johns, C. L., and Kukona, A. 2014. Low working memory capacity is only spuriously related to poor reading comprehension. *Cognition*, **131**(3), 373–403.

van Rij, J., van Rijn, H., and Hendriks, P. 2013. How WM load influences linguistic processing in adults: A computational model of pronoun interpretation in discourse. *Topics in Cognitive Science*, **5**(3), 564–580.

Varma, S. 2016. The CAPS Family of Cognitive Architectures. In S. E. F. Chipman, (ed.), *The Oxford Handbook of Cognitive Science*. New York: Oxford University Press, p. 49.

Vasishth, S. 2015. *A Meta-analysis of Relative Clause Processing in Mandarin Chinese Using Bias Modelling*. MSc thesis, School of Mathematics and Statistics, University of Sheffield, UK.

Vasishth, S. 2020. Using Approximate Bayesian Computation for estimating parameters in the cue-based retrieval model of sentence processing. *MethodsX*. https://doi.org/10.1016/j.mex.2020.100850.

Vasishth, S., Bruessow, S., Lewis, R. L., and Drenhaus, H. 2008. Processing polarity: How the ungrammatical intrudes on the grammatical. *Cognitive Science*, **32**(4), 685–712.

Vasishth, S., Chen, Z., Li, Q., and Guo, G. 2013. Processing Chinese relative clauses: Evidence for the subject-relative advantage. *PLoS ONE*, **8**(10), e77006. https://doi.org/10.1371/journal.pone.0077006.

Vasishth, S., Chopin, N., Ryder, R., and Nicenboim, B. 2017b. Modelling dependency completion in sentence comprehension as a Bayesian hierarchical mixture process: A case study involving Chinese relative clauses. In *Proceedings of the 39th Annual Meeting of the Cognitive Science Conference*, London.

Vasishth, S., and Drenhaus, H. 2011. Locality in German. *Dialogue and Discourse*, **2**(1), 59–82.

Vasishth, S., and Gelman, A. 2019. *How to embrace variation and accept uncertainty in linguistic and psycholinguistic data analysis*. Submitted.

Vasishth, S., Jäger, L. A., and Nicenboim, B. 2017a. Feature overwriting as a finite mixture process: Evidence from comprehension data. In M. K. van Vugt, A. Banks, and W. Kennedy, eds., *Proceedings of the 15th International Conference on Cognitive Modeling*. Coventry: University of Warwick.

Vasishth, S., and Lewis, R. L. 2006. Argument-head distance and processing complexity: Explaining both locality and antilocality effects. *Language*, **82**(4), 767–794.

Vasishth, S., Mertzen, D., Jäger, L. A., and Gelman, A. 2018. The statistical significance filter leads to overoptimistic expectations of replicability. *Journal of Memory and Language*, **103**, 151–175.

Vasishth, S., Nicenboim, B., Engelmann, F., and Burchert, F. 2019. Computational models of retrieval processes in sentence processing. *Trends in Cognitive Sciences*, **23**, 968–982.

Vasishth, S., Suckow, K., Lewis, R. L., and Kern, S. 2010. Short-term forgetting in sentence comprehension: Crosslinguistic evidence from head-final structures. *Language and Cognitive Processes*, **25**(4), 533–567.

Vehtari, A., Gelman, A., and Gabry, J. 2017. Practical Bayesian model evaluation using leave-one-out cross-validation and WAIC. *Statistics and Computing*, **27**(5), 1413–1432.

Vehtari, A., Ojanen, J., et al. 2012. A survey of Bayesian predictive methods for model assessment, selection and comparison. *Statistics Surveys*, **6**, 142–228.

Bibliography

Villata, S., and Franck, J. 2016. *Similarity-based interference in agreement comprehension and production: Evidence from object agreement.* Manuscript.

von der Malsburg, T., Kliegl, R., and Vasishth, S. 2015. Determinants of scanpath regularity in reading. *Cognitive Science*, **39**(7), 1675–1703.

von der Malsburg, T., and Vasishth, S. 2011. What is the scanpath signature of syntactic reanalysis? *Journal of Memory and Language*, **65**(2), 109–127.

von der Malsburg, T., and Vasishth, S. 2013. Scanpaths reveal syntactic underspecification and reanalysis strategies. *Language and Cognitive Processes*, **28**(10), 1545–1578.

Vosse, T., and Kempen, G. A. M. 2000. Syntactic structure assembly in human parsing: A computational model based on competitive inhibition and lexicalist grammar. *Cognition*, **75**, 105–143.

Wagers, M. W., Lau, E. F., and Phillips, C. 2009. Agreement attraction in comprehension: Representations and processes. *Journal of Memory and Language*, **61**(2), 206–237.

Warren, T., and McConnell, K. 2007. Investigating effects of selectional restriction violations and plausibility violation severity on eye-movements in reading. *Psychonomic Bulletin and Review*, **14**(4), 770–775.

Warren, T. C., and Gibson, E. 2005. Effects of NP-type on reading English clefts. *Language and Cognitive Processes*, **20**(6), 751–767.

Wasserstein, R. L., and Lazar, N. A. 2016. The ASA's Statement on *p*-Values: context, process, and purpose. *American Statistician*, **70**(2), 129–133.

Watkins, O. C., and Watkins, M. J. 1975. Buildup of proactive inhibition as a cue-overload effect. *Journal of Experimental Psychology: Human Learning and Memory*, **104**(4), 442–452.

Waugh, N. C., and Norman, D. A. 1965. Primary memory. *Psychological Review*, **72**, 89–104.

Weger, U. W., and Inhoff, A. W. 2007. Long-range regressions to previously read words are guided by spatial and verbal memory. *Memory and Cognition*, **35**(6), 1293–1306.

Wells, J. B., Christiansen, M. H., Race, D. S., Acheson, D. J., and MacDonald, M. C. 2009. Experience and sentence processing: Statistical learning and relative clause comprehension. *Cognitive Psychology*, **58**, 250–271.

Wu, F., Kaiser, E., and Vasishth, S. 2017. Effects of early cues on the processing of Chinese relative clauses: Evidence for experience-based theories. *Cognitive Science*, **42**, 1101–1133.

Yadav, Himanshu, Smith, Garrett, Paape, Dario, and Vasishth, Shravan. 2020. Modeling individual differences in sentence comprehension. In *Proceedings of the Architectures and Mechanisms for Language Processing Conference*, Potsdam, Germany.

Yee, E., Blumstein, S. E., and Sedivy, J. C. 2008. Lexical-semantic activation in Broca's and Wernicke's aphasia: evidence from eye movements. *Journal of Cognitive Neuroscience*, **20**(4), 592–612.

Yngve, V. H. 1960. A model and an hypothesis for language structure. *Proceedings of the American Philosophical Society*, **104**, 444–466.

Zurif, E. B., Swinney, D., Prather, P., and Love, T. 1994. Functional localization in the brain with respect to syntactic processing. *Journal of Psycholinguistic Research*, **23**, 487–497.

Index

3CAPS, 180
4CAPS, 10

ABC, 66
accessibility, 74
ACT-R, 1, 10, 17, 20, 49
  based model, 172
activation
  level, 54
  model, 164, 167
adaptive control of thought rational, 49
adversarial priors, 46
agnostic priors, 46
agreement attraction, 32, 34
ambiguity advantage, 5
animacy, 108
antilocality, 54
aphasia, 178
approximate Bayesian computation, 63, 66
Armenian, 34
artificial intelligence, 10
associative strength, 56
attend-word, 120
average behaviour, 10

backward-looking processes, 6
base-level activation, 55
Bayes' rule, 65
Bayesian methods, 15, 45
Bayesian parameter estimation, 64
benchmark empirical tests, 18
bilingualism, 3
binary match, 84
binding theory, 38, 39
Broca's aphasia, 178

capacity constrained resource deficit, 180
capacity differences, 6
case marking, 34
categorical match, 84
CELEX database, 126
centre embedding, 2
Chinese, 167
chunks, 50

clinical trials, 15
cluster analysis, 194
cognitive
  psychology, 21
  science, 10
community of priors, 46
competing models, 18
computational cognitive models, 8
computational
  model, 52
  modelling, 8
confusability, 32
connectionist models, 8
constraint-based models, 8
construal, 150
content-addressable, 162
  memory, 49
  search, 23
contrastive focus, 108
cross association, 90, 91
  cue, 85
  level, 86, 88
cross-modal lexical priming, 184
cue combinatorics, 108
cue overload, 55, 56, 76, 162
cue-based
  retrieval, 32, 38, 49, 52
  search, 23
cue-confusion, 72
cue-feature associations, 74

decay, 7, 49, 50, 104, 186
  parameter, 50
decision processes, 8
declarative
  knowledge, 50
  memory, 50, 54
dependency
  completion, 23
  locality theory, 6, 9, 187
depth hypothesis, 2
direct-access, 20
  model, 161, 165, 167

222 Index

discourse
  referents, 9
  saliency, 108
  status, 75, 107
  topic, 94
distance
  account, 168
  effects, 54
distractor
  activation, 104
  prominence, 75
drift diffusion process, 33
dynamical systems approaches, 8

E-Z Reader, 10, 20, 116
early processes, 40
EMMA, 20, 117
encoding, 22
  interference, 170, 172
English, 167
exit-time-out, 127
expectation, 141
expert opinion, 45
eye-movement control, 10
eyetracking, 19, 40, 171

facilitatory
  effect, 104, 171
  interference, 41, 47, 58, 60, 75, 83
  interference effect, 79, 170
fan effect, 21, 29, 30, 37, 51, 56, 57, 76, 81,
    86, 104, 164, 168
feature
  overwriting, 32, 172
  percolation, 172
    account, 171
    model, 174
find-next-word, 120
first mention, 108
first-pass regression, 128, 147
focus of attention, 50
forward-looking processes, 6

garden path, 11
  sentences, 134
Gibbs sampling, 65
good-enough processing, 44, 148

Hamiltonian Monte Carlo, 65
heterogeneous variances, 169
  model, 174
high
  attachment, 5
  capacity, 6
  feature co-occurrence, 108
high-capacity readers, 149

high-level surprisal, 125
homogeneous
  variance model, 174
  variances, 169

illusion of grammaticality, 31, 171
individual differences, 17, 20
individual-level
  behaviour, 10
  differences, 20
inhibitory effect, 104
inhibitory interference, 21, 26, 29, 57,
    60, 162, 164, 167
  effects, 170
integrate-word, 120
interference, 21, 186
  effect, 75
item prominence, 63

k-fold cross-validation, 165, 169

language processing, 52
late closure, 4, 11
latency
  exponent, 57
  factor, 52, 57, 126
lexical variables, 116
limited capacity, 50
local coherence, 176
lognormal race, 30
long-term memory, 50
low attachment, 5
low feature co-occurrence, 108
low-capacity, 6
  readers, 149
low-level surprisal, 125
low-precision, 16

marking and morphing, 32
match quality, 90
mathematical modelling, 8
maximally discriminative cues, 94
maximum associative strength, 51
MCMC, 65
memory
  access process, 162
  load, 7
  processes, 21
  retrieval, 106, 117
meta-analysis, 28, 61
Metropolis-Hastings, 65
mildly uninformative priors, 45
minimal attachment, 4, 11
mismatch
  penalty, 89
    parameter, 51

Index

223

misretrieval, 21, 30, 32, 57, 79
Monte Carlo Markov chain, 65
multi-associative cues, 20, 62, 63, 74, 84,
    88–90, 98, 106, 108, 109

negative polarity items, 54
noise, 50
non-agreement subject-verb dependencies,
    101
null
    hypothesis significance testing, 16
    null results, 13, 14, 39
number agreement, 31, 32

object
    relative, 167
        advantage, 168
object-extracted structure, 141
ORC, 143, 144

p-value, 16, 37
paired t-test, 13
parallel, 6
    word processing, 116
parsing architecture, 54
partial
    feature match, 24, 30
    matching, 30
posterior
    distribution, 65
    predictive distributions, 65
postlexical processes, 116
Potsdam sentence corpus, 125
power, 11, 13–15, 20, 37
    simulation, 13
precision, 13
predictions, 3
predictive processing, 6
principle A, 39
prior
    distribution, 64
    knowledge, 45
    predictive distributions, 65
proactive, 27
    interference, 21, 24, 25, 27, 38, 98
probabilistic
    grammar, 6
    knowledge, 3, 7
    parsing models, 8
    predictions, 146
procedural knowledge, 50
processing deficit, 178
production rule, 50
prominence, 20, 22, 62, 72, 74, 89, 93, 98,
    106, 108

quantitative
    modelling, 9
    predictions, 9

race process, 30, 58, 77
ranked parallel, 6
rapid integration failure, 134
re-reading time, 128
reactivation, 21, 50
reanalysis, 20, 140
    interface, 160
recency, 106
reciprocals, 95, 101
reflexives, 38, 39, 101, 105
region of practical equivalence, 15,
    16, 106
regression path duration, 128
regularizing priors, 45
rejection sampling, 66
relative clause, 5, 167
representational deficit, 178
retrieval, 23
    cue, 161, 163
    interference account, 171
    latency, 57
    time, 163
retroactive, 27
    interference, 21, 24, 25, 27, 38, 98
root-mean-square deviation, 122, 136
ROPE, 15, 106

saliency, 74
    component, 93
sample size, 11
sceptical priors, 46
Schilling corpus, 126
self-paced
    listening, 19
    reading, 19, 171
sentence processing, 161
serial order, 52
    position, 49
    processing, 116
short-term buffers, 50
similarity-based interference, 7, 26, 50, 51
SOAR, 10
speed-accuracy tradeoff, 162
spreading activation, 30, 55, 56, 86, 92
SRC, 144
    structure, 143
standard
    error, 13
    hierarchical linear model, 169
statistical facilitation, 58, 77
stop-reading, 120

224 Index

storage cost, 3
structural
  complexity, 2
  prediction, 117
subcategorization, 35
subject relative, 167
subject-extracted structure, 141
subject-verb number agreement, 101
subvocalization, 141
surprisal, 14, 124
SWIFT, 10, 116
SYNCHRON, 180
syntactic complexity, 2
  cue weighting, 110
  position, 107
  prediction locality theory, 6
  surprisal, 124
  weighting, 107

target
  match, 57, 60, 79, 103
  -match configuration, 62
  mismatch, 57, 60, 75, 103
  -mismatch configurations, 62
Time Out regression, 124, 127, 129
topic, 74

total fixation time, 128
trace deletion hypothesis, 179
Type
  M, 13, 14
  S, 13, 14

uncertainty, 12
underpowered studies, 11
underspecification, 4, 5, 7, 20, 32, 140, 160, 176
  interface, 153
UNIFICATION SPACE model, 181
uninterrupted reading, 152

verb-final, 3
verb-particle constructions, 3
verbally stated models, 8, 9

Wernicke's aphasia, 178
working memory, 1, 2, 7, 50, 168, 186
  capacity, 2, 7, 17, 110, 150, 152, 153
  limitations, 3, 5
  models, 10
wrap-up effects, 133

ziji, 88, 95